The
EVERYTHING®
Torah Book

Dear Reader:

One of Charles Schultz's famous *Peanuts* cartoons portrays Charlie Brown facing a history test. The single question reads, "Explain World War II. Use both sides of the paper if necessary."

Providing "Everything Torah" in several hundred pages is a similarly daunting task. According to traditional Jewish thought, the Torah is nothing less than "the Blueprint of Creation." The Written Torah is merely the beginning; the full Torah tells us why God Created the world, and what we should hope to accomplish now that we're here. In a way, "Everything Torah" is redundant—for *Everything* is in *Torah*.

As a broad introduction to the Torah Path, I do hope that every reader finds this book a valuable source of insights and understanding. For those Jews unfamiliar with the idea of ongoing Torah study and discovery, I hope this will be a starting point in your Jewish learning, and lead to much more—because it is critical to our Jewish future.

Torah study is a never-ending process. I look forward to meeting you, receiving your feedback, and corresponding with you, at *www.everythingtorah.com*!

The EVERYTHING® Series

Editorial

Publishing Director	Gary M. Krebs
Managing Editor	Kate McBride
Copy Chief	Laura M. Daly
Acquisitions Editor	Gina Chaimanis
Production Editors	Jamie Wielgus
	Bridget Brace

Production

Production Director	Susan Beale
Production Manager	Michelle Roy Kelly
Series Designers	Daria Perreault
	Colleen Cunningham
	John Paulhus
Cover Design	Paul Beatrice
	Matt LeBlanc
Layout and Graphics	Colleen Cunningham
	Erin Ring
Series Cover Artist	Barry Littmann

Visit the entire Everything® Series at *www.everything.com*

THE

EVERYTHING®

TORAH
BOOK

All you need to understand the basics of
Jewish law and the Five Books of the Old Testament

Rabbi Yaakov Menken

Adams Media
Avon, Massachusetts

In memory of my father-in-law, Rabbi Dr. Azriel Rosenfeld z"l.

An Everything® Series Book.
Everything® and everything.com® are registered trademarks of F+W Publications, Inc.

Published by Adams Media, an F+W Publications Company
57 Littlefield Street, Avon, MA 02322 U.S.A.
www.adamsmedia.com

ISBN: 1-59337-325-2
Printed in the United States of America.

J I H G F E D C B

Library of Congress Cataloging-in-Publication Data
Menken, Yaakov.
The everything Torah book / Yaakov Menken.
p.   cm.—(An everything series book)
Includes bibliographical references and index.
ISBN 1-59337-325-2
1. Judaism—Sacred books. 2. Judaism—Essence, genius, nature. 3. Judaism—
History. 4. Bible. O.T. Pentateuch—Commentaries. I. Title. II. Series: Everything series.
BM496.6.M46 2005
296.1--dc22
2005009552

This book is available at quantity discounts for bulk purchases.
For information, please call 1-800-872-5627.

Contents

Acknowledgments

My parents, Dr. Matthew Menken and Prof. Jane Menken, sent me out to get an education and to value the truth. Rabbis beyond mention helped me find it, but Rabbis Nosson Tzvi Finkel, Dovid Gottlieb, Yisroel Rakowsky, Yisroel Simcha Schorr, Yaakov Eliezer Schwartzman, and Avraham Teichman shlit"a all made different extraordinary and lasting contributions. Rabbi Moshe Silberberg shlit"a and family take hospitality to the next level, and provided constant guidance and support.

Rabbi Azriel Rosenfeld z"l, and yblctv"a his wife Chava, made me truly a part of their family when I married their daughter. My father-in-law was both a leading computer scientist and a Torah scholar at the same time, and his encyclopedic knowledge and sharp insights would have been a great help as I wrote this book—which is dedicated to his memory, HaRav Azriel Yitzchak ben HaRav Avraham Tzvi z"l.

My children bring joy to our house every day, and were more than patient as their father worked away each evening. Above all, I thank my wife Tova, without whose ongoing support projects like this book would never come to be.

Top Ten
Torah Aphorisms for Life

1. Love your neighbor as yourself. —Leviticus 19:18

2. Serve God with joy. —Psalms 100:2

3. In accordance with the effort, is the reward. —Fathers 5:23

4. The past is gone, the future is yet to come, and the present is like the blink of an eye—so why worry? —Rabbi Avraham ibn Ezra

5. Look not at the vessel, but at what it contains. —Fathers 4:20.

6. Who is Wealthy? He who is happy with his lot. —Fathers 4:1

7. Fix your own problems first, before you correct everyone else. —Talmud Bava Metziah 107b

8. Educate Each Child According to His Way. —Proverbs 22:6

9. Silence is an aid to wisdom. —Fathers 3:13

10. The entire world is but a narrow bridge—and the key is not to be at all afraid. —R' Nachman of Breslov

Introduction

▶ A NON-JEW once came to the master teacher and Sage, Hillel, and said, "Convert me, on condition that you teach me the entire Torah while I stand on one foot." Hillel told him, "That which is hateful to you, do not to your fellow man. This is the entire Torah; the rest is commentary. Now go and learn!"

It seems almost inconceivable that this Torah, which has had an unequaled impact upon the entire world, should come from a people that is, even today, tiny among the nations. But it's true: the Jewish Nation, who—according to the Book—received the Torah 3,300 years ago, represent barely 0.2 percent (merely 2 in every 1,000) of the world's population.

Not only is this the case, but most Jews today don't observe the Torah's laws as did the Prophets and Sages. While most Jewish people followed the Torah 200 years ago, that is much less common now. So while many people are familiar with the text itself, far fewer know much about the beliefs of those who revered, studied, and argued about Torah for millennia.

If you are Jewish, you will probably be surprised to learn how different the Torah's traditional philosophy and worldview is from what you may have learned as a child, or through classes taught by those with a more liberal perspective. Not only are many of the practices of traditional Judaism foreign to many Jews, but the beliefs themselves are often very different—and in many cases, you may recognize in yourself, your synagogue, or your community a search to recapture what, in fact, was always yours.

For those who are not Jewish, understanding the Torah's religious world-view—as traditional Judaism understands it—may give you a better understanding of your own faith, even if you have never so much as met a Jewish person, much less entered a synagogue. Jesus learned from the early Sages of the Mishnah, while Mohammed encountered post-Talmudic Judaism. The Seven Universal Laws given to Noah were known to many scholars, and were quoted by Sir Isaac Newton—but if you are like most people, you'd probably never heard of them before picking up this book.

But above all, in *The Everything® Torah Book* you'll be asked to think and to probe, and—quite possibly—to argue. As you will discover, the Talmud encourages the reader to question and challenge every statement, and every premise, in the search for understanding. That's why the Everythingtorah.com Web site is intended for you, even more than for those who haven't yet bought the book. On the site, you'll find opportunities to ask your questions, pose your challenges, and read the thoughts of others.

Jewish Sages taught, thousands of years ago, that the Torah is what preserves the Jewish Nation. Today many Jews have lost their attachment to Torah, and a corresponding weakness in Jewish identity has followed. So if you are Jewish, but have not had much of an opportunity to learn Torah, this is a special—and very important—opportunity.

So dive in—a wide "sea of Jewish learning" awaits you!

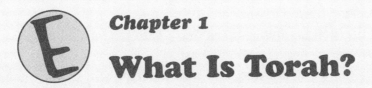

Chapter 1

What Is Torah?

What's the Torah? Why, the Torah is the Five Books of Moshe, the first five books of the *Tanach* (the Jewish Bible, which Christians call the Old Testament). But if that were the whole answer, you wouldn't need an entire book about Torah. You could just read the Bible.

Torah simultaneously refers to something far greater than a single written document. Torah, which means "instruction" in Hebrew, is the totality of God's directions to the Jewish People, and includes all areas of Jewish religious knowledge.

God, Torah, and the World

Torah has given birth to religious views that now cover most of the globe. Two thousand years ago, every European worshiped a panoply of gods, from Odin in the north to Zeus in the south. The earliest Americans, from Native Americans to the Mayans of the Yucatan Peninsula and the Incas of Chile, similarly bowed to a range of gods great and small. But today, the majority of the world's population shares a faith in One God, the God of a band of early Hebrews in the Middle East.

Do you believe that the One God, too, is but a myth? Or do you believe that perhaps there is a God, but He is not directly involved with the world, and certainly doesn't care about little ol' you? This book may challenge your assumptions, and have you probe inwardly to think about those beliefs. You will see a vision of history in which God's role is ever-present, and encounter a rich theology that answers many of the questions people have about why we're here in the world.

Torah Today

The past several decades have seen an extraordinary revolution in Torah learning and living. Everywhere you turn—in the Torah-observant Jewish community, among the more modern, liberal Jews, or even among non-Jews—there is renewed interest in studying the Torah, as well as a desire to examine or even to observe its many Commandments.

The Growth of Yeshivos

The study of Torah has grown dramatically within the traditionally observant community. Over the past two decades, the number of adult students in *yeshivos*, traditional Torah academies, has doubled. Whereas the largest such academies just twenty years ago might have had 1,000 students, today the Mirrer Yeshiva in Jerusalem is home to over 5,000, equivalent to a midsize private college.

These numbers are bolstered, in part, by the *Ba'al Teshuvah* movement. The term *Ba'al Teshuvah*, or "Master of Return," was previously used in reference to someone who abandoned Torah practices and then readopted them.

In modern times, however, it is used to refer to those raised in nonobservant families who, as adults, took upon themselves the obligations of Torah observance. Before the 1950s, this was almost unheard of. Today, however, the population of Ba'alei Teshuvah in both the United States and Israel is adding significantly to the size of Torah academies and observant communities.

Torah Learning Across the Spectrum

While traditional Jews have always emphasized Torah learning and observance, other Jewish groups now recognize the importance of Torah study to the Jewish future. The most recent platform of the Reform movement, adopted in 1999, encouraged "the ongoing study of the whole array of mitzvot [Commandments]." The Conservative movement also called for all members to begin reading a chapter of the Bible every day—an obvious duplicate of the successful *Daf Yomi* program, in which Orthodox men worldwide cycle through the Talmud at the rate of one page per day.

The Noahides

Outside the Jewish community, some non-Jews have gone so far as to reject any other religious affiliation, in favor of classifying themselves as "Noahides," followers of the Torah's Commandments for non-Jews, originally given to Noah upon his exit from the Ark after the Flood. Noahides may observe some Jewish holidays, but otherwise worship together and study those portions of Torah relevant to their observance of the Seven Universal (or Noahide) Laws.

Something for Everyone

Most religions teach that everyone should adopt that religion. The religion of the Torah is very different—it spends most of its time describing how God gave the Jewish Nation a special job to do, and outlining the rules that the Jewish People should follow. But at the same time, the Torah also tells us that every human being was created in God's image. The Torah says that God spoke to Noah, the father of everyone alive today, and gave him his own set of rules to follow after exiting his famous Ark.

The Torah Speaks to Non-Jews, Too

That means that when it comes to faith and belief, the Torah says that everyone should believe in the One God who Created us all. But when it comes to practice, it says that most people—the overwhelming majority of the human race—don't have to follow all the rules of the Torah. If they want to, they can join the Jewish Nation, but they don't have to do that in order to be God-fearing people.

The Unique Mission of the Jewish Nation

At the same time, the Jews do have a unique mission—to spread knowledge of God throughout the world. According to the fullness of Torah thought, this isn't merely a general call for *tikkun olam*, "Repairing the World," however you might define that. No, the Torah calls for something much more difficult: *tikkun atzmo*, "Repairing the Self." As the Talmud says, "Correct yourself, and then correct others."

Being "a light unto the nations" doesn't mean to lead demonstrations, get A's in all your classes, or excel at sports. It means to be the best human being you can be—and the Torah claims that it can help you to reach that goal. When you read above about people who don't believe in God, did you say, "Well, that's not me"? Okay then! If God Created you, and Created the Torah, and the Torah claims it can help you to perfect yourself . . . you have to believe it. God's more reliable than people are, right? God *always* keeps His promises.

A Tapestry of Customs, but Unified Beliefs

When people see the different customs of Chassidic Jews with their long caftans and round fur hats, Ashkenazic Jews (from Northern Europe) in business suits, and Sephardic Jews (from Spain and Northern Africa) with long white robes, they tend to focus upon the external differences of custom. They will point to these obvious differences, and tell you that this isn't the Judaism of 2,000 years ago. But—as Jewish communities around the globe are realizing today—Judaism doesn't depend upon lox and bagel, or kibbeh and felafel.

Different Customs

Each community has its own customs, the result of living apart for hundreds of years—and the differences may seem profound. It is customary, for example, for a Torah-observant person to not merely avoid mixing meat and dairy in the same meal, but to wait after a meat meal to allow the meat to digest, or after hard cheeses to allow the dairy products to be consumed. But while the observant person from Eastern Europe might wait six hours between one and the other, a sincere and pious individual from Germany might wait only three—and one from the Netherlands, a mere seventy-two minutes!

On the holiday of Passover, the law demands that one not eat leavened products, breads made from wheat, barley, rye, spelt, or oats. In the Ashkenazic community, a well-established custom bars legumes and rice as well—either to prevent confusion or because of a concern that wheat or barley kernels might have gotten mixed in at the market. The Sephardic authorities never made any ban on these products, so even the most devout person from Sephardic lands will happily eat a meal with rice, lentils, or peas during Passover, while an Ashkenazic follower of Torah never would. So it may seem strange to say that the two are both observing the same Torah.

The Ties That Bind

In this book, you'll learn about the core beliefs and history that have tied the observers of Torah together, regardless of geographical location, the type of government, and the circumstances where they live—and even what era they live in. These beliefs have survived and held the population of exiles together; according to tradition, they've held the Jews together ever since Sinai.

Faith and Reason

Most religions teach that religious faith is something that either you've got or you don't. "Faith" is belief in something that can be neither proven nor disproven, so it is immune to the sort of critical analysis that we apply to other decisions that we make in our lives. In this view, "theological truths" are not things that we determine to be true by using the standard tools of rational decision-making, but rather are arrived at by liberating oneself from the limitations of rationality.

The Torah, and Judaism in general, do not support this distinction. On the contrary, Jewish literature consistently suggests that belief in Torah is based upon facts and rational arguments. The Torah appears to argue that one can arrive at these beliefs using the same decision-making process that we use in every other area of our lives.

Maimonides begins his legal code by saying, "The foundation of all foundations and pillar of wisdom is to know that there exists a First Being." He does not say that this is a belief, or a faith, but rather a fact that one should know to be true.

This being the case, the Torah subjects itself to an extremely high level of critical analysis. If faith cannot be proven or disproven, there is nothing to argue. But traditionally, Judaism never shared the view that the Torah is merely poetry of faith. If these are alleged to be facts, then one can attempt to prove them wrong.

Names, Languages, Pronunciation, and Perspective

As you read this book, some of the familiar names you recognize from the Bible may look, well, unfamiliar. For those who have seen Hebrew before, the transliterations may also look different. And even the ideas expressed may be dissimilar from what you've learned from other sources—even Jewish ones. So a few notes of explanation will help get you oriented toward the rest of this book.

What's in a Name?

Those reading the Bible in English are usually more familiar with the translated names of Biblical figures: Abraham, Isaac, and Jacob rather than *Avraham*, *Yitzchak*, and *Yaakov*. Today, however, we live in a multicultural society, and it is worthwhile—for any number of reasons—to become conversant with the original names. Many names you find in the Bible have meanings, and were chosen on that basis: Yaakov, for example, was holding onto the *akev*, heel, of his brother Esav (Esau) when he was born. The original Hebrew names are emphasized throughout this book; often the translation is provided alongside, and in any case it is provided in the Glossary.

Languages of Torah

When studying a text, reading in translation is always inferior to reading it in the original. Nuances of language in the original text can be lost, as well as relationships between two words that have no connection once rendered into another language. There are literally dozens of different English-language translations of the Torah from Jewish and Christian authors—but there is only one original Hebrew version.

Torah study is so complex in part because only the Written Torah, as well as most books of the Jewish Bible, are written in ancient Hebrew. In order to be a Torah scholar, one must be able to read the Mishnah, Talmud, and commentaries, so one must know several different dialects of at least two different languages:

- **Biblical Hebrew**: This is the language of the Torah and most of the Jewish Bible.
- **Mishnaic Hebrew**: This is the Hebrew of the Mishnah, which, though very similar, shows that the language developed over time and was influenced by other languages, such as Aramaic.
- **Aramaic**: This is the language of the Babylonian Talmud, though a fair amount of Aramaic is also found in the Book of Daniel and other Biblical texts. It is closely related to Hebrew, but is a different language nonetheless.
- **Rabbinic Hebrew**: This is the language of the commentators, from the time that the center of Torah scholarship moved from Babylonia to Europe and Northern Africa. The change back to Hebrew can probably be attributed to the fact that many of the earliest Jewish occupants of these lands came from Israel rather than Babylonia. For the past thousand years, this has been the primary language of Torah scholarship, with generous use of Aramaic terms and phrases from the Talmud.

Interestingly enough, the Modern Hebrew language isn't quite any of the above. Modern Hebrew was created primarily by an early Zionist named Eliezer Ben-Yehudah, early in the twentieth century. His sixteen-volume *Dictionary of Ancient and Modern Hebrew* omits Aramaic and other foreign words used in Rabbinic texts, and adds new words that he coined to meet modern needs.

ALERT!

Ben-Yehudah's goal was not the revival of rabbinic Hebrew—on the contrary, biographers describe him as openly anti-religious. Some argue that the usage of Modern Hebrew by Israelis causes problems in studying their Torah and Talmudic texts since many of the words in Modern Hebrew don't mean precisely the same thing in earlier literature.

Dialects and Pronunciation

To further confuse matters, 2,000 years of exile have brought with them vastly different pronunciations of the same Hebrew and Aramaic. Usually one community or the other has lost the ability to distinguish between two consonants or vowels, and now pronounces them the same way. Originally, six letters of the Hebrew alphabet were pronounced differently depending on where in a word they appeared. Today, only Yemenite Jews have preserved two different pronunciations for all six letters. Ashkenazic Jews retain them for four letters, and Sephardic Jews for three. Within Ashkenazic Jewry, those from Galicia and Hungary pronounce vowels differently from those who stem from Poland or Lithuania, while German Jewry's dialect is slightly different from the latter.

In this book, you will find transliterations (English-letter renderings of the Hebrew words) that follow the standard Ashkenazic pronunciation—so the word for house will be transliterated as *bayis*, rather than the Sephardic *bayit* or Yemenite *bayith*. It's all the same word, and even those familiar with one of the other pronunciations will most likely not be confused.

A Matter of Perspective

What may confuse some readers—particularly Jewish readers exposed primarily to more liberal views on the Torah and tradition—is the perspective you will find in this book. You won't find "but we don't really believe that" in these pages, or "those thoughts came from a more primitive time." On the contrary, you may find material here that challenges those viewpoints.

The Torah, as traditionally taught and observed, has much to tell you about life, God, and Judaism. Prepare to learn about the beliefs and history of Torah, and about the scholars who brought the wisdom of Torah down to us today. Read on, for there's much to discover!

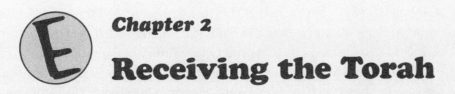

Chapter 2

Receiving the Torah

According to Torah thought, the existence of the Torah, in human hands, helps fulfill the purpose of Creation. The Torah says, "Moshe commanded us the Torah, an inheritance for the Congregation of Jacob" (Deut. 33:4). Ever since Sinai, it has been treated like an inheritance. Each generation reads it, studies it, and transmits it on to the next with the utmost precision and care. Although the Torah is thousands of years older than the printing press, you can be confident that what you are reading is almost exactly as it originally was.

Torah Before Sinai

According to Jewish tradition, the Torah not only existed before the Jews came to Mt. Sinai; it preceded the universe itself. It even preceded the creation of time—for the entire world was created in accordance with the Divine Plan, and this plan is found in the Torah. The *Medrash* (Beraishis Rabba, 1:2) says, "He looked at the Torah and created the world." Like any good architect who creates the blueprints before starting work on a building, God first created His blueprint before Creating the world.

The Talmud teaches that the forefathers of the Jewish People, Abraham, Isaac, and Jacob (or, in the original Hebrew, Avraham, Yitzchak, and Yaakov), all followed the precepts of the Torah. This was possible only because Avraham correctly identified not only who God is but what He wanted human beings to accomplish during their time on earth.

Rabbi Shlomo Ibn Aderes, the *Rashba*, explains that the Torah's guidance enables a person to perform acts that have a spiritual impact, even without a full comprehension of Kabbalah and the spiritual realms. The forefathers, in their tremendous wisdom, achieved the necessary level of spiritual awareness to recognize the appropriate deeds on their own, and performed them correctly.

Not only did the Jewish forebears observe the Torah, the Medrash says that they initiated several practices that later became Rabbinic decrees. For example, Avraham initiated the practice of praying every morning. Yitzchak added an afternoon prayer, and Yaakov followed with an evening service as well.

FACT

Early commentators wrote that the forefathers even observed the Jewish festivals, eating *Matzah* (unleavened bread) on Passover and building a *Sukkah* (booth) on Sukkos. Even before the Jewish people experienced the events now tied to these holidays, they detected and responded to the unique spiritual energies present during those seasons.

This is not to say that all of their descendents were saintly people—in fact, we know that the opposite was true. The long years of Egyptian slavery caused most of the Jews to worship idols and engage in all the immoral practices of their taskmasters. In fact, mystical sources teach that there are fifty levels of spiritual impurity, and the great-grandchildren of Jacob descended through forty-nine of them—the Medrash says that if God had not taken them out right when He did, it would no longer have been possible to redeem them.

It was at that point that God intervened more obviously in human history than at any other time since Creation itself. Remembering His promises to Avraham, Yitzchak, and Yaakov, He pulled their descendents from Egypt to create an entirely new nation.

A Nation Hears the Voice of God

In the beginning—no pun intended—the Torah's revelation stories are similar to all the others. You're told that God spoke with Adam, Noah, Avraham, Yitzchak, and Yaakov, but you have no way to verify these stories. How do you know that they happened? The source of those stories is the Torah—so generally speaking, only those who believe that the Torah is the Word of God believe that these revelations of God actually transpired.

Once the Ancient Israelites arrive at Sinai, however, something entirely different takes place: Over a dozen different Biblical passages refer to a prophetic experience shared by the entire Jewish Nation. This was no private ceremony! Approximately three million people reportedly saw the mountain on fire—and heard not thunderclaps or mere rumblings, but the clear voice of God. Furthermore, these witnesses were not some unnamed group in a far-away nation; they were the grandparents of the Jewish people holding onto the document.

The Torah often emphasizes that the Jewish faith does not rely upon miracles performed by Moshe or other Prophets—in fact, the Torah even speaks of false prophets who will perform miracles and try to lead people astray. On the contrary, the Torah relies upon the Revelation at Sinai for its credibility.

This is a story like no other. While a thorough examination of all the details could be a book unto itself, a careful study of human history shows that this story is unparalleled.

> When you will please ask about the earliest days that came before you, from the day that God Created man upon the earth, and from one end of the heavens to the other, has there been anything like this great thing, or has anything like it been heard? Has any nation heard the Voice of God speaking from inside the fire, like you heard, and lived? Or has God ever undertaken to come and take to Himself a nation from the midst of a nation, with trials, signs, and wonders, with war, a strong hand, and an outstretched arm, and with great and awesome deeds, like all that *HaShem* your God did to you in Egypt, before your eyes? (Deut. 4:32–34)

Why is this story unique? If a revelation story is an obvious benefit—if not an outright necessity—for a new monotheistic religion, it is equally obvious that a public revelation is better than a private one. So if this story could have been created by just anyone, you have to wonder why "just anyone" never did.

The Chosen People?

One Torah concept that can cause misunderstanding is the idea of a "Chosen People," selected by God. Notions of racial superiority come to mind, with all their sorry and bloody history. So it is important to clarify what this concept means in Torah.

Two Kinds of "Chosen"

Sometimes to be chosen means to be preferred: a "select" wine is one considered of superior quality to the others. At other times, however, the selection is based upon suitability to task rather than inherent value—while red wines are chosen to accompany meat dishes, this does not imply that red wines are superior to white.

When soldiers are chosen for a dangerous mission, it is true that they will be deemed heroes if they are successful. The potential consequences of failure, though, may leave their bunkmates quite happy to have been left out.

The Mission

In this case, God chose the Jewish nation for a mission. This mission involves changing their daily lives, and abstaining from ordinary worldly behavior in many different ways. Yes, it is an honor and a privilege to be chosen, but it is hardly free from costs—and being chosen in this fashion also presents new opportunities to stumble that otherwise would not exist.

Or, as Rabbi Kalman Packouz writes, "The concept of Chosen People means both chosen and choosing. Chosen for the responsibility to be a light unto the nations, to be a moral signpost for the nations of the world. Choosing means that the Jewish people accepted on Mt. Sinai to fulfill this mandate and to do the will of God. We are not chosen for special benefits; we are chosen for extra responsibility."

Anyone Can Join

Any individual can come close to the Almighty, and everyone can participate in the divine mission in accordance with the way that God has provided for him or her. In the words of the Talmud, "the Righteous of All Nations have a share in the World to Come."

At the same time, the ultimate relationship with the Divine comes through entering the Covenant of Abraham and fulfilling God's Torah. This special relationship is open to any member of humanity who wishes to enter the Covenant, irrespective of race, gender, or national origin.

The Written Torah

The Five Books of Moshe are frequently referred to as *Torah Shebichtav*, or the Written Torah, in order to specify the document itself. The unique claim of this document is that unlike even the Books of the Prophets, which were written by Divinely Inspired human beings, the Torah declares itself to be the literal word of God.

Concerning Moshe, the Torah says, "And God spoke to Moshe face to face, like a man speaks to his friend" (Exod. 33:11). During the forty years of the Exodus, God told Moshe what to write in the Torah, word by word, and Moshe wrote as instructed. While the Prophets wrote by Divine Inspiration, Moshe wrote by Divine Dictation.

The Book of Deuteronomy is devoted primarily to the teachings of Moshe shortly before his death. "These are the words which Moshe spoke to the entirety of Israel on the far side of the Jordan . . ." (Deut. 1:1). Nonetheless, the Torah teaches that what material was written, and how it was recorded, was determined by God alone.

Because of this important distinction, Jewish scholars subject the Torah to a far higher level of scrutiny than that accorded to the Prophets, Writings, or any other text. No letter is deemed superfluous; even what might appear to be the most trivial choice of phraseology is plumbed for hidden meaning.

Preservation of Torah

The Torah has always been written by hand, and passed down for thousands of years—according to Jewish tradition, ever since God gave it to Moshe in the Sinai desert. So it is logical to question how closely the version used today matches the original work. A number of factors, however, have worked together to preserve this document, and it most probably remains nearly identical to its original form.

Writing a Torah Scroll

Every synagogue must have one or more Torah scrolls for regular use. A Torah scroll is a series of panels made from the skin of a Kosher land animal, such as a cow, sewn together in a single long scroll (see Appendix for an explanation of Kosher). Both ends are wrapped around wooden posts, and then the scroll is covered in a cloth cover or wooden box. The scrolls are stored in a special *Aron Kodesh*, or Holy Cabinet, at the front of the synagogue.

The scribe who writes such a scroll must be specially trained for the task. He must use only certain varieties of ink and a quill pen. In order for a Torah scroll to be valid for public use, the scribe must work directly from an existing text, reading and copying each word exactly. No deviation in the text is tolerated. If a single letter is written incorrectly or broken by chipped ink, the entire scroll is rendered invalid and cannot be used for public readings until it has been repaired.

It goes without saying, then, that even a single misspelled word renders the entire scroll invalid. This applies even to Hebrew letters that merely indicate how a word should be pronounced, without any change in form or meaning. Even with regard to these, the scholar Maimonides writes in his Code that "this document is invalid, and it does not have the holiness of a Torah Scroll at all; rather like any copy of the Pentateuch from which children are taught" (Laws of the Torah Scroll, 1:11).

Constant Duplication

According to the Talmud and as codified throughout Jewish legal works, every individual is commanded to write or obtain a copy of the Torah. Today a Jewish person can fulfill this obligation with a printed text, but before the era of the printing press this meant an extraordinary number of copies of this one work. The volume of texts available for comparison meant that when discrepancies were discovered, it was easy to find many other copies in order to determine which reading was accurate.

Torah Readings

The reading of the Torah remains a constant feature of synagogue life. On at least three days out of every week, and often more, one will find the Torah read in any traditional synagogue. Combined with individual study, this annual repetition keeps the text of the Torah familiar to every regular synagogue attendee.

The Torah is divided into fifty-four portions: twelve in Genesis, eleven in each of Exodus and Deuteronomy, and ten in Leviticus and Numbers. One or two of these portions is read on each Sabbath throughout the year, so as to finish (and begin again) during the "Gathering on the Eighth Day," a holiday at the conclusion of Sukkos, the Jewish Festival of Booths. There are special readings designated for all Jewish holidays; those for major holidays interrupt the regular order, but the following week the regular cycle will resume from where it left off so that every portion is read each year.

Sukkos, the Festival of Booths, is mandated by the Torah itself, "In order that your generations know that I placed the Children of Israel in Booths when I took them out of Egypt, I am the Lord Your God" (Lev. 23:43). The Talmud says that the "Booths" were the Clouds of Glory that surrounded Jewish People during the Exodus.

The greater the sanctity of the day, the greater the number of people called to read from the Torah during that day's morning service. We find this in the Mishnah, the earliest written record of Jewish Oral Law:

> On Mondays, Thursdays, and Sabbath afternoons three people read; one may not subtract and one may not add to them . . . On the New Months and the Intermediate Days of Festivals four read . . . On holidays, five read; on Yom Kippur, six read. On the Sabbath seven read; we do not subtract from this number, but we may add to it. (Mishnah Megillah 3:1–2)

Although each person is called to "read" the Torah, common practice is to have a specially trained reader—the individuals called merely follow along with him. One consequence of this is to subject the Torah scroll to constant scrutiny. A well-trained reader has carefully reviewed the text in advance; many, in fact, know it by heart. As a result, they are likely to immediately spot errors in the scroll that may invalidate it, at which point the scroll must be sent back to a scribe for repair.

Preservation

Because of the level of care, precision, and re-examination of the Torah text used every time it is copied or even read, there is every indication that the text we have today remains remarkably true to the original. This is further demonstrated when we look at the existing variations in different Jewish communities.

For hundreds of years, the Jewish communities of Europe interacted only rarely with those in Northern Africa and the Middle East. Yemenite Jewry has been a separate and distinct community for at least 1,500 years, with its own prayer book and unique customs. Yet in all of these communities, there are no more than fifteen tiny variations in the Torah texts they deem authentic.

What qualifies as a variation? Many of the differences are mere spaces between words: in English, an example would be "wellbeing" in one text versus "well being" in another. Other changes are letters used merely as pronunciation guides, as mentioned earlier. The Ashkenazic community writes one word in Deuteronomy ending with a letter "aleph," while the Sephardic community ends it with a "hey." But both letters are silent at the end of a word, so both pronounce the word the same way.

It may seem impossible, but even today, after thousands of years, no community accepts a Torah text with even a single word transposed, added, or subtracted from that used by any other. No word has a different meaning, or would even be pronounced differently were the same person to read both texts—although at the same time, the various Jewish communities have developed very different dialects.

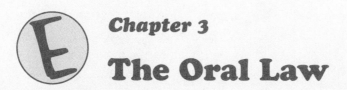

Chapter 3

The Oral Law

According to Jewish tradition, the Oral Torah is as much a part of Torah as the Written one. It, too, was given to Moshe on Mt. Sinai, and has been studied, shared, and transmitted from generation to generation for thousands of years. It enables a much deeper and more profound understanding of the Written Torah—and beyond that, most of our understanding of the Torah belief system, holidays, and daily observance comes from outside the written text.

The Missing Link

Despite its greatness and its profound spiritual teachings, it is clear that in the Written Torah alone, something is lacking. As you will see, the Torah's Commandments have a profound effect upon the daily life of one who observes them. From arising in the morning until going to bed at night, the teachings and practices of the Torah have a constant impact on the life of the Torah-observant individual. All the details necessary for following a system of this nature, even in one era, could not be contained in just five short books.

Throughout the Torah, you find hints that something has been left out. Many times it refers in passing to a commandment or instruction, but never fills in the details. At other times, two passages apparently contradict each other. And in some cases, even the meaning of the words cannot be understood except with the help of a teacher.

Words Without Vowels

Our Rabbis taught: there was a non-Jew who came in front of Shammai, and asked "how many Torahs do you have?" And he answered him, "Two: the Written Torah, and the Oral Torah."

The Non-Jew said, "concerning the Written, I believe you, but concerning the Oral, I do not believe you. Convert me on condition that you will teach me the Written Torah." Shammai rebuked him and pushed him out with anger.

He came to Hillel, and he converted him. On the first day he taught him the Hebrew alphabet: *Aleph, Bais, Gimmel, Dalet*; but on the next day he reversed the order. The non-Jew protested, "but yesterday you did not teach it to me like this!" Hillel said, "so were you not relying upon me? Concerning the Oral Torah also, rely upon me." (Talmud Shabbos 31a)

Hebrew is an unusual language, in that it was originally written without vowels—the vowel markings are a relatively modern invention. Torah scrolls are always written by hand, without vowels. Sometimes the lack of these markings makes it impossible to accurately know the meaning of the text without someone to teach you the correct pronunciation.

For example, in three places (Exodus 23:19 and 34:26, Deuteronomy 14:21) the Torah says that "you shall not cook a kid in its mother's milk." Yet the word for milk is spelled precisely the same as the word for animal fats, which are entirely prohibited, as in "all the fats of an ox, sheep or goat you may not eat" (Lev. 7:23). We only know that dairy consumption isn't prohibited, while fats are only prohibited when served with the meat of that animal's child, because someone explained the words to us.

FACT

Not having vowels is often not a problem. n mst css, t s nt ncssr t hv vwls t ndrstnd th sntnc! Today, both Rabbinic texts and Modern Hebrew books and newspapers are usually printed without vowels. Prayer books, as well as study versions of the Torah and other Biblical works, are the exceptions—they almost always have vowels, at least for the text if not the commentaries.

Was God Confused?

The Torah contains a number of passages that beg further explanation. The quotation above that prohibits consuming milk and meat together is found, as mentioned, three times in the Torah. One time should be enough, leaving us wondering what the Torah intended to teach us by repeating itself.

At other times, passages in the Torah appear to flatly contradict each other. Exodus 34:18 reads, "The holiday of *Matzos* (unleavened bread) you shall guard, for seven days you shall eat *Matzos* as I have Commanded you . . ." Yet in Deuteronomy 16:8 we are told, "For six days shall you eat *Matzos*, and on the seventh day it shall be a gathering . . ." On the surface, it certainly appears that if one of these is correct, the other must be mistaken.

In Numbers 15:37–38, the Israelites are instructed to "make fringes on the corners of their garments, throughout their generations, and to put onto the fringes at the corner a twist of blue wool." Yet Deuteronomy 22:11 says, "You shall not wear a forbidden combination, wool and flax together."

The Torah merely says that the combination is prohibited, implying that it is possible to wear a shirt made of flax. But the verses in Numbers, to the contrary, appear to require a twist of wool at the corners of every garment.

Someone with a flaxen shirt should either be failing to observe the obligation of "making fringes . . . [with] a twist of blue wool," or, alternatively, observing that rule and in so doing violating the prohibition of "a forbidden combination."

The next verse in Deuteronomy, 22:12, says, "You shall make tassels at the four corners of your clothing, with which you cover yourself"—which apparently refers back to the fringes in Numbers. This simply makes the contradiction more obvious.

ALERT!

This is hardly an exhaustive list of the contradictory and confusing passages found in the Torah. You will probably come across others in your studies. It is important to remember that you are on extremely well-traveled ground, and there's probably a commentary, written many centuries ago, that can provide you with a good answer.

There are also references to instructions that were never given. In Deuteronomy 12:21, God says that animals must be slaughtered "as I have Commanded you" before being eaten. Yet there is no such instruction anywhere in the Torah explaining how an animal should be killed.

Further Instructions Required

The case of slaughtering is exceptional only because it clearly refers to instructions not found in the text. There are countless examples of Commandments in the Torah where further instructions are obviously needed, yet were never given in the Five Books themselves.

"For six days work shall be done, and on the seventh day it is a Holy Sabbath to God. All who do work on the Sabbath day shall surely die" (Exod. 31:15). Clearly, working on the Sabbath is no minor sin—yet there's no definition of "work" provided. Is moving a piano called work? If using a computer is called work, does that even apply to games? If a Rabbi teaches Torah for a living, why is he allowed to give sermons on the Sabbath?

Clearly, something more is required in order for "observance" of Torah to be possible—an Oral Law, another body of material that fills in all of the missing details.

FACT

The Karaites, a group dating back to the ninth century c.e., rejected the Oral Law. Since the Torah says, "Fire shall not pass throughout your homes on the Sabbath day" (Exod. 35:3), they extinguish all fires before the Sabbath. The Oral Law, however, specifies that lighting, moving, and extinguishing fire is prohibited, but it's OK to leave the heat on.

Why Not Write It Down?

So let's say that at this point, you see that there is a lot missing from the Written Torah. You see that all these details are missing, and you're willing to accept the idea that there must've been something else to go along with it—something that explains the details and helps people understand what they are actually supposed to do.

At this point, your next question should be: Why not write it down? There are obvious benefits to having a written record, one that is more detailed than what we find in the Written Torah. So why depend upon oral transmission of that detail, which is of course not going to be perfect? There are several reasons why, in this case, having an Oral Torah was actually the ideal.

Writing Isn't Error-Free

While it is true that there can be errors with an oral transmission, the truth is that writing leaves room for even greater levels of misunderstanding. When going over a subject in oral discussion, it is easy to detect errors and go back and correct them. If you have ever carried on a discussion by e-mail or other written correspondence and then finally used the telephone or a face-to-face meeting to resolve confusion over various issues, then you have already seen for yourself how much more effective oral communication can be.

For further proof, one need only look at what happened when finally, as you will read later on in Chapter 8, it became necessary to write down the Oral Law to prevent its being lost. First the Sages wrote down the Mishnah, a brief catalog of laws meant to remind everyone of what they needed to know. Over the ensuing centuries, various issues of confusion came to light, and extensive clarifications were needed, eventually resulting in the Babylonian and Jerusalem Talmuds. Later on, additional commentaries were written to clarify the Talmud's intent, and many of these commentaries disagree about particulars. This process has continued until this very day.

Speaking the Language of the Day

Throughout history, human circumstances have changed—yet the Torah is Eternal. Its lessons apply in every era. But the Oral Law would certainly be easier to understand if all of its discussions were couched in today's language.

The Talmud talks about an ox goring a cow. But we could certainly relate much more quickly to a discussion about an automobile accident, or your neighbor's Doberman chasing your cat up a tree. Instead of just discussing what day laborers are allowed to eat while on the job, we could talk about using office supplies and doing personal e-mails. Instead of bloodletting and healing baths, we need to relate to organ donation, in vitro fertilization, and cloning.

A Walking Torah Scroll

God Commanded the Jewish People to study the Torah constantly. "The words of this Torah shall not be lost from your mouths, and you shall delve into it day and night" (Joshua 1:8). Yet people have other activities. They move around, they work at tasks—they cannot constantly be reading from texts.

By according full status to the Oral Torah on par with the Written, a person can be involved in Torah study even while doing other things. Today one can drive while listening to classes, discuss Torah concepts while walking, and think about Torah while working around the house.

In the final analysis, keeping an Oral Torah is crucial to the very goal of Torah itself: to transform a person. The ideal for the Jewish nation is to be a walking repository of Torah ethics and knowledge, and for men this translates into the deepest possible understanding of the Torah's logic and the methods for derivation of Torah Law.

Dissecting the Torah

If it is true that there is an Oral Law, and it is somehow related to the Written Torah, you should wonder how the two are related. To the Sages, the Torah is almost like a letter between spies—although the words and sentences have clear meaning all by themselves, many additional messages lie beneath the surface, coded into the text. The messages overlap each other, so the decoding process is often very complex.

Whenever you find two verses that appear to contradict each other, or a passage of laws that seems too vague to be understood correctly, you can be certain that the Sages of the Talmud took those verses apart, juxtaposed them against others, and derived a host of additional lessons that seem obvious only in retrospect. In the commentaries, you will discover that no verse is left without notes to explain and elucidate what the Torah is telling us therein.

Thirteen Principles of Hermeneutics

"Hermeneutics" is the theory and methodology by which texts are interpreted, especially Scripture. Rabbi Yishmael, one of the Sages of the Mishnah, provides a list of thirteen rules for Torah Hermeneutics:

1. Inference from a lenient case to a more grave one
2. A received tradition that draws a connection between the use of the same word in a new context
3. A general principle built upon one verse, or upon two verses
4. A generalization followed by a specific instance
5. A specific instance followed by a generalization
6. A generalization, followed by a specific instance, followed by another generalization—in which case one can only apply a rule to things similar to the specific

7. A generalization that requires specific detail, or a specific that requires generalization

8. Something that was included in a general rule and was then singled out for instruction; is not intended to teach merely about itself, but to serve as an example

9. Something that was included in a general rule and was then singled out to apply a condition similar to the general rule; was singled out in order to be lenient and not to be more strict

10. Something that was included in a general rule and was then singled out to apply a condition dissimilar from the general rule; could be singled out to be more lenient and/or to be more strict

11. Something that was included in a general rule but was then singled out and treated as a new case; cannot be returned into the general rule until a verse does so explicitly

12. Something understood from its context, and something understood from the following passage

13. Two verses that contradict each other, until a third verse comes and reconciles them

Admittedly, reading this list is probably more confusing than enlightening, at least at first. These are the complex rules that decode the multilayered messages of the Torah. Examples should make the rules and their usage more clear, but one of the most important lessons is, "Don't try this at home!" The Sages had an enyclopedic knowledge of every verse of the Jewish Bible, and thus knew how and when to apply each principle.

Some Applications

The first rule is to infer from a lenient case to a more grave one. It's only logical that if a lenient situation has a particular stringency, then a more stringent situation should have that same stricture. For example, if a person must pay damages when his animal eats someone else's grain—even though it intended no harm—it is only logical that the owner must pay when his animal was deliberately destructive (Talmud Bava Kama 4a).

The second rule, by comparison, operates not from simple logic, but when there is a received tradition (going all the way back to Sinai) that the use of two similar words in two contexts is intended to connect the two. In Numbers 28:2, God says that the daily offering should be brought "in its proper time" (*b'moado*), which is understood to mean even on the Sabbath or Festivals. So the same word "b'moado" in the context of the Passover offering (Num. 9:2) is used to teach that it, too, should be brought even on the Sabbath.

The sixth rule is more complex—it concerns a general rule followed by a specification, which is then followed by another generalization. In discussing a special fine for stealing, the Torah says "for any matter of wrongdoing," which is very general. Then it specifies "for an ox, donkey, sheep or garment" but then appends another generalization, "for any lost thing" (Exod. 22:8). In this case, the sixth rule tells us to include everything that is similar to the specific—since animals and garments are both movable property, this law is applied any time that someone steals movable property, but not when someone steals real estate (which doesn't move) or contracts (which lack intrinsic value).

A final example: The twelfth rule holds that when one comes across a passage of Torah that is difficult to understand, it may be understood in context. For example, one of the Ten Commandments says, "Thou Shalt Not Steal." Now, is this talking about stealing money, property, or a person? If you look at the previous and following verses, they say "Thou Shalt Not Kill" and "Thou Shalt Not Commit Adultery." Both of these are, according to the Torah, capital crimes. So what sort of theft fits that context? The answer is that theft of a person—i.e., kidnapping—is a capital crime, and therefore must be the variety of theft discussed here.

Laws Given to Moshe, from Sinai

Despite all of the above, there is a rare class of laws that are simply part of the oral transmission of Torah, laws that cannot be found in any verse of the Written Torah. These are called "Laws Given to Moshe, from Sinai." For example, the Torah never says that certain holy texts must be written in black ink on a prepared animal skin, yet there is a received tradition that this is so.

So in reality, the Torah comprises three varieties of laws:

1. Those that are explicit in the Torah
2. Those that can be derived using the rules of hermeneutics
3. Those given to Moshe, from Sinai

Maimonides points out that whereas two courts can disagree about the application of the laws of hermeneutics, there can be no conflict about that which is explicit in black and white, or that which is a received tradition. So everywhere one finds an argument, it always has to do with the application of the rules of hermeneutics in the most logical fashion.

Arguments in Torah Law

You may have heard of the Talmud before, even before reading Chapter 8 in this book. In that case, you've probably heard that this massive work is essentially filled with arguments. And it is encyclopedic in size and scope, covering most areas of Jewish law. So isn't it obvious that the Rabbis really weren't sure about what the Law was originally? Isn't it all a fabricated collection of individual opinions?

There is a relatively straightforward fallacy in this line of reasoning. While it is true that the Talmud is filled with arguments, they occur only when one gets down to the "details of the details." There are no arguments about the basics of Jewish belief or Jewish law, or even about the basics of their implementation.

The Art of Argument

Imagine an art instructor giving three students a photograph of a field and a forest, with mountains in the background, and asking them to paint the scene. Two of the students depict a field and a forest, complete with the mountains in the background. The third, however, paints an imaginary tank battle, which of course looks nothing like the scene that they were instructed to draw.

Faced with a failing grade, the third student complains when he hears that the other two were both commended for their work. He points out that one of the other two paintings is inaccurate as well: In the second student's work, the wind seems to be coming from the South, while in the photograph the wind is coming from the West!

The failing student is correct that the second student made an error. The first student's painting is accurate with regard to this detail, whereas the second's is not. But it is obvious that the art instructor's tolerance for this minor slip does not imply that a student can paint whatever he or she desires and expect to pass the course.

What Are They Arguing About?

With this analogy in mind, we can take another look at the type of arguments found in the Talmud. Is it true that everything is a matter of opinion, that the scenes are as different as a field of trees versus a tank battle? Or does everyone agree on almost everything, save which way the wind was blowing?

Let's look at what is considered to be one of the greatest arguments in the Talmud: whether something can be prohibited because of an undesired effect. This concerns, for example, a person dragging a bench across a lawn on Saturday afternoon, when the bench legs might create furrows while being dragged. Since the person doesn't want the furrows—he simply wants the bench on the other side of the lawn—Rebbe Shimon says yes, he may drag the bench, but Rebbe Yehudah says no.

There are many other examples when the unintended effect of doing something might be prohibited, but what the person actually wants to do—in this case, moving the bench from point A to point B—is absolutely fine. Whether or not a person is allowed to do this is truly one of the most far-reaching arguments in the entire Talmud.

Unintended effects come up all the time. As another example, the Torah prohibits wearing linen and wool together. So if a salesman wants to show off garments of both types, can he put them on if his intention is to show his wares rather than to cover his body? That's another case of the same underlying argument.

So the question that must be answered is: Does this argument involve changing the entire picture, or merely what the tips of the trees look like? To answer that, let's look at some of the things the Rabbis agree about:

- There is a God.
- God created the world.
- God created human beings.
- God took the Israelites out of Egypt.
- God gave the Torah to Moshe (Moses) at Mt. Sinai.
- God gave the Written Law during the forty years in the Sinai desert.
- God gave an Oral Law along with the written.
- The day of rest begins on Friday at sundown and ends Saturday at sundown.
- "Creative labor" is determined from the work required to build the Tabernacle.
- Creative labor is prohibited on the Sabbath.
- There are thirty-nine categories of prohibited creative labor.
- One of those thirty-nine categories is creating a furrow suitable for planting.
- It is prohibited to *intentionally* create a furrow not only with a plow, but even with a bench.

To return to our analogy, all the Rabbis of the Talmud certainly agree upon the same basic picture. They even agree where the trees are! This "great" Talmudic argument is truly analogous to the direction the wind is blowing. This argument actually reinforces the solidity of the core beliefs of the Oral Law—for one thing is for certain: were there any argument at all about anything more fundamental, the Talmud would certainly have recorded that argument, and in great detail.

Chapter 4

 Kabbalah, Mysticism, and Meaning

Why are we here? What is the Purpose of Creation? Is there a World to Come, and how do we get there? These are but a few of the basic questions that are answered in the Talmud, the Medrash, the *Zohar*, and other books of Jewish thought. The Judaism of the Torah is both profound and all-encompassing, touching upon every area of life. While it is impossible to summarize an entire way of life in just a few thousand words, this chapter should help you understand several basic elements of the Torah's philosophy and worldview.

Everything Has a Purpose

As mentioned in Chapter 2, the Medrash teaches that God "looked at the Torah and created the world." This means that everything in the world has a spiritual purpose. If the mosquito did not have a reason to exist derived from the Torah, then there would be no mosquitoes.

Of course, this does not mean that we can immediately understand the purpose of everything. Only in recent years have biologists begun to understand the complex balance of animal and plant life that forms an ecosystem, and to realize how the absence of even one species can disrupt all forms of life in the region.

Humans Are Takers

Within all ecosystems and food chains, there is a constant balance of give-and-take. Vegetables and animals exchange oxygen and carbon dioxide. Animals that eat vegetables are consumed, along with animals that eat insects, by other animals. When these animals die, they are eaten by yet other animals—and by insects that end up as food.

Human beings are an exception to the rule. We take, but we do not give back. We consume everything—plants, land animals, birds, fish, even insects. We encourage the growth of life by cultivating crops and raising animals, but we do this to meet our own physical or emotional needs—we do not contribute our own selves back into the ecosystem. Even in death, many utilize cremation, enbalming, or burial in mausoleums, tombs, or permanent caskets.

ALERT!

The Torah says that the world was created to benefit man, so you don't have to "apologize" for consuming the world's natural resources. However, it's still appropriate to be responsible stewards of the world and its blessings.

Top of the Heap

The story is told of a group of philosophers who came together to analyze all forms of life in the world and to determine the purpose of each one. After many months of study, they came to the surprising conclusion that everything exists for the benefit of Man. All of the vegetation, the animals, and the inanimate objects form systems that help us to live out our lives.

Having reached this determination, the philosophers made a feast to celebrate having achieved such a complete understanding of our world, and their realization that everything exists for the benefit of Man. One member of the group, however, turned their delight into confusion with one simple question: What is the purpose of Man?

Who Is Happy in This World?

The Torah says that God exists, God is both good and all-powerful, and He wants the best for mankind. But in order for all of these things to be true, it must also be true that this world is not all there is.

God wants good things for human beings, says the Torah. But who has a truly peaceful and joyous life in this world, without pain and sorrow? Do we see that good is rewarded, and evil is punished? On the contrary, all too often it looks like a world where "good guys finish last." As the Psalmist wrote, "The days of our lives are seventy years, and with strength eighty years, and their pride is toil and deception" (Ps. 90:10).

If this world were the end of the story, it wouldn't even make sense for human beings to be the top of the heap, the ones created "in the image of God." Rabbi Gershon Weiss of the Yeshiva of Staten Island asked the following deceptively simple question: "Who do you think is happier: you or Bessie the Cow?" When you think about it, it's pretty obvious that Bessie has you beat, because her instincts and drives are far more in tune with what she needs to be happy.

The Sages say that "jealousy, lust and the desire for honor remove a person from the world" (Chapters of the Fathers 4:21). These instinctive human traits not only conspire to make us unhappy, but they actually run counter to our most basic instinct: survival. If we follow our desires, we often make ourselves worse off in the end. Bessie has no such problems, lives in accordance with her instincts, and is satisfied with her life.

Jealousy

How much better off would we be if we never saw what anyone else had? If all we had to worry about was our own property, we'd be fine. But when your neighbor drives up in his new car, you want a new car. When your friend starts dating the most popular guy or girl in school, you can't stand being "single."

A ten-year-old car may run fine, but the owner wants a newer car. The guy with a car from two years ago wants a brand-new model. The guy with the brand-new model wishes he could have a foreign sports car like his neighbor. The neighbor wishes he had a yacht like his boss. The boss wishes he had a mansion like his golf buddy . . .

Meanwhile, the guy with the mansion is going insane, because he found out that money really doesn't buy happiness. Trying to make the *Forbes* list of wealthiest entrepreneurs, people take ridiculous risks with their money and their health, and jeopardize their very survival.

ALERT!

There's one sort of jealousy the Talmud tolerates: jealousy for Torah. "The jealousy of scribes increases wisdom," it says. If no one has a brand new car, no one is jealous—and everyone is happy. But there should always be more Torah, and Torah makes people happier.

Bessie never has these problems. She wants an ample supply of grass and a warm bed. It doesn't bother her that the cow on the other side of the fence has greener grass and pillows in a climate-controlled barn.

Lust

Bessie has a mating season, which only starts when she's old enough to handle raising a calf. She goes into heat, a bull finds her, they do what they need to do, and the game is over.

Human beings, on the other hand, are interested in reproduction—or, at least, the *act* of reproduction—long before it's good for them, and then it never ends. We want more than one partner: We fall in love, then we fall out of love and we move on—or else we seek out partners without any deeper feelings for them at all.

QUESTION?

What's this about Kosher sex?
The Torah does not call for celibacy—on the contrary, it says, "Be Fruitful and Multiply," and calls marriage the ideal, saying "It is not good for Man to be alone." Between husband and wife, relations are not only appropriate (Kosher), but one of a husband's obligations to his wife.

Honor

The desire to be honored is often related to jealousy, but is nonetheless not the same thing. You can look for honors that no one else has, and you can demand respect from your spouse or children. These have nothing to do with jealousy, but they can be just as unhealthy.

Bessie doesn't run around looking for respect—but human beings do. Humans will commit suicide rather than face public dishonor and humiliation. Wars are fought and soldiers die for the sake of honor. You don't see animals abuse and sacrifice their bodies and minds in the elusive search for honor and glory.

These are only a few of the disadvantages that we humans have. Animals don't seem to become ill as often as human beings. They don't have the same problems humans do making peace with each other, and so on. As the great philosopher Rabbi Moshe Chaim Luzzatto remarked, "Even one in a thousand doesn't find that the world has provided him with pleasure upon pleasure and true serenity, and even he, should he reach the age of 100, has already passed and is nullified from the world."

The Soul

What sets human beings apart is that we, unlike animals, have souls. The soul is that within us that is attracted to the intangible. We possess within us a desire for spiritual heights, for acts of dedication and altruism, and for an attachment to the Divine—desires that no animal would understand. And we also have base, materialistic desires that no animal must face.

In Jewish philosophy, the soul is far greater than the physical shell that we can perceive. The body is to the soul as a shoe is to the body—a mere covering, a physical container that, at best, holds within it a tiny fraction of the whole.

The Divine soul within us is what gives us the ability to reason and to philosophize, and to accomplish things that no animal could imagine. At the same time, it is our souls that are dissatisfied with the mere physical world around us, and that search for meaning.

Rabbi Luzzato compared the soul in this world to a daughter of the royal family who has married a simple villager. He can bring her the best that his village has to offer, but it means nothing to her—she is a princess, used to fine jewelry, furnishings, clothing, and foods that reach far beyond what the villager could hope to provide.

In the Chapters of the Fathers 4:22 it says, "Against your will you are created, and against your will you are born." This, says Rabbi Luzzato, is because the soul does not love this world at all—in fact, it is repulsed by it.

The World to Come

What the soul desires is a level of spiritual pleasure that cannot even be found in this world. The ultimate purpose for which we were created is, in Rabbi Luzzato's words, "to rejoice in God and to derive pleasure from the radiance of the Divine Presence, for this is the true joy and the greatest pleasure that can be found. And the place where this pleasure can truly be found is in the World to Come."

The World to Come is the soul's natural habitat. There, the soul is truly at home. It is the palace where the princess can find all the fine things to which she is accustomed.

In addition, the soul in the World to Come doesn't find itself pulled in two directions by contradictory instincts. There are no physical desires, nothing to draw the soul away from the spiritual. Everything is truly good, and the only desire is for good.

So the World to Come is the ultimate goal. We can experience a level of spiritual joy in the next world that is beyond imagination. "One hour of spiritual bliss in the World to Come is greater than the entire life in this world" (Chapters of the Fathers 4:17).

The World Is Like a Corridor

After reading all of that, you may be wondering: If the World to Come is so great, why does God make us suffer with this world first? Couldn't He simply skip to the good parts, and let us enjoy ourselves?

Can't We Be Angels?

The truth is that this is essentially what the angels experience. They don't have all the pains of physical existence, and they have no contradictory or evil desires or instincts. Even the Angel of Death, says the Torah, is simply doing the will of God.

But in Jewish mysticism, human beings are higher than angels. Even the spiritual universe was created for the sake of humans. The Torah was given to humans, not angels. Obviously, there must be some reason why we need to experience this world before proceeding to the next.

Which $100 Is More Valuable?

Imagine that you meet a stranger on the street and she gives you $100. She says, "Here, I don't need this money—go spend it on anything you want."

First of all, you'll be worried that something is wrong: the money is counterfeit, you are being set up for something, or the woman busy handing her money away is simply insane. Only when you know it is safe to really spend it will you be able to do so, and even then you'll probably be nervous.

But now imagine that the same stranger gives you a very difficult task to accomplish, and offers you $100 to do it. With serious effort you're able to do the job, and she pays you—with the very same bill that she simply handed to you in the first situation.

Now, of course, you aren't worried about spending the money at all. You don't worry every time you get paid that you are getting counterfeit currency, and you certainly don't think the person who paid you is mentally unstable. The work that you did was obviously something that the stranger was willing to pay $100 to have done, and since you were the one who did it, you got the $100.

But in addition, this $100 bill is worth much more to you than the first one. You *earned* this money. She didn't simply drop it into your lap—you had to sacrifice time and energy to get the money, and so you know that to you, this $100 was worth the effort. Getting something for nothing simply isn't as valuable.

Earning the Reward

In Jewish thought, spiritual satisfaction works the same way. Yes, you could enjoy closeness to the Divine Presence simply because God lets you experience it, but the closeness is much more valuable if you earn it.

So the Sages say that this world is the place where we get ready. "Today is for performing, and tomorrow is for receiving their reward."

The Chapters of the Fathers says, "This world is like an entryway leading into the World to Come. Prepare yourself in the entryway, so that you may enter the banquet hall" (4:16). This world provides us with an opportunity to earn our place, rather than simply having good handed to us.

This is why we experience so many contradictory instincts in this world—in order to earn reward for making the right choices. If a person follows his base desires, warns Rabbi Luzzato, then he distances himself from true good. Good and evil battle within a person throughout his or her life. "For everything in the world, be it good or bad, everything is a test for man."

In the world of Jewish mysticism, every person finds within him- or herself two warring forces: the *Yetzer HaTov* and the *Yetzer HaRa*, Good and Evil Inclinations. You've probably seen those images of a person standing with an angel and devil hovering over each shoulder whispering in each ear—according to Torah, that's not far from the truth. The Good Inclination wants you to do what benefits your soul, while the Evil Inclination wants to get worldly pleasure. A person is capable of training even his or her Evil Inclination to serve God—for example, have it thinking, "Learn more Torah, so everyone will respect you!"

"And if he shall be a valiant warrior," says Rabbi Luzzato, "victorious in this war that surrounds him on all sides, then he shall be the complete man who merits to cleave to his Creator, and proceed from the entryway into the palace to experience the light of life. And in accordance with the level to which he conquered his desires and lusts and distanced himself from those things that distance him from good and strove to cleave to Him—so shall he find Him and rejoice in Him."

The Meaning of Life

Have you ever wondered what we are doing here, why we exist, and what we are supposed to accomplish? From the preceding sections, the Torah's answer to these great existential mysteries becomes clear. We exist, says the Torah, in order to take advantages of the opportunities we have in this world to improve ourselves, improve the world, and attach ourselves to the Divine.

The Goal

In his introduction to the Chapters of the Fathers, Maimonides describes our goal in life as "attaining the knowledge of God, as far as it is possible for any human being to know Him. All of man's actions and words, whether at work or at leisure, should be aimed at this goal so that no action is senseless and pointless."

Rabbi Luzzato writes that our goal is "to rejoice in God and to derive pleasure from the radiance of the Divine Presence," but describes the place for this level of attachment as the World to Come:

> But the path to get to our desired destination is via this world… and the methodologies which bring a person closer to this goal are the Commandments which the Holy One, Blessed be He, Commanded upon us.

And the place for performance of the Commandments is only this world. For this reason a person is placed first into this world, in order that by way of the methods which are available to him here, he can reach the place prepared for him, which is the World to Come. (Path of the Just, Ch. 1)

These two definitions are in actuality quite similar. The better we know God through our efforts in this world, the better we will be able to rejoice in God in the next. Performance of the Commandments brings a person to knowledge of the Divine through concrete action, and Torah study—which is direct attainment of knowledge of the Divine—is the greatest of the Commandments.

Following the Commandments

According to Jewish thought, the Torah is filled with Commandments—not just the famous Ten, but a total of 613. Without understanding the Torah's perspective on the world and our goals within it, it is easy to imagine that 613 Commandments add up to a huge mountain of restrictions or burdens. The Torah, on the other hand, understands them as 613 opportunities, methods through which the goal of attachment to the Divine can be attained.

ALERT!

The "Ten Commandments" are so named only by non-Jewish sources. In Hebrew they are referred to as the *Aseres HaDibros*, the Ten Declarations, and there are actually fourteen or fifteen distinct Commandments found therein.

There is an old parable used to describe a life under the "yoke of Torah." There was once a merchant who asked a friend to bring a package for him from another city. Since the package contained diamonds, it was both extremely valuable and extremely small.

On the day the package was due to arrive, he looked out his window, and saw his friend approaching—struggling under a tremendous burden. He rushed out the door to his friend, yelling "You must have the wrong package! My package is light, and easy to carry!"

This, explain the Sages, is how Jewish philosophy looks at observing the Commandments. It is supposed to be easy, enjoyable, and tremendously satisfying. If a person is struggling under a burden, something is wrong!

Does God Need My Prayers?

When looking at the Commandments, you may wonder: Does God really care if I observe this or don't do that? Why would an all-powerful God be hurt if I ate a cheeseburger?

In Jewish thought, however, the Commandments don't exist to address what God needs. God is complete, and doesn't need our prayers, study, or observance at all. Instead, the Commandments exist to address what *we* need. And in this regard, God is like any parent who wants to see his or her children succeed.

Connecting the Dots

While observance of the 613 Commandments is a crucial part of Jewish philosophy, this is not enough to complete the picture. As described above, the Commandments are to help a person travel a path to Godliness. As the Torah says, "You shall be Holy, for I, the Lord your God, am Holy" (Lev. 19:2).

It's possible to fulfill the technical details of all the Commandments and yet, by trying to get by with just the minimum, manage to be an unkind or even vulgar individual. This is clearly not what the Torah has in mind.

You probably remember connecting the dots in order to create a picture when you were a child. Without necessarily understanding what you were going to accomplish, you drew lines from one number to the next. Before you knew it, you had a picture of a rabbit, a bicycle, or a toy. Perhaps you also tried to see what would happen if you connected the dots out of order. You connected sixteen to seven, just to see what would happen—and instead of a pretty picture, you ended up with a mess.

In a similar vein, it's not enough to say that you intend to observe the 613 Commandments. You have to "connect the dots" in the right order. Let the instructions guide you, and they can transform you into a far more spiritual individual.

Chapter 5

Maimonides' Thirteen Principles

Every religion has its credo, a set of core beliefs that distinguish that faith from others. One of the clearest definitions of the Torah Credo—and certainly the most commonly known and accepted—is that of Rabbi Moshe Maimonides. By studying his Thirteen Principles of the Jewish Faith, you will acquire a basic understanding of what a follower of Torah is expected to believe.

The Torah Credo

The Commentary on the Mishnah was the first major work of Rabbi Moshe ben Maimon (1135–1204 c.e.), about whom you will learn more later in this book. He is called "the *Rambam*" by most Jewish scholars from the acronym of his name, while others in the English-speaking world call him "Maimonides" after his father.

He wrote his Commentary on the Mishnah in Arabic—the common language of Mediterranean Jewry in his day—in order to make his work accessible to the common man. And when he came to the Mishnah in Tractate Sanhedrin (about which you will learn more in Chapters 8 and 9) that hints to several core beliefs of Judaism, he added a major section to his work in order to dispel several common mistakes, and then to provide what became known as his Thirteen Principles of the Jewish Faith.

Required Fundamentals of Faith

According to Maimonides, each and every Principle is a prerequisite for authentic Jewish belief. He writes that these are the central points, the foundations of the Torah faith. So it is clear that he intended to include only the most critical beliefs, setting aside those that, while important, were not part of the core definition of Judaism.

Are All Truly Mandatory?

Other early authorities questioned the inclusion of some of these points as core beliefs, or their division into thirteen distinct parts. As you read, you will probably notice that some of the Principles could be combined by, for example, requiring belief in an "Eternal, Unified, Non-Corporeal God" instead of stating four separate principles.

Others digested the basic requirements of the Torah faith to as few as three core beliefs—combining some and excluding those that were deemed not so critical as to exclude anyone who denied them from the realm of the faithful.

It is important to emphasize that everyone agreed that these were all Torah beliefs. No Rabbi said that any of Maimonides' Principles were wrong. What they argued about was merely whether a person who didn't believe one or another of these points could still be considered a believer in Torah Judaism.

Does every Jew follow these Principles today?
Although the traditionally observant community follows the Thirteen Principles, the modern, liberal movements do not accept the view of Maimonides and adopt beliefs contrary to many of the Principles. Many who self-identify as Jews have probably not considered the Principles as carefully as you shall by the time you complete this chapter!

Studied for Seven Centuries

Today, the Thirteen Principles may be found in all traditional Jewish prayer books in two forms. An abbreviated definition of each Principle is found at the end of the morning service, which many pious Jews recite each day. In addition, the Principles were condensed into a thirteen-line song by Rabbi Daniel bar Yehudah of Rome in the early fourteenth century C.E. This too is found in traditional prayer books worldwide, and is sung in most synagogues—especially on the Sabbath and major holidays. While the poetry is lost in translation, the song provides us with a brief summary of the Thirteen Principles, which will be discussed in greater detail in this chapter.

1. Great is the living God, and praised;
   He exists, and there is no time [limit] to His existence.
2. He is One, and there is no Oneness like His;
   Hidden, and there is no end to His unity.
3. He has no image of a body, and is non-corporeal;
   One cannot make comparison to His holiness.
4. He preceded all things that were created;
   He is first, and without beginning.
5. Behold, He is master of the world to all that is formed,
   Displaying His greatness and His majesty.

6. The bounty of His prophecy he bestows
   Upon men of His choice and glory.
7. There will not arise in Israel another like Moshe,
   A prophet who saw His image.
8. God gave a true Torah to His nation,
   By the hand of His prophet, the trusted of His house.
9. God will not switch nor replace His Law,
   Forever, for anything else.
10. He sees, and knows our secrets;
    He sees to the end of a thing at its beginning.
11. He grants kindness to a person in accordance with his deeds,
    He gives evil to the wicked, in accordance with his wickedness.
12. He will send our Messiah at the End of Days,
    To redeem those who await His final salvation.
13. God will revive the dead in His great compassion,
    Blessed be His praised Name forever and ever.

The Nature of God

What do you imagine when you think of God? You may think of God as one who originally created the world but who has since left it to run on its own. Some even define God as the product of our collective consciousness.

If the Torah is a book about God and the world He created, you would probably expect it to define God. In many respects, though, the Torah assumes rather than states this definition. Maimonides digests the Torah's understanding of God down to four fundamental points—the first four of his thirteen fundamentals.

1. There Exists a Complete Being

The Rambam writes, "The first fundamental is to believe in the existence of the Creator, Blessed be He—and this [belief] is that there is a Complete Being." He goes on to explain that this one Being is complete and perfect in every way, in every facet of what it means to exist. Maimonides doesn't say God, but rather "Complete Being"—because this more clearly expresses the image of God he wishes to convey.

What he means is not merely that God's existence is complete and absolute, but that this is one of the differences between the Creator and all that He Created. "All created things find the establishment of their existence in Him, and their establishment is from Him."

In his Code of Law, Maimonides refers to God as the "First Being," emphasizing a different facet of the same understanding of God: He who existed before anything else, and who Created everything else.

Maimonides says that if we were to imagine the absence of God, then everything else would also disappear, and nothing would remain. The converse, however, is not true: were all else to vanish, God would still exist.

The Rambam directs you to the words of the Prophet *Yirmiyah* (Jer. 10:10): "The Lord, God, is Real." Nothing else, says Maimonides, is real in the sense that God is.

2. God's Unity Is Absolute

When you speak about one single person, you will say "him" or "her" instead of "them." But the truth is that a person can be divided, subdivided, and subdivided again: the head versus the arms, the brain versus the eyes, the cerebellum versus the temporal lobe, and so on right down to the subatomic level.

This is not the nature of God. It is not enough to say that God is not a member of a pair or a group. God is both infinite and continuous, a Unity like no other. This is what the Torah means when it says, "Hear O Israel, the Lord our God, the Lord is One" (Deut. 6:4).

At the beginning of his legal code (Foundations of Torah 2:10), Maimonides discusses the Oneness of God at the metaphysical level. As a human being, you and what you know are not the same; you are not defined by what you know. If you learn something, or forget something you knew yesterday, you are still the same person. Similarly, you and your life are things that you can consider separately. But God, on the other hand, truly is the All-Knowing and the Eternal: He, His knowledge, and His existence are all one thing. God would not be God if He did not know everything or were not eternal—they are all part of His Unity.

Of course, the Unity of God precludes the belief in multiple deities. In order for there to be "room" for more than one god, each would have to be limited, bounded in some way. The God of the Torah is entirely without boundary or limitation.

3. God Is Non-Corporeal

God has no body, physical attributes, or physical limitations. God can be in two places at once, and is restrained by no force, even by time.

If you read the Bible, however, you will find many instances where we refer to God in anthropornorphic terms—the hand of God, God's throne, and other such physical references appear frequently. These are only intended as metaphors, designed to help us understand God's attributes. This is why the Talmud says (Brachos 31b), "The Torah speaks in the language of man."

4. God Is Eternal

The Fourth Principle teaches that God is without beginning and without end—in fact, God created time. Nothing else is eternal and above time as He is.

This means that from God's perspective, time is completely irrelevant. God is creating the world, teaching Moshe the Torah, watching you read this book, and seeing the coming of the *Moshiach* (Messiah), all at the same "moment."

In his Guide for the Perplexed, Maimonides elaborates on this concept:

> Even time itself is among the things created by God. Time depends upon motion. In order for motion to exist, we must have things that move. And all things were created by God. (Guide for the Perplexed 2:13)

FACT

Maimonides stated a relationship between matter and time 700 years before Einstein and his theory of relativity. Today, the concept that time is related to motion and matter (things that move) is a well-established scientific fact, but the Rambam and Torah sources made this observation at a time when everyone else believed that time was constant and unchanging.

What about Angels?

The existence of angels is supported throughout Torah thought. So you could wind up thinking that you can ask these ministering angels to intercede as advocates on your behalf. Or, as many did in ancient times, you could venerate the sun because of its tremendous life-giving benefit to the world.

5. Prayer Is Only for God

Maimonides says that our prayer, praises, and allegiance must be directed to God alone, and not to anything beneath Him, for they have neither the ability to judge nor free will to argue, as it were, with God. So one can neither pray to them nor ask them to be advocates for us. "To Him alone should one direct his thoughts, and he should leave aside all else but Him," says Maimonides—and this is his Fifth Fundamental Principle.

What Could Go Wrong?

In his Code of Law, the *Yad HaChazakah*, the Rambam elaborates upon how requests to stars or angels might quickly lead to idolatry. He explains that idolatry started in the days of Enosh, grandson of Adam and Eve.

In the days of Enosh, people made a great error, ignoring the advice of the wise men of their generation—and Enosh was among those who made this mistake.

Their error was that they concluded that since God created stars and constellations to guide the world, and placed them on high and gave them honor, and they serve those who serve before Him, therefore (they believed that) it is appropriate to praise and glorify them and to give them honor. And this (they thought) is what God, Blessed be He, desires—for us to honor and praise those who honor and praise Him, as a (human) king wants to honor those who stand before him, and that is the honor of the king.

Since this idea entered their hearts, they began to build temples to the stars, to offer sacrifices to them, to praise and glorify them with words, and to bow down before them. All this was in order to achieve God's will, according to their erroneous reasoning.

This is the foundation of idol worship, and this is what the idolators who know its source will say. (Laws of Idol Worship 1:1)

The Existence of Prophecy

Have you ever met a prophet? Unless you are part of a religion that grants this title to its leaders, you should most certainly answer no. Give this answer either because you truly believe that you have not met one, or because you expect your neighbors to doubt your sanity otherwise.

Frankly, your neighbors are right. There are no prophets today. But it would be unwise—and contrary to a basic principle of Torah thought—to say that this has always been the case.

6. Prophecy Exists

In earlier eras, there were multitudes of people who, having ascended to an exalted spiritual level, attained the level of prophecy. They had to be individuals of sterling character and great intelligence, and masters over their impulses, but until the age of prophecy ended in the early years of the Second Temple period (approximately 300 B.C.E.), such people were able to connect to the Ultimate Intellect and receive Divine Inspiration.

ALERT!

According to Jewish sources, the Prophets mentioned in the Bible are but a tiny fraction of those who ever lived. There were over a million! Most, though, spoke only to the people of their time. The Books of the Prophets were preserved because their messages were applicable to future generations as well.

7. Moshe Was the Ultimate Prophet

Moshe was the Father of all the Prophets. Whether they preceded him or followed him, none achieved, or will ever achieve, his level of connection to the Divine. Maimonides goes on to differentiate the prophecy of Moshe from that of all other Prophets, in four ways.

Moshe Had No Intermediary

First and foremost, God spoke to other Prophets only through an intermediary, an angel who brought the message to the Prophet. Moshe, however, heard directly from God without an intermediary. Only concerning him does God say in the Torah, "Mouth to mouth I will speak to him" (Num. 12:8).

Moshe Was Wide Awake

All other Prophets could receive prophecy only when sleeping, whether at night or by falling into a trance. Genesis 20:3 says, "God came to Avimelech in a dream at night," and there are many similar quotations in the Torah and Prophets. Even if they received prophecy during the day, the other Prophets would fall into a sleeplike trance—they didn't see or hear what was around them, and their minds were empty of active thought. This was called a "vision"—for example, when the Prophet Yechezkel (Ezekiel) described being brought to Jerusalem "in visions of God" (Ezek. 8:3).

Moshe, however, spoke to God while fully awake. God says: "Hear now my words, when there will be Prophets of God, in a vision I will appear to him, in a dream I will speak to him. Not so my servant Moshe, who is trusted in all my house. Mouth to mouth I will speak to him, and I will appear to him, not in a dark vision, and the image of God he will see" (Numbers 12:68).

Moshe Could Stand It

When prophecy came to a Prophet, even though it was in a vision by way of an angel, it would terrify him and make him very weak, nearly to the point of death. Daniel says that when the angel Gavriel spoke with him in a vision, "no strength was left in me, and my appearance was overturned . . . I was in a trance, on my face on the ground" (Dan. 10:8).

Moshe, on the other hand, experienced no fear or trembling. As the verse says, "And God spoke to Moshe face to face, like a man speaks to his friend" (Exod. 33:11). This means that just as you are not afraid to speak with your friend, Moshe was unafraid to speak with God, even though it was "face to face."

Moshe Started the Conversation

No Prophet could receive prophecy whenever he or she wanted it, but only when God wanted to give it. A Prophet could wait days or years and not receive prophecy. He could ask God to reveal something prophetically, and then wait to prophesy—it might be after several days, or after several months, or perhaps the answer would never come at all.

Moshe, on the other hand, could say whenever he wanted, "Stand, and I will hear what God will command you" (Num. 9:8). When God tells Moshe, "Speak to Aharon your brother, that he not come at all times into the holy place" (Lev. 16:2), the Sages say in the Midrash (*Sifrei*) that Aharon could not come whenever he wanted—but Moshe could.

The Nature of Torah

The next two Principles explain the centrality of the Torah. In Judaism, the difference between the Torah and any other work—even one of the Books of the Prophets—is even more profound than the difference between Moshe and any other writer. For while the other Prophets were conveying their understanding of the prophetic visions that they had received, Moshe was transmitting God's Law itself—and doing so with the clear vision that he alone enjoyed.

8. The Torah Is God's Word

In Torah thought, the Torah is not the work of man, whether Divinely Inspired or otherwise. It comes entirely from Heaven, from the mouth of God. In the words of the Rambam, "Moshe was like a scribe that you would read to and who would write down what you said. Moshe recorded all of the occurrences during his days, the stories, and the Commandments of the Torah in this fashion."

So, Maimonides continues, it doesn't matter whether the words are "the children of Ham were Cush and Mitzrayim" (Gen. 10:6) or "I am the Lord your God" (Exod. 20:2)—every word of God's Torah has the highest level of holiness, and comes directly from God.

This includes not only the Written Torah, but the Oral Torah as well. "The received explanation of the Torah is also from the mouth of God." What the Jewish religious articles are and how they are to be used—for example, the Sukkah booth constructed for the holiday of Sukkos, the *Shofar* (ram's horn) blown on Rosh HaShanah, and *tzitzis* fringes on garments—all are done the way that God told Moshe that they should be done.

ALERT!

Many of the Jewish observances, such as building a Sukkah or blowing a Shofar, are from the Torah, while others, such as lighting Chanukah candles or reading *Megillas Esther* (the Scroll of Esther) on Purim, come from the Rabbis. Most every person who observes Torah, though, learns quickly which are which.

9. The Torah Is Eternal

Some things in the world change; others, however, stay the same. The earth's rotation, gravity, and the speed of light don't change (tiny variations notwithstanding). Human nature and human urges are the same today as they were thousands of years ago. After all of our efforts to advance civilization, the twentieth century C.E. proved itself to be even more bloody than those that preceded it.

The Torah is God's code for how the Jewish People should interact with His world. If God is eternal and timeless, that means He was able to deliver a Torah that speaks to the constants of human existence. It doesn't need revision every time new circumstances arise; rather, the existing tools of the Oral Torah are brought to bear upon the new situation.

In his Commentary on the Mishnah, Maimonides quotes Deuteronomy 13:1: "You shall not add to it, nor subtract from it." In his legal code, he provides many more verses to show that the Torah considered itself eternal and unchanging, such as "the revealed things are for us and for our children forever, to do all the words of this Torah" (Deut. 29:28). Many times in the Torah, Commandments are called "an eternal statute, throughout your generations."

God and Man

Some philosophers have suggested that God created the universe but left it alone once He set it in motion. This isn't a new concept—even in the days of the Prophets, there were people who said "God has abandoned the land, and God does not see" (Ezek. 9:9).

Whether at a conscious or subconscious level, this provides an escape mechanism for those who want to misbehave. If they are free from God's oversight, then they can believe in God and still do as they wish. In his next two Principles, Maimonides clarifies that God is All-Seeing, and that there is indeed Reward and Punishment.

10. God Observes Our Actions

The Torah speaks of a God who knows all of our actions and thoughts. This is related to the Unity of God, for it is impossible for God to be infinite, All-Knowing, and All-Encompassing, if He does not know any part of His universe—and that includes you.

Maimonides takes this to a profound philosophical level. He writes in his code (Foundations of Torah 2:10) that God "is He who knows, that which is known, and the knowledge itself—it is all One . . . Therefore He does not recognize and know the created things as creatures like we know them; rather, He knows them because of Himself. Because He knows Himself He knows everything, because everything is dependent upon Him for its existence."

11. Reward and Punishment

Hearing some mention of "God's Judgment" may conjure up images of fire and brimstone in your mind. While the Torah does speak about reward and punishment, it also teaches that the average, decent individual will end up enjoying the radiance of the World to Come. Exclusion from this reward is considered in Torah philosophy to be the greatest of punishments, reserved for only the truly wicked.

This is not to say that any wrongdoing is simply ignored—on the contrary, the Torah teaches that even the tiniest misdeed is recorded. In Torah thought, the soul of a person who sinned will require cleansing after death, if he or she did not abandon that sin and was not already punished in this world. But after a period of cleansing of up to a year (for all but the worst offenders), the soul eventually enters the World to Come.

The End of Time

Maimonides' final two Principles concern the future—what will happen at the end of time. Judaism teaches that there will be a Messiah, and at the end of time the dead will return to life.

12. The Messianic Age

Torah thought indicates that there will be a Moshiach, a Messiah, who will bring an end to the exile of the Jews. This Messiah will be a human being, but an extraordinarily pious and holy individual—one who not only observes the Torah's Commandments himself, but inspires others to do so as well.

The mission of the Moshiach is to restore the kingdom of David and rebuild the Holy Temple in Jerusalem. At that point, all of the laws of the Torah will be observed as they were originally, including those that currently cannot be fulfilled in the absence of the Temple or the Davidic monarchy.

The Moshiach does not need to perform signs or miracles, or bring the dead back to life. He proves himself to be the Messiah simply by fulfilling his mission. Rebbe Akiva, one of the great Sages of the Mishnah, believed that a man named Bar Kochbah was the Messiah, until the latter was killed. By dying before the job was complete, Bar Kochbah proved himself not to be the Moshiach.

ALERT!

The word *Moshiach*, Messiah, does not mean "savior" or "redeemer." Moshiach merely indicates one who was anointed—including all the High Priests and Kings. In Jewish tradition, the Messiah will be an anointed King from the line of King David, who will rule over the third and final Jewish kingdom in the Land of Israel.

The Messiah will not change any of the Torah's eternal laws. As discussed in the Sixth Principle, one who performs signs and wonders and then encourages people to stray from performance of the Torah's Commandments is to be ignored. The Moshiach will merely restore the world—and the Land of Israel in particular—to a state in which everything can be properly performed.

13. The Resurrection of the Dead

The last of the Thirteen Principles is the belief that in the future, the righteous will be resurrected. The many references to this Resurrection in the Prophets, the Talmud, and prayers are not metaphors, but references to something that will actually happen.

Maimonides wrote a separate essay on the topic of the Resurrection. In it, he explains that the body and soul will be literally reunited. As the Prophet Daniel records, "Many who sleep in the dust will awaken, some to everlasting life, and some to embarrassment and eternal shame" (Dan. 12:2).

In Maimonides' understanding, life after the Resurrection will be similar in many ways to our lives today. People will eat and drink, marry, and have children, up until the end of time itself.

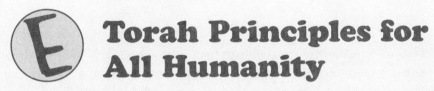

Chapter 6

Torah Principles for All Humanity

Most religions actively seek converts. The Torah, on the other hand, teaches that "the righteous of all nations have a place in the World to Come," rather than expecting all to adopt Judaism.

What does the Torah expect of a non-Jew? What does it mean to "accept the yoke of His Kingship" if the Commandments don't apply? In fact, the Torah offers principles that all can appreciate, as well as a path toward spiritual growth and service of God.

How Does the Torah View Non-Jews?

It is clear from the Torah itself that it does not expect everyone to convert to Judaism. On the contrary, the Torah teaches that the Jewish People have a unique mission, and are to exist as but one among many nations in the world. How, then, does the Torah regard the non-Jews, the vast majority of humanity?

The Torah teaches that man and woman were created in the image of God. Every person, regardless of race or nationality, is a child of Adam and Eve—and carries God's image. Every person contains a soul, a spark of the Divine, and the Talmud teaches that "the Righteous of all nations have a share in the World to Come" (Sanhedrin 105a).

FACT

The term *gentile* comes from the same Latin root as the word "gentle," but it is used by various groups to refer to someone of a different faith, and can sometimes be considered disrespectful. The Hebrew term *goyim,* though it literally means simply "nations," is often used in a pejorative sense and should be avoided. "Non-Jew" is therefore the term chosen for this book.

When King Solomon built the Holy Temple in Jerusalem, he asked God to hear the prayers of all who pray toward His Temple. "Also a non-Jew who is not of your people Israel, but will come from a distant land for Your Name's sake . . . and will come and pray toward this Temple, may You hear in Heaven Your dwelling-place, and do according to all that the non-Jew calls out to You . . ." (I Kings 8:41–43).

Who Is a Jew?

The Jewish nation traces its roots back to its forefathers, Avraham, Yitzchak, and Yaakov. Yaakov had twelve sons; he and all of his children and grandchildren were the people who went down to Egypt, and who were enslaved for 210 years before emerging in the Exodus. The *Kohanim*, the Priests, are male descendents of Aharon, Moshe's brother from the tribe of Levi.

Jewish tradition says that the mother alone determines the Jewish status of her children. If a non-Jewish man and a Jewish woman have a child, the child is Jewish, while in the opposite case the child is not.

The Reform movement decided in 1983 that a child born of one Jewish parent, whether it is the mother or the father, may be considered Jewish, but that Jewishness must be demonstrated by "appropriate and timely" Jewish acts. This, however, was a deviation from traditional Jewish law, as will be discussed in Chapter 14.

Others may join the Jewish nation by undergoing *geyrus*, or conversion to Judaism. This is a complex process, as described below, and is not necessary in order to live a fulfilling spiritual life in accordance with God's wishes. The primary focus of this chapter is, instead, to understand the Torah's expectations of non-Jews.

Adam, Eve, and the Commandments of God

Adam and Chava were created as spiritual beings in physical bodies. They had no innate desire to do evil, as people do today. And they only had one Commandment: not to eat of the Tree of Knowledge of Good and Evil. "And the Lord God commanded Adam, saying: 'Of every tree in the garden you may surely eat. But from the tree of the knowledge of good and evil you may not eat of it, for on the day that you eat of it you shall surely die'" (Gen. 2:16–17).

Jewish scholars have offered several candidates for the physical fruit on the Tree of Knowledge, ranging from the *Esrog* (citron) used on the holiday of Sukkos, to wheat kernels. None, however, suggest it was an apple tree.

After violating this Commandment, they were reduced from what they were initially. Ever since that time, man has had good and evil desires fighting within him. By choosing the good, a person elevates his or her soul, and God provided Laws to guide us toward the good.

Six out of the Seven Universal Laws that the Torah traces to Noach (Noah) actually were first given to Adam. We know this because his children were expected to follow the moral ways of God, and the world was judged when they did the opposite.

The Flood

Concerning the state of the world before the Flood, the Torah says, "And the land became corrupted before God, and the land was filled with wickedness" (Gen. 6:11). The classical Biblical commentator Rashi (Rabbi Shlomo Yitzchaki) teaches that "corruption" refers to sexual immorality and idol worship, while "wickedness" refers to thievery.

Noah and his sons were spared because they avoided the degradation that surrounded them. "Noah was a righteous man in his generation; Noah walked with God" (Gen. 6:9).

The inhabitants of the Ark lived in constant touch with God. Their vessel held far more animals than it could possibly contain, and had far less food than all of them would need. Their life was one miracle after the next, while those who had corrupted the world were swept away.

Seven Universal Laws

After the waters receded, God reiterated the Seven Laws for Noah and his family. As Noah left the Ark, God told him that he could eat meat—but not while the *nefesh* (soul) of the animal remained in its blood, meaning that a limb or blood taken from a living animal is prohibited. Murder is also forbidden, and Noah was told to set up courts to judge murder and other crimes.

All told, Judaism teaches that God gave a basic moral code of seven laws (or, more accurately, seven categories of legal obligations) that are incumbent upon all humanity. These laws were first given to Noach and his sons; later, God informed Moshe and the Jewish People that these laws were to be observed by all humanity.

The majority of these are prohibitions, but this does not mean that the experience of observing them is negative. On the contrary, it is what we refrain from doing, even more than what we do, that differentiates a civilized society from savage anarchy.

1. To refrain from idolatry
2. Not to curse the name of God
3. Not to murder
4. To avoid forbidden sexual relationships
5. Not to steal or rob
6. Not to eat a limb or meat that was severed from a live animal
7. To establish courts of justice, to pronounce and mete out decisions for all mankind, and to ensure observance of the previous laws.

Seven Categories, Many Details

If you were surprised to learn that Judaism finds not Ten but 613 Commandments in the Torah, then you will be less surprised to learn that sixty-six of these Commandments are subsumed in the Seven Universal (or "Noachide") Laws for all humanity. Each of the seven laws is considered to contain all of the relevant laws specified separately in the Torah. Thus the nineteen Commandments related to civil courts are all part of the Noachide Law on Establishing Courts of Justice. Only one Universal Law contains but a single *Mitzvah* (Commandment) within it: the prohibition against murder.

This is explained by Rabbi Aaron HaLevi of Barcelona in his *Sefer HaChinuch*, The Book of (Mitzvah) Education, Mitzvah 416: "My son, do not err in this numbering of 'Seven' Commandments of the Children of Noah, which are known and recorded in the Talmud. Because in truth, those Seven are types of general categories, but they have many details."

What about Other Commandments?

The Torah was given to the Jewish People, but any person who wants to do so is welcome to perform most of the Commandments in order to receive reward. There are only two main exceptions to this rule, mentioned by Maimonides in his legal code (Laws of Kings 10:9): the Sabbath and study of the Oral Law.

The Jewish Sabbath is a special sign between God and the People of Israel. While non-Jews can offer special prayers on that day, a non-Jew should not rest from all of the creative labor that is prohibited to Jews.

Similarly, because the Torah was given as a unique inheritance to the Jewish People, a non-Jew is encouraged to study only those sections of the Oral Law that are relevant, meaning those that pertain to the Seven Universal Laws. This includes, in actuality, a tremendous amount of material.

The Medrash says that Moshe was commanded to write the Torah in all seventy languages then in use; some say that the reason for this was to enable interested non-Jews to read and be familiar with the Written Torah. All of the Prophets focus upon the Unity of God and the need to follow His ways, and therefore it is appropriate to study them. All of the sections of Talmud, commentaries, and Medrash pertaining to the Universal Laws (and the sixty-six relevant Commandments) are appropriate to study as well.

To examine each of the Seven Universal Laws in detail could, as a result, easily involve years of study. The next several sections of this chapter are intended to provide a basic overview of each. For further study, several books and Web sites are suggested in Appendix B.

Respect for God

God is everyone's Creator and everyone's Father, and the acknowledgment of Him lies at the root of the Seven Universal Laws. Maimonides begins his legal code with the following words: "The Foundation of all Foundations and pillar of wisdom is to know that there exists a First Being, and he brings into existence all that exists" (Foundations of Torah 1:1).

Not everyone, of course, chases after wisdom. The Torah does not expect everyone to develop a profound knowledge of God—but it does call for the rejection of false gods, and for people to refrain from blasphemy (cursing God's Name).

Avoiding Idolatry

As discussed in the last chapter, Maimonides says that idolatry began when people observed the heavenly bodies, and decided that it was appropriate to pray to God's "assistants." This devolved into idolatry, as people began to worship God's creations as deities without acknowledging their Creator.

The prohibition of idolatry includes not only idols of wood and stone, but also worship of the sun, moon, or stars, or worship of a human being—such as a cult leader who declares himself to be a god. At the same time, it is important to recognize that idolatry has declined over time, as monotheism has grown around the world.

Rejecting Blasphemy

The ultimate act of hatred that one person can commit against another is to try to kill him. One cannot, of course, kill God. The worst that one can do is, simply, to curse Him. The Talmud considers this idea, just the concept, to be so terrible that it consistently uses the euphemism "to bless God" rather than to actually express the opposite.

While idolatry denies God as the Creator by ascribing supreme power to another, the act of blasphemy denies that God is entirely good and wants nothing other than our benefit. A person with a healthy understanding of God's greatness and beneficence could never imagine repaying such kindness with an act of hate.

Respect for Humans

The Talmud records that a prospective convert came to the scholar Hillel, and demanded to be taught the entire Torah while standing on one foot. "That which is hateful to you, do not do to your neighbor," replied the scholar. "All the rest is commentary—now go and learn."

Of course, one hardly needs to convert to Judaism in order to attempt to fulfill this important principle. On the contrary, many of the most basic demonstrations of human brotherhood and consideration are required of all descendants of Noach.

Not to Murder

One of the most obvious and fundamental forms of respect for others is respect for their lives. Maimonides writes that not only is a direct act of murder prohibited, but it is also forbidden to force someone in front of a lion, for example. In our day, of course, the lion would more likely be a car, but the principle is the same.

While perhaps the prohibition on murder is obvious, the same cannot be said for all of its corollaries. The level of sanctity accorded by the Torah to every human life is occasionally at odds with modern Western views. Euthanasia, for example, runs contrary to the Torah's understanding of the value of life, as does the denial of care or a feeding tube to a comatose patient. Abortion is also not in accordance with Torah values in most cases.

FACT

In cases where carrying a fetus threatens a mother's life, Jewish law mandates an abortion. This comes from the general rule that when one person is bent upon causing the death of another, one is supposed to save the second person—even by stopping the first with lethal force when there is no alternative. The fetus is, in effect, "pursuing" the mother in this situation.

To Avoid Forbidden Sexual Relationships

In an era where permissive behavior is the norm, the Torah's emphasis on sexual restraint may seem an anachronism. The Torah, however, acknowledges the strength of sexual desire, and notes that it can lead a person to behave in unhealthy ways. These behaviors may be destructive to others, and also to one's self—certainly no less so today than they were in earlier eras.

The Medrash also says that proper conduct in this area has profound spiritual benefits. Leviticus 19:2 reads, "Speak to all of the Congregation of the Children of Israel and say to them, you shall be Holy, because I am Holy, HaShem Your God." The Medrash comments, "You shall be Holy—separate yourselves from immorality and sin, because every place where you find boundaries of moral sexual conduct, you find Holiness."

Maimonides (Laws of Kings 9:5) writes that six relationships are forbidden to a man:

1. His mother
2. His father's wife—i.e., his stepmother
3. A married woman
4. His sister
5. Another man (homosexuality)
6. An animal (bestiality)

All of these, with the exception of a sister, are derived from a single verse in Genesis (2:24) following the formation of Adam and Eve: "Therefore a man shall abandon his father and his mother, and cleave to his wife, and they shall be one flesh." The Talmudic Sage, Rebbe Akiva, explains this as follows:

- *A man shall abandon his father:* This refers to his father's wife
- *And his mother:* As it seems, meaning literally his mother
- *And cleave to his wife:* And not to his friend's wife
- *And cleave to his wife:* To woman, and not to another man
- *They shall be one flesh:* With whom he can become one flesh, excluding animals because man and beast cannot become one flesh

Not to Steal or Rob

Finally, God requires of all humanity that we respect the property of others, by not taking it as our own. Contained within this are all of the various Commandments to the Jewish People concerning theft.

The Torah contains separate Commandments for stealing while hidden (e.g., breaking into a home or car or pickpocketing) versus openly (mugging), as well as moving property marks, cheating, and other financial crimes. There is even a law prohibiting us to covet another person's property in our heart, even if we make no effort to obtain it—the *Sefer HaChinuch* explains that this desire may, if left unchecked, motivate us to attempt to acquire it improperly. This, and all of the other Mitzvos related to theft, are contained in the Universal Law prohibiting stealing.

Respect for Creation

Have you ever seen someone swallow a live goldfish? According to Torah thought, this isn't merely gross—it promotes a callous attitude toward God's Creations.

"Every moving thing that lives, it shall be food for you, just as the green plants, I have given you everything. But flesh with its living soul, its blood, you shall not eat" (Gen. 9:3–4). This does not mean that blood is prohibited, but instead prohibits humanity from eating any part of an animal that is still alive.

Rabbi Samson Raphael Hirsch explains that the blood is that which ties the body together as an organism in service of its living soul, and it effectively "serves" the soul by keeping all of the organs alive. After death, the blood is no longer in service of the soul, and then the entire animal may be consumed.

To Establish Courts of Justice

The one precept given to Noach requiring positive action was the establishment of courts of justice. This is not as simple as it seems; in fact, this is the law that includes the most Commandments beneath it—nineteen in all.

For it is not enough to simply appoint judges. One must have judges who are familiar with the laws, and who will uphold them. They cannot take bribes, and can neither favor the wealthy nor pity the poor when it is time to determine which party is in the right.

Every person is required to give honest testimony to these Courts. The idea of swearing to tell "the truth, the whole truth, and nothing but the truth" has roots in Torah Law, where a person could be called upon to swear that he does not owe another person money.

The duty of the courts is, of course, to enforce observance of the other laws. A state or nation that observes the Seven Universal Laws will provide a civil society for all its inhabitants, where people will respect the rights of others instead of merely their own.

Maimonides says (in Laws of Kings 8:11) that a wise person could realize on his or her own that these laws are requirements for a civil and just society. The Torah considers it a greater feat, though, to recognize that God

Commanded these Seven Universal Laws (both to Noach and later in the Torah given to Moshe), and to undertake to do them properly and carefully because they represent God's Will. Such a person, says Maimonides, is classified among the elite group of *Chassidei Umos Ha'Olam*, the Pious among the Nations of the World, and has a portion in the World to Come.

Conversion to Judaism

As we said at the beginning, the Torah does not call for evangelism to those born outside the Jewish Nation. The Torah calls upon the Jewish People to perform a unique service for God and the world, yet sees every human being as created in the image of God. It is not necessary to join the Jewish People in order to serve God and gain a share in the World to Come.

Maimonides writes in the Laws of Kings 8:10:

> Moshe Rabbeinu (Rabbi Moshe) did not give the Torah and the Commandments to anyone but Israel, as the verse says, "The Inheritance of the Congregation of Jacob." [It was also given] to anyone from the other nations who desires to convert . . . but we do not force anyone who does not want [to accept them] to accept the Torah and the Commandments.

For some people, though, learning about and observing the Noahide Laws will not satisfy them. They will want to take on all of the obligations of Torah observance in exchange for the spiritual rewards. If you find yourself in that group, then this simple, four-step guide should prove especially helpful.

Step One: Reconsider

Seriously! Conversion to Judaism is not for most people. It is perhaps more similar to citizenship in a new nation than to conversion to most other religions. The Torah governs every area of life, so Torah observance involves changing your entire lifestyle.

Following the Torah means a life without cheeseburgers, pork, Friday night parties or television shows, and a host of other limitations on a "normal" life. Besides leaving work early every Friday during the winter, you will also miss several days each year in the middle of the week—possibly enough to consume your vacation time.

Question why you are contemplating this drastic step. As you read in this chapter, it is possible to live a fulfilling spiritual life by observing the Noahide Laws, and to gain a share in the World to Come. The only valid reason for *geyrus* is, in the words of Maimonides (Legal Code, Issurei Biah 13:4), "to enter into the Covenant and to dwell under the wings of the Divine Presence."

ALERT!

Conversion must not be undertaken for an ulterior motive, such as in order to marry a Jewish partner. Some modern Jewish groups have reached out to non-Jews for purposes of conversion, but this is an extremely controversial deviation from Torah practice.

And in addition, there's no turning back. Some countries allow you to "renounce" your citizenship, but the Torah does not. Once you promise to follow the Laws of the Torah as your own, you will be bound by that promise for the rest of your life—and, if you are a woman, all of your future children will be Jewish as well. So it is extremely important that you think carefully about what you are planning to do, and then, when you're absolutely sure, think it over again for good measure.

Step Two: Find a Rabbi

Geyrus is not merely the adoption of a new set of religious beliefs. Rather, the convert joins the Covenant between God and the Jews, and like any other change of citizenship, this must be conducted in concert with the appropriate authorities.

You therefore would need a Rabbi to mentor you through the process, recommending appropriate study materials and testing your knowledge. Just as important, however, is the guidance your Rabbi will give as you adopt Jewish practices. The Rabbi will determine whether and when you are ready to convert. At that point, he will represent to a *Bais Din*, a religious court, that you are prepared and ready to undertake life as a Jew.

Step Three: Study and Practice

Conversion to Judaism is a process that takes not months, but years to complete. You will read books, study with the Rabbi, and attempt to put your learning into practice. This will, of course, give both you and your Rabbi the opportunity to see whether this is really the right path for you.

You can't become a Jew in a vacuum, and you can't learn properly about Judaism without living in an observant community. If that's not possible for you, then you will probably need to wait until you can move into such a community.

FACT

While the Torah recognizes the possibility of joining the Jewish People, there's no exit. A Jewish person can adopt Christianity, Buddhism, and Islam, declare him- or herself an atheist, do it all over again, and never cease to be Jewish.

Step Four: Conversion Itself

The actual conversion ceremony, like most traditional Jewish services, is done with minimal pomp or fanfare. A male convert must undergo circumcision, or, if already circumcised, the drawing of a symbolic drop of blood.

Then, a group of three Rabbis again ask prospective converts if they are certain that this is the course for them. Once again, they go over a few of the Commandments and ensure that the individual is certain that he or she wishes to perform them until the end of his or her lifetime.

Finally, they watch as the person immerses in a *mikvah*, a ritual bath, or if the convert is a woman, a woman supervises as she goes in. At that point, the individual becomes a *ger tzedek*, a righteous convert, and is welcomed into the Jewish People.

The Partnership

In the world today, we see that individuals have special talents and responsibilities. Doctors save lives when people become gravely ill, but we do not believe that everyone should become a doctor. Others become judges and policemen to help maintain a civil society, but no one thinks we should all be judges.

The Torah's view of the relationship between the Jewish Nation and the other nations of the world is similar. With the Giving of the Torah, God chose the descendants of Avraham, Yitzchak, and Yaakov to fulfill His Torah and the 613 Commandments.

When one undertakes to become a doctor, years of constant study and practice are required—one cannot expect to become a judge at the same time. Doctors and judges need each other.

Jews and non-Jews also need each other. Jewish law requires that Jews abstain from creative labors on the *Shabbos* (the Sabbath) and on holidays. Although power can be kept running in hospitals in order to save lives (which takes precedence over the Sabbath restrictions), without the partnership of non-Jews whole neighborhoods could go dark until nightfall—because maintaining fires and electrical circuits are prohibited as creative labors. Meanwhile, the Jewish People were commanded to bring the Torah into the world and, by observing such an extensive array of Commandments, to encourage all to follow God's view of morality and justice. In a way, the diverse religions based upon Torah, including Catholic, Protestant, Mormon, and Muslim faiths, have all helped to bring the Torah's message to the world.

The Mosaic and Noachide Laws are bound together. Humanity is obligated to fulfill the Seven Universal Laws because they were given on Mount Sinai, and the Children of Israel are commanded to teach the Seven Commandments to the righteous non-Jews who come to learn.

Chapter 7

The Chain of Transmission

For nearly 1,500 years, the Oral Law remained just that—an oral transmission from Rabbi to students, generation after generation. Throughout the centuries from Sinai until the recording of the Mishnah, there was never a time when the Jewish People lacked Sages who were able to transmit the Law from one generation to the next.

From Sinai to the Present

After God gave the Torah to Moshe on Mt. Sinai, Moshe taught the Torah—that is, all of the understanding of the Oral Law—to others. First among these was his devoted student Yehoshuah (Joshua), who became leader of the Jewish People following the death of his teacher. Maimonides explains this in the introduction to his legal code:

> All of the Torah, Moshe our Teacher wrote it in his own hand before his death. And he gave a Book to each and every tribe, and one Book he gave to be placed in the Ark of the Covenant for eternity . . . But the Commandment, which is the explanation of the Torah, he did not write down. Rather, he commanded it to the Elders and to Yehoshuah, and to all of the rest of Israel . . . Although the Oral Torah was not written down, Moshe our Teacher taught it in its entirety in his Legal Court to the Seventy Elders. And Elazar and Pinchas and Yehoshuah, these three received it from Moshe. And Yehoshuah, who was the student of Moshe our Teacher, to him he transmitted the Oral Torah, and commanded him concerning it.

This was the beginning of a long and unbroken chain of *Mesorah*, of transmission, as outlined by Maimonides in the same introduction. In each generation, there were many great scholars—but, nonetheless, each had one or more giants of Torah learning who were recognized as the leading authorities of the era. The transmission of the Oral Law continued without interruption until it was recorded in 3948 (188 C.E.), 1,500 years after it was given.

The Elders

Yehoshuah, Joshua, was not merely a military leader who conquered the Land of Israel with his army. Yehoshuah was Moshe's primary disciple, and he taught the Torah from Moshe's death in the year 2488 (1272 B.C.E.) until his own passing twenty-eight years later.

The Talmud says, "The face of Moshe was like the face of the sun, while the face of Yehoshuah was like the face of the moon" (Bava Basra 75a). This means that Yehoshuah reflected the light of the Torah, as taught by Moshe.

The Elders received the Torah from Yehoshuah. These were some of the same elders who heard the Torah from Moshe himself, such as Calev ben Yephuneh (see Num. 13:6) and Pinchas ben Elazar (Num. 25:7). These Elders, also known as the Judges, led the Jewish nation from the time of Yehoshua until the Torah leadership was passed to the Prophet Shmuel (Samuel) in 2871 (889 B.C.E.).

This is not to say that before Shmuel, there were no Prophets—on the contrary, Yehoshua and Pinchas ben Elazar were both Prophets, as were Devorah and Shmuel's parents, Elkanah and Chanah. So while there were many Prophets at the time, the greatest scholar and greatest Prophet were not necessarily one and the same, and in transmission of Torah, the Judge, the leading scholar, took precedence.

An interesting story in the Talmud emphasizes this point. When Moshe passed away, people realized after the period of mourning that they no longer were certain about a large volume of laws. Osniel ben Kenaz used the principles of Jewish hermeneutics to recover them, and others verified that his determinations were correct.

The question that must be asked is why this responsibility fell to Osniel rather than Yehoshua, who was of course the leader at that time. Our Sages record that Yehoshua felt that were he to answer, people might believe that he was answering as a Prophet rather than as a result of his scholarship. Only Moshe received the Torah through Prophecy; since then, the Torah "is not in Heaven" (Deut. 30:12), but here on earth to be studied and understood to the best of human ability.

On a larger scale, the mantle of leadership passed from Yehoshua to the Judges. Only when civil rule over the people was given to the Kings, beginning with David, did the Jewish People find that the leading scholar of that era was a Prophet as well. The Book of Judges lists the following leaders—with the assistance of recent scholars, such as Rabbi Zechariah Fendel (*Legacy of Sinai*) and Meir Holder (*History of the Jewish People: From Yavneh to Pumbedisa*), we are able to attach approximate dates when the nation was in the hands of each:

Judge	Began to Rule (from Creation)	Modern Calendar B.C.E.	Book of Judges
Osniel ben Kenaz	2516	1244	3:11
Ehud ben Gera	2556	1204	3:30
Shamgar ben Anas	2636	1124	3:31
Devorah & Barak ben Avinoam	2636	1124	5:31
The Midianites	2676	1084	6:1
Gideon (Yerubaal)	2683	1077	8:28
Avimelech ben Gideon	2723	1037	9:22
Tola ben Puah	2726	1034	10:2
Yair HaGiladi	2749	1011	10:3
Ammonites & Philistines	2770	990	10:8
Yiftach HaGiladi	2788	972	12:7
Ivtzan (Boaz)	2792	968	12:9
Elon HaZevuloni	2797	963	12:11
Avdon ben Hillel	2806	954	12:14
Shimshon (Samson)	2813	947	15:20

Legacy of Sinai, *Rabbi Zechariah Fendel, p. 67.*

Obviously, what we know of these individuals is limited to what we know from the books of the Tanach, the Jewish Bible, and a few stories that survived to be recorded in the Talmud and Midrash. Nonetheless, it is clear that there was a solid chain of transmission throughout this period.

Eli was the *Cohen HaGadol*, the High Priest. He was also the leading scholar and Judge who received the Torah from Shimshon. On the same day that Eli was appointed Judge in 2832 (928 B.C.E.), a woman named Chanah came to the Tabernacle in Shiloh to pray for a son, because she was childless. Because most people of that time prayed aloud, Eli mistakenly believed that the silent woman moving her lips was simply drunk. When he realized his error, Eli blessed Chanah: "Go in peace, and the God of Israel will give as you have asked, that which you have asked from Him" (I Samuel 1:17).

To this day, the central prayer of the Jewish service is said standing in silent concentration, following the model of Chanah established nearly 3,000 years ago.

She bore a son a short time later, and named him **Shmuel**, Samuel. As soon as he was weaned, she brought him to Eli for him to raise and educate. The Prophet Shmuel learned the Torah from Eli and his court, and carried it in his generation. From this point until the close of the era of prophecy, 1,000 years after the Revelation at Sinai, the Prophets were also recognized as the leading scholars of each generation.

The Prophets

As already mentioned, there were several Prophets mentioned in the Bible whose works, if any, are unknown to us. More than that, says the Talmud: During the 1,000 years of prophecy, there were *millions* of Prophets—twice as many Prophets as the number of people who left Egypt.

A Prophet had to dedicate himself totally to God. He had to have total mastery of his Evil Inclination, not letting it ever lead him astray. And he also had to have great intelligence and wisdom, to achieve this level of holy communication with the Divine. To achieve prophecy, however, did not mean that the person would write a book for future generations. Most, as we know, did not. Only prophecies that were relevant for future generations to read and study were recorded and canonized into the Tanach.

King David

Shmuel anointed **David** as King over Israel, forefather of all future kings, and Eli and his religious court transmitted the Torah to David. For although David was a King and courageous military leader, he was even more a devoted scholar, leader of the *Sanhedrin* (the supreme religious court), and a holy Prophet. From the time of Shmuel's death in 2884 (876 B.C.E.) until his own forty years later, David led the people not only as their King, but as the leading scholar and carrier of the Oral Torah.

Perhaps the most famous story from David's life is his battle against Goliath. When you look at the verses, though, you will see something that many of the secondhand sources seem to have glossed over: from beginning to end, David testifies that it is not he, but God, who will defeat Goliath.

The other Israelites were afraid, because they thought that they needed to fight on their own. David, though young and unfamiliar with weaponry, defeated a well-shielded, experienced warrior with one shot. This is because David devoted himself to God and Torah study. The Medrash says that God saw his devotion and said, "Involve yourself with Torah, and I will fight your battles."

The First Temple Era

King David's son Shlomo, Solomon, was both King of Israel and considered "wiser than all men" by the Sages. He was a brilliant, outstanding Torah scholar who also supervised the building of the First Temple in Jerusalem. But he was not, according to the records maintained by the Sages, the next scholar to carry the Mesorah after his father. It was **Achyah HaShiloni** who was the leading scholar after King David. According to the *Ra'avad*, a leading scholar of the twelfth century C.E., Achyah was himself a member of King David's religious court.

Achyah and his own court transmitted the Torah to **Eliyahu**, Elijah the Prophet. Eliyahu became so saintly during his lifetime that the Angel of Death could not touch him. The Medrash says, "Eliyahu, who did not sin, he is living and standing." According to tradition, it is Eliyahu who will come and announce the final redemption from exile, at the time of the Moshiach.

Eliyahu and his court transmitted the Oral Torah to **Elishah**, who was Eliyahu's devoted student. Elishah then gave it to **Yehoyada HaKohen**, who gave it to his son, the Prophet **Zechariah**.

The Talmud (Bava Basra 14b) says that four of the Prophets found in the Tanach were contemporaries: **Hoshea**, **Amos**, **Yeshayah** (Isaiah), and **Michah**, all of whom learned Torah from Zechariah. While Yeshayah's book of prophecy in the Tanach is many times longer than those of the others, in terms of carrying the Mesorah all were considered critical to the process. The Prophet **Yoel** received it from them.

Yoel and his court transmitted the Torah to **Nachum**, who gave it to **Chavakuk** (Habakkuk), who gave it to **Tzephaniah** (Zephaniah), who gave it to **Yirmiyahu** (Jeremiah), who foresaw the destruction of the First Temple as well as its rebuilding after a seventy-year exile.

The Babylonian Exile

In the year 3338, 850 years after the Jewish People entered the Land of Israel, King Nebuchadnezzar of Babylonia destroyed the First Temple and exiled the people to his homeland. During the exile, the leading scholar was **Baruch ben Neria**. Here again, the well-known Prophet—in this case, Daniel—is not the leading scholar who is considered the bearer of the Oral Torah. Both Neria and his son Baruch were Prophets, though their prophecies were not recorded—but it was Baruch ben Neria who carried the Torah through his age.

Baruch ben Neria was ill during his later years, and when the Jews were permitted to return to the Land of Israel, he was unable to travel. The Talmud says, "The Study of Torah is greater than building the Holy Temple, for as long as Baruch ben Neria was alive, Ezra would not leave him and go up [to Israel]" (Megillah 16b). After he passed away, however, his disciple **Ezra** left Babylonia in order to return to Jerusalem.

From Prophets to Sages

The return to Israel and rebuilding of the Temple began in 3390, but the Second Temple was only completed in 3408, after a fifteen-year interruption. The early years of the Second Temple were also the closing years of the era of prophecy. Never since that time has humanity seen people reach such an exalted state of spiritual elevation.

In Jewish tradition, it is axiomatic that while the progress of generations may bring incredible advances in knowledge of the world, the years also distance us ever further from the Sinai experience, and the knowledge of God. Thus the end of the era of prophecy also set the stage for the eventual need to write down the Oral Law.

Ezra and the Great Assembly

Upon his arrival in Jerusalem, Ezra set out to restore the spiritual life of the Jewish people in Israel. The centers of Torah study had moved to Babylonia during the exile, while in the Land of Israel itself, Torah was all but forgotten. The Talmud says that "Ezra was worthy that the Torah should have been given to Israel through him, were it not that Moshe had preceded him" (Sanhedrin 21b).

Ezra also helped to create the **Great Assembly**, which he directed. The Great Assembly included 120 of the greatest Sages of the era. Many Prophets, such as Daniel, Mordechai from the story of Purim (described in the Book of Esther), Ezra's student Nechemiah, and Malachi—described as the last of the Prophets—were part of this Assembly. They did not all live at the same time or even in the same place, but together the Men of the Great Assembly had a tremendous impact.

With the end of the era of prophecy, permanent instructions were required to replace the ongoing guidance that the Prophets had provided. Therefore, for example, the Men of the Great Assembly established the "Standing Prayer," a set of Eighteen Blessings recited in silent concentration during morning, afternoon, and evening services. The Men of the Great Assembly also canonized the Tanach.

The Great Assembly represented a major turning point in the life of the Jewish People; an entirely new era was at hand. The Mishnah, in describing the chain of transmission of the Oral Law, says, "Moshe received the Torah at Mt. Sinai, and he gave it to Yehoshua, and Yehoshua to the Elders, and the Elders to the Prophets. And the Prophets gave it to the Men of the Great Assembly" (Avos 1:1). As the Assembly comprised both Prophets and Torah Sages, it ensured the seamless transmission of the Oral Law even as the age of prophecy came to a close.

The earliest recorded words of the Oral Law come from the Men of the Great Assembly, who taught "three things: be patient in judgment, raise many students, and make a fence for the Torah" (Avos 1:1). Their obvious priority was to ensure that judges and teachers were able to preserve the observance and teaching of Torah on into the future.

CHAPTER 7: THE CHAIN OF TRANSMISSION

Rabbi Shimon the Righteous

Rabbi Shimon the Righteous was one of the last Men of the Great Assembly, and also served as the *Kohen Gadol*, the High Priest, in the Holy Temple. Thanks to Alexander the Great, he was also governor of the Land of Israel.

The Talmud explains: Initially Alexander decreed, in response to a request from the Samaritans, that the newly rebuilt Temple was to be destroyed once again. When Shimon the Righteous heard this, he—though still a young man—dressed in his Priestly raiment and set out with a group of Jerusalem notables, all holding flaming torches.

When they finally came face to face with Alexander himself, Alexander immediately descended from his chariot and prostrated himself before Shimon the Righteous! To his generals and advisors, he explained that the image of this man had appeared to him before every battle, assuring him of victory. Alexander both spared the Holy Temple, and appointed the High Priest—Shimon himself—to replace the Persian ruler as governor of the Land of Israel.

FACT

The Jews honored Alexander by naming all boys after him for the next year. This explains why the obviously Greek appellation "Alexander" remains a common Jewish name even today.

Antigonos of Socho

Antigonos of Socho inherited the role of leading Sage from Shimon, taking his seat as the head of the Sanhedrin. Antigonos taught: "Do not be like servants who serve their master in order to receive reward, rather, be like servants who serve not in order to receive reward" (Chapters of the Fathers 1:3). While Antigonos merely said that one should serve God out of simple love and devotion, his students Tzadok and Baysos distorted the meaning of his words. In their version, Antigonos had taught that there was no reward or punishment in the World to Come, and therefore one should indulge in the pleasures of this world.

They therefore denied the Oral Law and the authority of Sages to interpret the Torah, accepting only their own interpretations of Torah passages. They created divergent "movements," commonly called Sadducees and Baytusans, that threatened the cohesiveness of the Jewish community for centuries.

Also during this era, Ptolemy Philadelphus gathered seventy-two Sages and placed them in separate rooms to render collaboration impossible, and told them to translate the Torah into Greek. Their translations were all identical, even though each offered a modified translation to answer theological questions found in the Torah itself. This translation is known as the Septuagint, and is still available today.

Other sources refer to a later "Septuagint" translation of the Prophets and Writings. According to Jewish tradition, however, the seventy-two Sages only translated the Torah, and there is no similar voice of authority behind the translation of the other works.

The Pairs

A second officer, the *Nasi*, or President of the Sanhedrin, was added to the existing position of *Av Beis Din*, the Chief Justice, following the death of Antigonos. While it is not clear why this was done, Ptolemy III took the responsibility of tax collection from the Jews away from the High Priest just years earlier. It may be that the Sages of the time determined that another public officer with impeccable credentials would help counterbalance the influence of a potentially corrupt tax collector.

Yose ben Yoezer and Yose ben Yochanan

The first pair consisted of **Yose ben Yo'ezer** as Nasi, and **Yose ben Yochanan** as the Av Beis Din. They received the Oral Law from Antigonos, as did their contemporary Yochanan (no relation to Yose ben Yochanan), whose son Mattisyahu started the Hasmonean revolt. The famous "Yehudah HaMaccabee" (Judah the Maccabee) from the story of Chanukah was Mattisyahu's son.

FACT

Mattisyahu called for a revolt against the Greeks and Jews who had placed idols in the Temple. The Torah-true Jews entered and cleansed the Temple in victory, but found that all flasks of oil but one had been defiled. Miraculously, its oil burned for eight days, until more could be prepared. Seeing this demonstration of God's Hand, the Sages enacted that the dedication, or Chanukah, of the cleansed Temple should be celebrated every year.

Yehoshua ben Perachyah and Nittai haArbeli

The Nasi **Yehoshua ben Perachyah** and the Av Beis Din **Nittai haArbeli** were the next of the pairs. According to Maimonides, one of the other great Sages who transmitted the Oral Law during this generation was Yochanan, son of Shimon—who was one of the four brothers of Yehudah (Judah), known as the Maccabee. Judah and his brothers led the military revolt against the Greeks and Hellenized Jews that led to the miracles of Chanukah.

Yehudah ben Tabbai and Shimon ben Shetach

The third generation of "pairs" consisted of the Nasi **Yehudah ben Tabbai** and the Av Beis Din **Shimon ben Shetach**. Shimon ben Shetach defied the evil King Alexander Yannai, ensuring the survival of Torah.

Alexander Yannai was a King from the Hasmonean line. One of the sad postscripts of the Chanukah story is that although the sons of Mattisyahu were Kohanim (Priests, from the tribe of Levi), they took it upon themselves to rule over Israel following their successful revolt. This was a tragic error, because the right to be King of Israel was granted by God to the descendants of King David, who is from the tribe of Yehudah, for eternity.

During the following generations, the Hasmonean leaders were corrupted by their power, both taking upon themselves the title of "King" and also acting with increasing hostility toward the Torah Sages. Alexander Yannai was influenced by an evil advisor to have the Sages killed—but his wife, Shlomis Alexandra, ensured that her brother Shimon ben Shetach was spared.

Shemayah and Avtalyon

Shemayah and **Avtalyon** were descendants of righteous converts; they traced their lineage to the evil King Sancherev of Assyria, who tried to destroy Jerusalem. Nonetheless, they rose to the highest ranks of Torah scholars, becoming the Nasi and Av Beis Din, respectively.

Hillel and Shammai

The last of these pairs of scholars is the most famous of all—**Hillel** and **Shammai**. Shammai lived in the Land of Israel all his life, while Hillel was born in Babylonia and moved to Israel to learn Torah from the greatest scholars. Soon he himself became one of them. Hillel served as Nasi from approximately 3728 (32 B.C.E.) until 3768 (8 C.E.).

ALERT!

Shammai is dismissed by some for being too stringent, while Hillel is admired for taking a more lenient view. The truth is that Shammai was often more lenient, and the two were colleagues and friends dedicated toward the same goal of spreading Torah study and observance.

The Prosbul

One of the most well-known—and most misunderstood—enactments of Hillel is known as the *Prosbul*, which made it easier for people to borrow money. According to Torah Law, all debts are forgiven at the end of the seventh, Sabbatical year (which is explained in Chapter 9). This existed as Torah Law, however, only until several tribes were exiled during the First Temple era; afterward, it was observed by Rabbinic decree so that people would not forget the Law (Maimonides, Laws of the Sabbatical Year 10:9).

Observance of this law, of course, required a high degree of trust in God. Money that one lent near the end of the Sabbatical year might never be returned—and for this reason, when the spiritual level of the people declined late in the Second Temple era, they started to find excuses not to lend money. Not getting a loan, of course, was much worse for the poor than getting a loan that would need to be repaid.

To fail to lend money was itself a violation of Torah Law. Hillel saw that people were failing to observe a Torah Law because of the earlier Rabbinic enactment to forgive debts. With the approval of the Sanhedrin, he therefore enacted the Prosbul, by which people transferred their loans to the authority of a Jewish court. Since a loan under court authority was not vacated at the end of the Sabbatical year, people then felt free to lend money.

So contrary to how the Prosbul has sometimes been misinterpreted, Hillel did not circumvent Torah Law. On the contrary, he strengthened it, by preventing Rabbinic legislation from inadvertently causing transgression of the Torah itself. As Maimonides writes:

> The Prosbul is of no value except for the financial Sabbatical in our day, which is of Rabbinic origin; but concerning the Sabbatical of the Torah, the Prosbul is without value. (Laws of the Sabbatical Year 9:16)

This was Hillel—an outstanding scholar and innovative thinker, steadfast in his complete dedication to Torah observance in accordance with God's will. Hillel's family line continued to serve in the position of Nasi, one after the other, for the next thirteen generations, until Hillel the Second 350 years later. Hillel's sixth-generation descendent, Rebbe Yehudah the Nasi, produced the final text of the Mishnah, the first published text for study of the Oral Law.

The Houses of Hillel and Shammai

Both men had schools of disciples—the Houses of Hillel and Shammai—that persisted for at least a generation. They debated position after position, issue after issue, defending their view with both Torah sources and scholarly logic. Because the aim of both sides was to understand the truth of Torah, an environment of mutual honesty and love prevailed between the two houses. In the vast majority of cases, the *Halachah* (Jewish law) was decided in accordance with the House of Hillel; there were many exceptions, however, several of which are discussed in the Mishnah and Talmud in the first chapter of Tractate Shabbos.

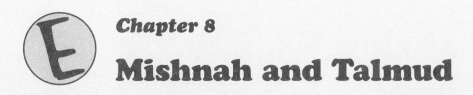

Chapter 8

Mishnah and Talmud

After 1,500 years of oral transmission, the Oral Law was recorded by Rebbe Yehudah, President of the Supreme Religious Court, a sixth-generation descendent of the great Hillel. This chapter explores why it was necessary to write down the Oral Law, identifies many of the major authors of the Mishnah, this first text, and further explores the writing of the Medrash, other works of the Mishnaic era, and both the Jerusalem and Babylonian Talmuds.

The Decline of the Generations

If you have studied science, history, or most any other field, you know that every area of research shares one fundamental trait: Knowledge is acquired over time. Civilization is advancing, and always has been. We know far more about biology, physics, linguistics, and even history than we did ten years ago. Knowledge in every field is continuously being amassed, acquired, and improved.

When it comes to Torah study, this characteristic of knowledge—that it is acquired over time—is turned on its head. In Jewish thought, the ultimate scholar, the greatest fount of Torah knowledge that ever lived, was Moshe Rabbeinu, Moshe Our Teacher. He knew more about Torah than any other human being ever has, or ever will. And with every passing generation since Sinai, knowledge is being *lost* rather than gained. Those who lived three generations ago were three generations closer to Moshe than we are today. The Talmud declares, "If the early generations were children of angels, then we are children of men, and if the earlier generations were children of men, then we are like donkeys" (Shabbos 112b). This concept is called *Yeridas HaDoros*, Decline of the Generations, the decline of Torah knowledge in the world.

Whenever we find new decrees and practices in the world of Torah study and Torah living, it is almost always in response to the perceived decline. New Rabbinic laws were issued because people were no longer able to operate in accordance with the Torah's dictates on their own. And, with the ongoing decline in knowledge, the Sages eventually decided that they must write down the Oral Law to prevent its loss.

Ideally, of course, the Oral Law should never have been recorded— the very name "Oral Law" tells you that it was intended to exist as oral teachings, with only the Written Torah as the guide to remind scholars of the laws. In the generations following Hillel and Shammai, however, arguments in Jewish law began to increase. While we know of only four cases in which Hillel and Shammai disagreed about a legal issue, there were 316 known disagreements between their disciples. The Talmud (Sanhedrin 88a) says that this was because the students did not listen to and serve their teachers with all the effort required, hence they forgot what their teachers had said.

The Tannaim—Sages of the Mishnah

The *Tannaim*, who laid out the Mishnah, lived and taught between the years 3770 and 3960 (10–200 C.E.). During a very tragic era in Jewish history, when the Second Temple was destroyed and thousands were slaughtered, these teachers compiled and recorded the totality of Jewish law, ensuring its preservation for millennia to come.

Yonason ben Uziel

Rabban Shimon ben Hillel succeeded his father to the post of Nasi, president of the Sanhedrin, and was followed by his son Rabban Gamliel *HaZaken* (the Elder)—but Yonason ben Uziel was considered the greatest of Hillel's disciples. He authored the *Targum Yonasan*, an Aramaic translation of the Torah and Prophets that provides explanations and clarifications of the text.

QUESTION?

Why are there so many different ways to say Rabbi?
The basic title in Hebrew is *Rav*, which means a teacher and scholar of Torah. During the age of the Mishnah and Talmud, only those who had received true *semichah*, a form of rabbinic ordination traced all the way back to Moshe and Mt. Sinai, were called *Rebbe* (pronounced REH-bee). *Rabban*, Our Teacher, was reserved for those who presided over the Sanhedrin.

Rabban Yochanan ben Zakkai

Yochanan ben Zakkai was the youngest disciple of Hillel. He became the Nasi—after Rabban Shimon ben Gamliel, son of Rabban Gamliel—at a crucial time: during the era when the Second Temple was destroyed at the hands of the Roman Empire. His negotiations with the Roman conquerors preserved the Torah itself, by ensuring that the invading army did not slaughter the members of the Sanhedrin, the supreme court that (until the destruction) sat on the Temple Mount.

Rabban Yochanan requested an audience with the Roman General Vespasian, and, according to the Talmud, began the meeting by predicting that Vespasian was to be the Emperor. Moments thereafter, a messenger arrived confirming the Rabbi's statement. Needless to say, Vespasian was inclined to listen to further statements from Rabban Yochanan. Rabban Yochanan then petitioned for permission to create a Torah academy in Yavneh, and that the Sages of the Jewish People who wished to join that academy be permitted to escape there through the Roman lines. Vespasian granted these requests, and in this way Rabban Yochanan ensured the survival of Torah scholarship.

Later, when he saw that the Romans were not pursuing the House of Hillel, Rabban Yochanan voluntarily stepped aside in favor of Rabban Gamliel II, Hillel's great-great-grandson. Besides keeping the position of Nasi within the "royal dynasty" of the family of Hillel, having a descendant of Hillel as Nasi sent the message to all Jewry that Torah learning would continue as before, despite their loss of national sovereignty and the Holy Temple.

Eliezer ben Hyrkanos

Rabban Yochanan ben Zakkai had five outstanding disciples, but Rebbe Eliezer ben Hyrkanos was the greatest of them all. He is also known as Rebbe Eliezer *haGadol* (the Great) because of his tremendous Torah knowledge. He authored the *Pirkei D'Rebbe Eliezer*, a work of Torah wisdom containing mysticism and stories from Talmudic Sages.

Rebbe Akiva

One of the greatest Tannaim of all started out as a barely literate shepherd. His wife, Rachel, saw greatness in him, but her wealthy father did not. Rachel's father was so distraught over her marriage to a simpleton that he left the couple to live in poverty. Later, he came to Rebbe Akiva, begged forgiveness, and the family was reunited.

Rachel always encouraged her husband to go learn Torah. At the age of forty, he was out in the fields, grazing the sheep, when he found a spring of water, and a stone that had been worn through by the water dripping onto it. He said to himself, "If water can penetrate even a stone, then words of Torah can penetrate my skull." He began to study, and did so with such incredible diligence that he became the leading scholar of his generation. Later, he told his thousands of students that all of his Torah, and all of *their* Torah, was to Rachel's credit.

Rebbe Akiva had many students, but only five survived him to carry the Torah forward. These five, known together as *Raboseinu ShebeDarom*, "our Rabbis in the South," were Rebbe Meir, Rebbe Yehudah bar Ilai, Rebbe Shimon bar Yochai, Rebbe Yose ben Chalafta, and Rebbe Elazar ben Shamua. It is remarkable that these five were ordained, because the Romans forbade semichah and killed the Rabbi, Rebbe Yehudah ben Bava, who ordained them. They themselves managed to escape from Roman territory until the decree against semichah was rescinded.

Rebbe Meir

Rebbe Meir was a disciple of Rebbe Akiva, and his opinion is quoted throughout all the books of the Mishnah. The Talmud says that his name was not really "Meir"—he was called this because the word means "enlighten," and "he enlightened the eyes of the scholars in Jewish law."

FACT

The Talmud also questions why, if Rebbe Meir was the greatest scholar of his day, his opinion is often a minority view—not followed by the majority. The Talmud answers that the other Rabbis were unable to understand the tremendous depth of his thinking, and Jewish law required following the majority in a debate of scholars.

Rebbe Shimon bar Yochai

Shimon bar Yochai was also a student of Rebbe Akiva. When the Romans attempted to stop Torah study in Israel, Shimon bar Yochai was forced to go into hiding. Together with his son Elazar, they hid in a cave for thirteen years, subsisting on little more than carobs, and studying Torah with a select group of students. He authored the Zohar, a major work of the Kabbalah, which you'll read more about in Chapter 12.

Rebbe Yehudah HaNasi, Editor of the Mishnah

Rebbe Yehudah was the son of Rabban Shimon ben Gamliel II, making his the seventh generation of the dynasty of Hillel. He learned Torah from his father and others, including Rebbe Shimon bar Yochai and the other students of Rebbe Akiva. Rebbe Yehudah is often referred to as "Rabbeinu HaKadosh," Our Holy Teacher, because of his sincere piety, or simply as "Rebbe," for he was everyone's teacher.

FACT

Rebbe Yehudah developed a warm relationship with the Roman Emperor Marcus Aurelius, and his son, Commodus. They were not merely friends, but confidants, and this resulted in a period of peace and tranquility for the Jewish subjects of the Empire. The absence of persecution of the Sages during this era made it possible for them to properly study and understand complex Torah subjects.

Recording of the Mishnah

From the days of Moshe himself, until the time of Rebbe Yehudah HaNasi, teachers and students kept notes of the Oral Law. These notes were not distributed publicly, but were recorded by each individual for his own use, to help him to remember what he had heard from his teachers. He would then teach orally, and his students would record their own notes.

Many years before Rebbe Yehudah, other teachers were already structuring their notes in various forms, and permitting others to benefit from them. Some trace the division of the Mishnah into six sections back to Hillel and Shammai. At least two of the smaller tractates were written by others, and incorporated by Rebbe Yehudah essentially in toto. The Talmud speaks of both *Mishnah Rishonah* and *Mishnah Acharonah*, earlier and later Mishnah, referring not to an entire collection, but individual paragraphs that existed in earlier forms.

Rebbe Yehudah HaNasi saw that thanks to Roman persecution, the number of Torah students was declining, while the circumstances in which they lived were getting worse—meaning that the smaller number of students would also be distracted from Torah study. He realized that the students would need a written guide, to help them quickly review the totality of Torah.

Although the recording of the Oral Law was not the ideal, the Law nonetheless permitted writing it down in a circumstance like this one. So Rebbe Yehudah gathered the lecture notes, decisions, and explanations of all of his colleagues, including what they had heard from their teachers—which went back several generations—in all areas of the Torah, and combined them into one work. He completed this great project, the Mishnah, in roughly 188 C.E.

ALERT!

Like your own notes from classes and lectures, the Rabbis' records were brief and even cryptic. The key requirement of oral transmission was preserved, because no one could understand the Mishnah without a teacher who already understood it and could explain it.

Medrash, Tosefta, and Braisa

The Mishnah was hardly the only work written during this period. Since the Mishnah was as concise as possible, a great deal of material was left out. Others wrote down this material, whether to explain the Mishnah in more detail, to clarify the Halachah (the law), or to explain the verses of the Torah, both the stories and the legal decisions that emerge from them.

Medrash

There are two major types of Medrash. The first, called *Medrashei Aggadah*, explain the stories of the Torah. Several of these were written by early *Amoraim* who are well known in the Talmud. There were other great scholars, however, who were known specifically for their involvement with the study of Aggadah, and their expertise in understanding it.

A Medrash Aggadah explains the stories of the Torah by filling in details not found in the text itself. Sometimes there are multiple traditions for what happened, all of which are recorded. Since, unlike in the legal areas, there is no practical ramification of accepting one version over the others, all are recorded and considered to have value for the lessons taught, even if all cannot simultaneously describe what happened.

The second type of Medrash is called *Medrashei Halachah*, and these explain the laws found in the verses. Examples of these are *Mechilta* on the book of Shemos (Exodus) and *Sifra* on the book of Vayikra (Leviticus). Some of these were written by Tannaim, others by Amoraim. The same expertise needed to argue the laws in the Talmud was obviously needed to write a Medrash Halachah, and all of the writers of Medrashei Halachah are known to us in either Mishnah or *Gemarah* (Talmud).

Tosefta and Braisa

The Mishnah consists of Halachic material that existed before Rebbe Yehudah HaNasi; Rebbe Yehudah organized and finalized this material into the Mishnah. It was designed to be as concise as possible, limiting explanations to the absolute minimum. There was, however, additional material that explains the Mishnah, provided either by Rebbe Yehudah himself or by one of his students. This material is called the *Tosefta*, a word that comes from the Aramaic for "adding on."

The *Braisa*, on the other hand, which comes from the Aramaic for "outside," is a work unto itself, but one that clarifies the words and opinions of the Mishnah by restating them with extra words. In Rabbinic terminology, various extra texts, including Medrashei Halachah, will all be referred to as "Braisos."

There is also a special class of Braisos called the *Masechtos Ketanos*, or "small tractates," also sometimes called the "external tractates." In some of these, one can find references to the Amoraim, teachers of the Talmud. Nonetheless, Sages agree that these tractates, like the others, were written by Tannaim of the Mishnah, but notes were added later to further explain their meaning.

The Talmud

The later scholarship of the Amoraim added extensive discussion and commentary on top of the Mishnah, explaining and elaborating upon its terse legal decisions. An *Amorah*, or Speaker, was the designated Rabbi in the academy whose job it was to recite the scholars' teachings before the public. The discussions of the Amoraim were recorded as the Gemarah.

Once the Mishnah was complete, having expressed majority and minority opinions, no later teacher could disagree with the Mishnah. Only a select few who lived at the end of the period of the Tannaim were considered Tannaim themselves, able to argue with the others.

The Jerusalem Talmud

Work on the Jerusalem Talmud commenced almost immediately after the Mishnah was complete. Rebbe Yochanan, who began the process, was a student of Rebbe Yehudah HaNasi. He studied and argued with his brother-in-law, Rebbe Shimon ben Lakish, and their frequent debates are recorded in both Talmuds. The yeshiva, the House of Study that Rebbe Yochanan established in the city of Teveriah (Tiberias), remained a leading institution until the Jerusalem Talmud was completed.

The Jerusalem Talmud is often called the Palestinian Talmud. Given that it was written primarily in Tiberias rather than Jerusalem, its most common name is not fully accurate!

Work on the Jerusalem Talmud continued for several more generations. Its language is very difficult—according to some, it was written in a then-current Syrian dialect, close to Aramaic but not the same. Further, the yeshiva of Rebbe Yochanan and all others in the Land of Israel, were subject to persecution by the Roman emperors. The later Sages thus were not able to make large changes to Rebbe Yochanan's work. Some speculate that ongoing discussion of certain sensitive topics, such as the Temple laws, would have caused the Romans to crack down on the academies, also obstructing further work.

For these reasons, the Jerusalem Talmud is considered a valuable resource, but not fully authoritative when arriving at an Halachic decision.

The Babylonian Talmud

While there had been a continuous Jewish presence in Babylonia ever since the first exile—over 550 years before the codification of the Mishnah—the persecution of the Jews in Israel now made it an attractive destination. Many who had come up from Babylonia to Israel during Rebbe Yehudah's tenure, when relationships with Rome were extraordinarily warm, decided to return soon thereafter. One of these was Abba Aricha, who returned to Babylonia some thirty years after the Mishnah was completed. He had once been the youngest member of the Supreme Religious Court of which Rebbe Yehudah was Nasi, or President, and now was simply called "Rav" in recognition of his great scholarship.

Rav in the city of Sura, and Shmuel in Nehardea, directed the two leading academies of Babylonia in their day—and thus began six generations of Torah scholarship, leading to the redaction of the Babylonian Talmud. The two scholars most directly responsible for its production were Rav Ashi, who led a yeshiva in Masa Machsya for over fifty years, and his colleague Ravina.

Today, we have only thirty-seven tractates of the Babylonian Talmud, and there is a dispute regarding whether the remaining tractates were lost or were simply never compiled. What remains is an authoritative work covering all areas of Torah life in our day (when the Temple is not standing), and a repository of Jewish wisdom as well as law.

The Discussions of the Talmud

A discussion in the Gemarah always takes a Mishnah as its starting point, which explains why a tractate of Talmud will contain the entire tractate of Mishnah, divided into the same chapters—just with extensive discussion following each Mishnah. In addition, the Gemarah will often digress. Most books are the individual thoughts of one individual. The Gemarah, on the other hand, is a record of discussions and debates—including many issues that Rabbis returned to literally over the course of centuries, recording the opinions expressed by each generation of Amoraim.

In the middle of debating one question, the Talmud may venture off into a complex debate about something else, simply because the conclusion of that argument will be applicable to the current discussion. If in the current Mishnah it appears that a particular Tanna is guided by an underlying principle of law, the Talmud will venture off into other opinions of the same Tanna to confirm or rebut the assertion that he was indeed guided by that principle. So following a complicated discussion in the Talmud is a tremendous challenge to the intellect, requiring that you not "overlook the forest for the trees"—that you retain an understanding of the central issue under discussion, while carefully examining each of the related statements or debates.

The Structure of Mishnah and Talmud

Looking at a page of the Talmud for the first time can be daunting. First of all, the material is all in an old dialect of Hebrew, or worse, Aramaic. There are commentaries running down both sides of every page, so initially it's hard to follow a single commentary from one page to the next. And in the middle of the page, you find short passages from the Mishnah interspersed with explanatory material. There is a structure to all of this—it's just not easy to follow at first.

Divisions and Subdivisions of Mishnah

When Rabbi Yehudah HaNasi compiled the notes of the Tannaim, he divided them into six sections, called *Sedarim*, a word meaning order or structure. Each Seder contains multiple Masechtos, or tractates—single books. For example, the tractate on the Sabbath, *Maseches Shabbos*, is one of twelve found in the order covering the holidays, *Seder Moed*. There are a total of sixty-three tractates in the Mishnah.

The concept of a *Seder,* an order or structure, is integral to Judaism. The festive ceremony and meal on the first nights of Passover is called the *Pesach Seder*, because it is a carefully structured service of fifteen steps. Similarly, the Prayer Book is called the *Siddur* because prayers are said in a particular order.

Each Masechta contains from three to thirty *Perakim* (chapters). The chapters limit themselves to one or a few subtopics, usually related to the topic of the tractate. Each of these chapters is further subdivided into two to a dozen or more *Mishnayos* (the plural of Mishnah, which can refer to a single paragraph-long section or to the entire work).

Not Every Mishnah Is Explained

Volumes of the Gemarah only exist for certain tractates. Some tractates are found only in the Jerusalem Talmud, some only in the Babylonian, while some are found in both and others in neither. It is apparent that the early European Sages had access to a Jerusalem Talmud on the order of *Kodshim*, Holy Objects—but it has since been lost.

In the following chapter, you will find short descriptions of each Masechta of the Mishnah. Each tractate will be listed in **bold**. If it is found in current editions of the Jerusalem Talmud, it will also be **<u>underlined</u>**, while if it is found in the Babylonian it will be ***italicized***. So ***<u>Brachos</u>***, for example, is both underlined and in italics because it is found in both Talmuds.

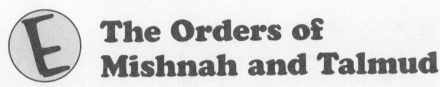

Chapter 9

The Orders of Mishnah and Talmud

The Mishnah is the collected Oral Law in its most concise form, while the Jerusalem and Babylonian Talmuds discussed and explained its teachings. The sixty-six volumes of the Mishnah contained in six Sedarim have been studied without interruption for nearly two millennia. A brief introduction to each order and volume of Mishnah displays both the scope and great depth of the Torah's Oral Law. (See page 98 for an explanation of the italicizing and underlining of the tractates.)

Seder Zeraim—The Order of Seeds

The first order of the Mishnah, *Seder Zeraim*, covers laws related to agricultural produce, most related to the Land of Israel in particular. This probably explains why none except the tractate on blessings are found in the Babylonian Talmud, while there is a volume of Jerusalem Talmud for every one.

A Book about Blessings

Brachos: Blessings. This tractate talks about the laws of blessings. It is not limited to the blessings over food; in fact, it begins not with blessings at all, but by discussing when one should recite the *Shema* in the evening.

The "Shema" consists of three short Torah passages that, according to tradition, are to be recited every morning and night. The first passage, Deuteronomy 6:4–9, begins *"Shema Yisrael"* ("Hear, Israel,"), thus its name. This passage is followed by Deuteronomy 11:13–21 and Numbers 15:37–41.

You may be asking two questions: (1) What do blessings have to do with a Talmudic order devoted to agriculture, and (2) What does the Shema, a selection of Torah passages, have to do with blessings?

Fortunately, Maimonides answers both questions in his introduction to the Mishnah. Medical care, he says, begins with choosing the right foods. Similarly, Rebbe Yehudah began by discussing how to impart a spiritual component into the food—by saying a blessing upon it. At that point, it became logical to discuss all blessings in order to have one tractate devoted to the topic.

The recitation of the Shema is the one Mitzvah, or Commandment, that applies every day. It would not be appropriate to begin discussing the blessings surrounding the Shema without discussing the Shema itself—and that is why the time for saying the Shema is the first topic discussed.

Why does the tractate start by discussing the evening recitation, if it is supposed to be said in the morning as well?
In the Torah, days begin and end at sunset. You find this at the beginning of Genesis: "And it was evening and it was morning, one day" (Gen. 1:5). So it's consistent for the tractate to talk about the evening recitation first, followed by the morning one.

The tractate then discusses the blessings on Shema, before turning to other blessings, such as the Amidah, the Standing Prayer, a series of blessings that lies at the heart of synagogue prayer services even today. It concludes with the blessings to be said upon food, bringing us to the agricultural laws that are the main subject of this Seder.

Produce in the Field

The next several tractates regulate how a farmer should handle produce in the field. There is a Jewish way (and time) to sow, and a Jewish way to reap, and these tractates explain the relevant laws.

Peyah: The Edge of the Field. When a farmer harvests his field, it is a mitzvah to leave the corner of the field untouched, for the poor to come and take it. The Talmud begins with this agricultural law, says Maimonides, because it is the only one that applies while the produce is still attached to the ground. This tractate also discusses other mitzvos concerning charity for the poor.

D'mai: Questionable Produce. What happens if a person isn't sure whether he removed the proper tithes from his produce? What if the produce comes from an unlearned merchant, who may have failed to take the tithes? This tractate discusses what should be done in various situations, depending upon the type of produce, the area(s) of uncertainty, and other factors. Maimonides explains that this tractate is included here, following Peyah, because the poor are able to consume D'mai like Peyah.

Kilayim: Forbidden Mixtures. In one of their famous comedies, Bud Abbott discovers Lou Costello planting corn and peas in the same row. He asks, "What are you trying to grow?" And Lou answers, "Succotash!" In this tractate, you learn that it is forbidden to plant many species in close proximity, and to graft many varieties. The Torah also forbids wearing a mixture of linen and wool. Cross-breeding (e.g., breeding mules from a horse and a donkey) is discussed as well.

Shevi'is: The Sabbatical Year. Every seven years, the Torah requires that all fields in Israel be left to lie fallow. This is the topic of a large portion of the Torah itself, and is discussed in this tractate. The Prosbul, which you read about in Chapter 7, is also described here.

Tithes and Offerings

The remaining tractates govern the various tithes and offerings taken from the produce.

Terumos: Harvest Portion given to the Priest. Because the members of the tribe of Levi, including the Kohanim, the Priests, did not receive a portion in the Land of Israel, responsibility for their support fell upon everyone. This was especially true of the grain harvest, a portion of which was set aside for the Priests. These support offerings were holy, and had to be treated with special respect.

Ma'asros: Tithe given to the Levite. While on the surface this harvest offering seems very similar to Terumah, the portion given to the Kohein, Ma'aser has its own regulations, which are substantially different. Like the English word "tithe," Ma'aser stems from the word Eser, which means ten. Indeed, this offering is the source of the concept of tithes.

Ma'aser Sheni: The Second Tithe. This additional tithe of food was either set aside or sold, and the resulting funds set aside, so that they could be consumed in Jerusalem, the holy city. This tithe ensured that everyone had funds for their holiday expenses when they went up to Jerusalem three times per year for the festivals—Pesach (Passover), Shavuos (the Festival of Weeks), and Sukkos (the Festival of Booths).

Challah: Dough Offering. When making dough in order to make bread, a portion of this dough was also set aside for the Kohanim.

Orlah: New Fruits. The first three years after planting a new tree, its fruits are forbidden. One important topic of this tractate is what happens when a forbidden object, such as "orlah" fruit, becomes mixed in with other permitted items (e.g., in a large barrel of fruit) and can no longer be distinguished. In addition, the fruit produced by a tree in its fourth year—called *Neta Revai*—has special holiness and must be treated akin to *Ma'aser Sheni*.

Bikkurim: The First Fruits. Each year, the first fruits from several species, all indigenous to the Land of Israel, were brought by landowners to the Temple in Jerusalem. There, the fruits were received by the Kohanim, as is discussed in this tractate.

Seder Moed—The Order of Sacred Days

Moed, though perhaps best translated merely as "appointed time," is the word used in the Torah and Bible to describe special days, those that are set apart from non-sacred days. This, the second order of Mishnah, discusses the holidays of the Jewish calendar.

Interestingly enough, there's one holiday you *won't* see mentioned or discussed here—*Chanukah*, the Festival of Lights. Chanukah is in actuality a minor holiday of Rabbinic origin, with very few associated laws. Although many American Jews seem to treat it with greater care than, for example, the festival of Shavuos, this probably has far more to do with Chanukah's location on the calendar—namely, in the month of December—than its inherent value.

The Sabbath

Shabbos: The Sabbath. When you ask someone about the most important holidays on the Jewish calendar, they will likely mention Rosh HaShanah, the Jewish New Year, and Yom Kippur, the Day of Atonement. Yet in many ways it is the Sabbath that is the most important holiday of all. Even in the Torah, the section describing the festivals begins with the Sabbath (Lev. 23:3). This tractate discusses the types of *melachos*, creative labor, that are forbidden on the Sabbath.

You may have heard that "work" is prohibited on Shabbos, but this is essentially a mistranslation. A Rabbi, for example, can't avoid giving his sermon on the grounds that Shabbos is supposed to be a day of rest!

The Sages learn from the Torah that there are thirty-nine categories of creative work that were performed when building and using the *Mishkan*, the Tabernacle in the desert. These include all of the necessary preparatory steps to build the Tabernacle and its curtains, prepare bread, and slaughter cattle. Just as God turned away from Creation of the world on the seventh day, the Jewish People are commanded to cease their own creative labor—defined by those same thirty-nine categories.

__Eruvin__: Combined Domains. Of all the thirty-nine "labors," one is exceptional in that it makes no change at all to any object (as do planting, sewing, or cooking). Rather, the act of transporting an object into or through a "public domain" is prohibited. Because it is often difficult to understand the difference between a true public space and a semi-public/semi-private domain, the Rabbis forbade carrying something in even the latter type of space—but permitted the creation of a virtual "enclosure" that can make even an entire town into a jointly-owned "private space" in which it is permitted to carry. If that sounds complicated, you may understand why this topic takes up an entire tractate, all by itself.

The Festivals

__Pesachim__: The holiday of Pesach, Passover. The festivals of the year are discussed in Leviticus 23, as mentioned earlier, and Passover is the first of the annual holidays discussed. Passover celebrates the liberation of the Jewish People from slavery in Egypt, when God passed over the Israelite houses while causing the death of every firstborn Egyptian. Most of this tractate covers the many laws associated with the Passover offering. The tenth and final chapter, however, discusses the Pesach Seder, the ceremony and meal on the first two nights, during which the participants talk about the redemption from Egypt, eat Matzah, unleavened bread, to commemorate the hurried departure, and eat *Maror*, bitter herbs, to remember the bitterness of slavery.

Shekalim: The half-*shekel* donation. Every year, each person gave a half-shekel coin to the funds of the Holy Temple in Jerusalem, to help pay for the communal offerings. The new funds were used beginning in the month of *Nissan*, the month of Passover. As this subject is closely tied to the Temple's existence, it is unsurprising that this is the one tractate within *Seder Mo'ed*, this order of the Talmud, that has no Babylonian Gemara commentary to accompany it.

Yoma: Yom Kippur, the Day of Atonement. The Yom Kippur service in the Holy Temple was truly unique. The *Kohein Gadol*, the High Priest, entered on this day only into a special chamber called the Holy of Holies, offering a special incense-offering of atonement for sins. The complete service of the Day of Atonement is the topic of this tractate.

Sukkah: Sukkos, the Festival of Booths. For this holiday, the Jewish People are commanded to build a temporary booth outside, in which to eat and sleep (when possible) for seven days. It must have at least three walls, the roof must be composed of natural plant life (tree branches, bamboo, etc.), and the roof should provide shade, but should also be sparse enough that those inside can see light.

Beitzah: An Egg. The laws applicable to all of the three Pilgrimage Festivals—Pesach, Sukkos, and Shavuos (the Festival of Weeks)—are discussed in this tractate. This includes whether one can cook a freshly laid egg on the morning of these holidays, thus the unusual title.

FACT

All of the major holidays have tractates devoted to them, with one exception. Since Shavuos, which celebrates the day that the Torah was given on Mt. Sinai, has no special, unique commandments, there is no separate tractate to discuss it.

Rosh HaShanah: The New Year. The Jewish New Year is also the Day of Judgment, when the deeds of every person are examined by God. The result is a day that is simultaneously somber and happy. Going to court is always an ordeal, but when the judge is your Father, you know He's looking out for you! There are other, separate starting dates on the calendar for other purposes, such as when a new tithing period begins for grain and fruit—these are covered in this tractate as well.

Minor Holidays

Ta'anis: The Fast Day. The Prophets instituted several fast days, during which neither food nor drink should be consumed from sunrise until nightfall. While they might not be particularly *happy* days, these opportunities for reflection and redirection are special days on the calendar nonetheless.

Megillah: The Scroll. The Purim holiday, celebrating the defeat of the first plan to eradicate the Jewish population, is the topic of this tractate. It features the reading of *Megillas Esther* in the synagogue. This scroll, which is one of the books of the Bible, describes Haman's plot to kill the Jews and his ultimate downfall.

Mo'ed Katan: Smaller Days. The holidays of Passover and Sukkos share a common feature: Between the holy days at the beginning and end, there are intermediate days that have holiness, but the full laws of holiday observances do not apply. This tractate discusses the rules governing which laws apply and under what circumstances.

Chagiga: The Festival Offering. On each of the major festivals, the pilgrims who came up to Jerusalem brought a special *chagiga* offering in the Holy Temple. Maimonides explains that this tractate was left to the end because, unlike all of the other holiday observances, this one was limited to the men who were expected to travel, as specified in Exodus 23:17.

Seder Nashim—The Order of Women

An entire section of the Mishnah and Talmud is devoted to laws governing the relationship between men and women. Because those studying these laws were men, the order is appropriately named after the other party in the relationship. It is a relatively short Order, with only seven tractates—but, on the other hand, it is also the only Order that has both Jerusalem and Babylonian Talmuds for every tractate.

Marriage, Both Mandatory and Optional

Yevamos: Levirate Marriage. In Deuteronomy 25:5–10, the Torah commands that if a married man dies without children, his brother should marry the widow in order to continue his brother's name. This marriage is called *yibum*. If no brother wishes to do this, then the widow and one brother perform a ceremony called *chalitzah* to free them of the obligation.

Kesubos: Marriage Contracts. The Torah provides a model for the support of a wife, widow, and/or ex-wife that is thousands of years old. In the *Kesubah*, the prenuptial contract, the husband-to-be promises financial and other support to his bride during their marriage, as well as a substantial payment afterward. The Kesubah takes precedence over the children's inheritance—even those from another marriage—and most other debts that the departed might have had.

Vows and Oaths

Nedarim: Vows. This tractate discusses vows and oaths that a person can make, as well as how they can be annulled. While married, the Torah was concerned that a wife could make a vow that would bother her husband or otherwise disrupt the marriage, and permitted the husband to annul the vow immediately. According to Maimonides, this is why tractate Nedarim follows Kesubos. The husband has no such escape route—if his wife objects, he'll need to ask a Rabbi about annulment of the vow.

Nazir: the Nazirite Vow. A vow of *Nezirus* is a unique variety of oath, during which the Nazir could not cut his or her hair or drink wine. The husband could nullify this vow as well, another reason for this tractate to follow Nedarim.

Divorce and Betrothal

Gittin: Divorce. Taking a middle road between the complete rejection of divorce by some other religious viewpoints and the casual attitude toward divorce in Western society, the Torah and Talmud teach that a successful marriage is a goal to be achieved. If, on the other hand, the marriage does not succeed, then the couple are not stigmatized, but rather given extraordinary support. When a marriage fails, the husband gives the wife a document called a *Get*, thus entitling her to receive her *Kesubah* and to marry another.

Sotah: The Suspected Adulteress. Let's say a husband saw his wife frequently socializing with another man, and they even secluded themselves together in a home or office. The husband would be in a jealous rage, but there is a way to save the marriage if the wife did nothing wrong (if she admitted adultery, the marriage would end through divorce, which is why Sotah follows Gittin). She could go to the Temple, and drink water into which God's Holy Name had been erased. If she was innocent she would not be harmed, and the Torah would bless her as well. But if she compounded the sin of adultery by lying and causing God's Name to be destroyed, then she would be poisoned by the water. The Talmud says that God preferred to see His Name erased in order to preserve a marriage!

Kiddushin: Sanctification of Marriage. The first stage of getting married is an act of Kiddushin, betrothal, that sanctifies the marriage. In the Jewish wedding ceremony, this is why the first thing the groom does is give his wife the ring. According to Maimonides, Kiddushin was not included before Kesubos in order to keep Levirate and regular marriage together. Kiddushin was then left until after Gittin, divorce, because the verse says "She left his house, and she went and was married to another man" (Deut. 24:2).

Seder Nezikin—The Order of Damages

This, the third order, concerns itself with the court system, crime and punishment, and financial matters of all kinds, including real estate transactions, theft, the return of lost property, and damage caused by man or animal. This is the sort of interpersonal legislation that any society must have in order to avoid anarchy, and forms a very important part of Talmudic Law; it is the largest of the six orders of the Talmud.

Three Gates

According to one opinion, the first three tractates in this Order were originally one long, thirty-chapter tractate, which was then divided into three. Within this section one finds all of the basic discussions of civil laws, rights, and responsibilities found in the Mishnah.

Bava Kamma: The First Gate

This tractate deals with all sorts of damages that a person can cause. Maimonides explains that this is the first topic covered among the financial laws, because removing a potential risk is an urgent and important duty of a court. This tractate focuses upon four basic causes of harm:

1. Direct damage or injury caused by a person him- or herself
2. Damage caused by his or her animal, whether it was merely grazing or doing intentional harm
3. Digging a pit and leaving it uncovered in a public place
4. Setting a fire which then spreads to someone else's property

You may have read the Torah passage that says "A life for a life, an eye for an eye, a tooth for a tooth." While a literal version of this may have been good enough for Hammurabi, it wasn't for the Rabbis. While murder is indeed a capital crime, they said that "an eye for an eye" simply demands a financial payment equivalent to the value of an eye—rather than a barbaric court proceeding that would be of no benefit to the injured party. In God's eyes a person who does this *deserves* to lose his own eye, and therefore the assailant must beg forgiveness of the victim rather than merely paying the financial price. But nowhere in Jewish sources does any writer so much as speculate that "an eye for an eye" demanded poking out the attacker's own eye.

Bava Metziah: The Middle Gate

This tractate discusses the return of lost property, disputed claims to ownerless property, real estate transactions, labor and wage laws, borrowed and guarded objects, fraud, and more. Following the laws of damages, the Torah discusses four types of custodians over another person's property:

1. The unpaid guard
2. The paid guard
3. The renter
4. The borrower

These have ascending levels of responsibility should something happen to the object.

Bava Basra: The Last Gate

This Masechta covers the division of shared property, inheritance, buying and selling, guarantees, defective merchandise, and other topics. Maimonides points out that these topics are found exclusively in the Oral Law, which is why they were left for last.

FACT

The severity of oaths is so profound that Torah-observant Jews will go to great lengths to avoid them, even when telling the truth. U.S. courts routinely permit those observing the Torah to *affirm* rather than swear that they will tell "the truth, the whole truth, and nothing but the truth." The Torah says "Distance yourself from falsehood," which prohibits false testimony, even without an oath.

The Court Is in Session

Sanhedrin: The Court. Having covered the civil laws, the Mishnah now turns to the court system that resolves disputes and enforces judgment. This includes the Supreme Court of seventy-one Sages, which met in the Temple, and the lesser courts that referred to it the most complicated and difficult matters. The administration of the death penalty is also discussed here.

Makkos: Lashes. Following the death penalty, the Mishnah then turns to lesser penalties, such as corporal punishment. This tractate also discusses what to do when it is discovered that witnesses offered false testimony in order to harm an innocent victim.

Shavuos: Oaths. There are several types of oaths that a person can make. One is voluntary, such as a promise to do or not do something; there are also court-administered oaths when, for example, a single witness testifies that one person owes another money, and the accused must swear that he does not owe in order to avoid paying.

The Very Good and the Very Bad

Eduyos: Testimonies. The testimony of witnesses in court is, of course, the foundation upon which a justice system rests. Here, Rebbe Yehudah

HaNasi collects the testimony of reliable witnesses: the Rabbis! Eduyos is a collection of laws upon which Rabbis were able to testify with absolute certainty that they were passed down from Sinai. Perhaps because their testimony was so clear, there is neither Babylonian nor Jerusalem Gemarah discussion of this tractate.

Avodah Zarah: Idolatry. This tractate covers the many laws regarding the worship of idols. Adherence to idol worship has clearly declined over the millennia—the Rabbis say that the first patriarch, Avraham, had far more questions and situations than they did, and they themselves were dealing with Roman and Babylonian pagans! Maimonides says that this tractate is last among those related to the needs of judges, because idolatry is so rare.

Ethics and Errors

Avos: The Fathers. This tractate is a collection of important ethical advice given by the Sages of the Mishnaic Era, and is often published as "Ethics of the Fathers." It also provides a brief record of the chain of transmission from Sinai, which you read about in Chapter 7. Maimonides explains that the chain of transmission is what gives today's judges their authority, and thus belongs in this Order. Furthermore, he says, no one needs good character traits more than a judge—which is why the very first bit of advice given is to judges, telling them to "be deliberate in judgment."

Horiyos: This tractate is "batting clean-up" because its topic is clean-up: what to do when judges make an erroneous ruling.

Judaism has no doctrine of infallibility. On the contrary, it's considered impossible for a human being *not* to make mistakes—even a panel of learned judges. People turn to them because of their superior knowledge, not because they are perfect.

Seder Kodshim—The Order of Holy Objects

This tractate covers the various Temple offerings. The Babylonian Talmud has Gemarah discussion on all but the last two tractates, while none of them are found in the Jerusalem Talmud. Much of this discussion is currently "Torah for its own sake"—without a Temple, no offerings may be brought. But Torah study is always worthwhile . . . and considering that God promised that the Temple will be rebuilt, it certainly never hurts to be prepared!

Zevachim: Animal Offerings. This discusses the many types of animal offerings in the Temple.

Menachos: Meal Offerings. The offerings of flour are discussed next, which is in order of their appearance in the Torah.

Chullin: The Non-Sacred. This tractate is applicable today, because it covers Kosher slaughter of animals for "regular" eating. By keeping Kosher, refraining from forbidden foods, and ensuring that animals are slaughtered in the specified manner, the mundane act of eating can be transformed into service of the Divine.

Bechoros: The Firstborn. Although "regular" meat can be slaughtered and consumed at will, there is still a tithe of firstborn animals to be observed. This tractate also discusses the ceremony of "redemption of the firstborn," referring to children—since before the designation of the Kohanim as Priests it was the firstborn who led the Divine Service, each firstborn child must be "redeemed" with a payment to a Kohein.

Erachin: Values. When one promises the value of a particular object, or pledges an object that can be redeemed for money, he or she needs to know how much money is involved. That is the topic of this tractate.

Temurah: Exchanges. This tractate, on the other hand, discusses what happens when one inappropriately substitutes for an animal that was pledged to the Temple.

Kerisos: Excision. Certain transgressions were considered more severe than simple violations, for which the penalty was lashes, but did not warrant the death penalty. For these, the punishment is *Kares*, spiritual excision. Doing something of this nature put a barrier between the person and God—which required sincere repentance and a desire to do better. If one did one of these transgressions by accident a sin-offering was required, which explains why this tractate appears in *Seder Kodshim*.

Me'ilah: Misuse of Sacred Objects. If one misused a consecrated object, a guilt-offering was required. As this is less severe than a transgression requiring a sin-offering, this tractate appears after Kerisos.

Tamid: The Daily Offering. This tractate describes the daily offering, which was brought in the Holy Temple each morning and afternoon.

Middos: Measurements. This tractate describes the *Beis HaMikdash*, the Holy Temple in Jerusalem, and the structure and size of its elements. Maimonides says that these measurements will be needed in order to build the Third Temple, when the time comes!

Kinim: Bird Offerings. The topic of this tractate is relatively obscure, covering what to do if varieties of bird offerings were confused. This happened very rarely, and indeed the tractate itself is relatively short (and has no corresponding volume in either Talmud).

Seder Taharos—The Order of Purity

The final order is one that, with its many laws of spiritual and ritual purification, is often the hardest to understand. The one tractate of immediate relevance today—and the only one with Jerusalem and Babylonian Talmudic discussions—is *Maseches Niddah*, which covers "family purity."

How Things Become Impure . . .

Keilim: Vessels. This tractate discusses containers of various kinds, and how they can become *tameh*, spiritually impure.

Ohalos: Tents. Next, the Mishnah turns to a tent, building, or room containing a dead body, and how the other objects in the same enclosure may acquire spiritual impurity from the body.

Nega'im: Blemishes. This tractate discusses the spiritual blemish called *Tzara'as* (often mistranslated as leprosy), which could appear on a person, clothing, or house.

. . . And How to Purify Them

Parah: The Cow. After contact with a dead body, a person would have to undergo a seven-day purification ritual in order to enter the Holy Temple. The ashes of a red heifer are a required component of this ritual.

Taharos: Purifications. This discusses the necessary purification methods after contact with weaker forms of spiritual impurity than that of a body.

Mikva'os: Ritual Baths. How to properly construct and fill a ritual bath is the primary subject of this tractate.

Family Purity

Niddah: Menstrual flow. When a woman menstruates, Biblical law prohibits marital relations between her and her husband until she has finished and immersed herself in a mikvah, or ritual bath. As already mentioned, a dead body conveys the severest form of spiritual impurity, and in general the loss of live-giving capacity—such as menstruation, when a female egg is lost, or a male emission—conveys impurity.

The special laws of Niddah separation act to renew the intellectual bond between husband and wife, forcing each to discuss and reconcile arguments without the often-artificial closeness of physical contact. These laws also, of course, renew the physical bond when the couple is permitted to touch each other once again.

Other Tractates Regarding Spiritual Purity

Mach'shirin: Prerequisites. This tractate discusses what must happen to food products before they can acquire spiritual impurity.

Zavim: Discharges. Here, the Mishnah turns to a type of discharge that could afflict a person. This was a spiritual illness that is not found in our era.

T'vul Yom: One who Immersed Today. When a person undergoing purification from certain forms of *tumah*, spiritual impurity, immerses in a mikvah, he or she retains a level of impurity until nightfall. This tractate discusses the laws that affect a person during the daytime, after immersion.

Yadayim: Hands. Certain forms of impurity were decreed by the Rabbis to affect the hands of a person, requiring more careful contact with foods and holy items. Most of these laws do not affect us today, because, as mentioned earlier, nearly everyone has been in a building with a dead body at one time or another, and is therefore tameh anyway.

Uktzin: Stems. This final tractate discusses how the types of impurity that can affect foods can or cannot affect the stems of fruits.

Chapter 10

From Babylonia to Europe

In the centuries following the Talmud's completion, the Talmud became the central focus of Torah study. No longer were students listening to the oral recollections of their teachers—rather, they were jointly analyzing the text, the teacher explaining the disagreements therein and the conclusions reached. Babylonia had been a center for Torah learning since the First Temple's demise, but it soon declined in favor of Europe. A similar dramatic shift was not to occur again until the Holocaust, more than 1,000 years later.

The "Geniuses" of the Post-Talmudic Era

Following the completion of the legal decision-making in the Talmud in approximately the year 4260 (500 C.E.), there was a short period of the *Rabbonan Savorai*, which could be translated as "Elucidating Rabbis." They were called this because they did not add new legal material to the text of the Talmud, but added explanations and made small emendations to clarify its logic and meaning. During the last generation of *Rabbonon Savorai*, the "minor tractates" of the Talmud were redacted.

This was also a period of intense persecution of the Jewish community. Late during the end of the era of the Talmud, the academy of Sura was forced to close for approximately forty years; it reopened in 4276 (516 C.E.), but both yeshivos, in Sura and Pumbedisa, were closed again during this era and leading scholars fled to areas under Arab rule.

The reopening of the yeshiva of Pumbedisa in 4349 (589 C.E.) began the era of the *Gaonim*, or the Geniuses. Twenty years later, the academy in Sura reopened as well, and the title of Gaon was accorded to the leaders of the great academies from then throughout the next several centuries.

We have relatively little written material from this era. Rabbi Menachem HaMeiri of Provence (1249–1306 C.E.) explains that this was, paradoxically, the result of their great scholarship:

> The Academies were great and well-respected, and the students were many, constant in their study. All the more so, the Deans of the Yeshivos, who were titled for their "Genius," who would barely leave the Tent [of Torah study] day or night. And they would know the entire Talmud by heart, or nearly so, and the words of the entire Torah and Talmud were completely familiar to them like the "Shema" [one of the most common passages of the morning prayers].
>
> And because of this, they saw no reason for it to be necessary to write long works, because the entire explanation [of the Talmud] was on the tip of their tongues, and they viewed the writing of a long explanation, such as we write today, a waste of words. This caused them to write only small things, whether to explain or to decide the application of the law.

The era of the Gaonim continued until 4798 (1038 c.e.), when, with the passing of Rav Hai Gaon, Babylonia's time at the center of Torah scholarship came to an end. Fortunately, by then many scholars had moved to Europe, and Torah had taken root there and begun to flourish.

The Early European Communities

The group of scholars who comprised the "Early Authorities" lived during the ninth through the fifteenth centuries of the Common Era. Historians refer to this period as the Dark Ages, when there was little scholarly development in Western thought. This same period of time, however, was incredibly fruitful in terms of Jewish scholarship. Not only was literacy among Jewish commoners much more prevalent than the European norm, but the leading Rabbis of the time produced voluminous works that are still studied avidly.

By the end of the eighth century, clear differences in customs and prayers had developed between the Sephardic Jews of Spain and Northern Africa, who came largely from Babylonia, and the Ashkenazic Jews of France, Germany, and Italy, who came from the Land of Israel. Each group had its own leading authorities, and for this reason a number of legal decisions and Rabbinic decrees made by the Rabbis of each side were not adopted by the other. Nonetheless, the ongoing correspondence and discussion between the scholars of each group indicate that an environment of mutual respect and admiration prevailed.

Even within these groups, minor differences developed, reflected today in the different practices of Syrian versus Moroccan Sephardim, or German versus Italian Ashkenazim. Only in our day do we find joint projects between researchers thousands of miles apart. In the Middle Ages, new developments in one community might have no impact upon others until decades, if not centuries, later. During the period under discussion, there were four (or by some counts, five) different regional groups, each with its own unique strengths.

Torah in Italy

The Italian Jewish community predates the Common Era—there was contact between Jews in Rome with the Kings of Israel while the Second Temple stood. Following the destruction of the Second Temple, Italy was the first established center for Torah learning in the Diaspora outside Babylonia. It was the preeminent location for Torah scholarship during the early Middle Ages, after the decline of the Babylonian academies.

Today, we have no Torah or Talmud commentaries from early Italian scholars, but others mentioned their high reputation. As you will read in a moment, Italian Rabbis helped establish Torah academies in the Sephardic lands, and there is a similar story of a Rabbi from Lombardy who moved to Germany and brought advanced Torah scholarship along with him. Rabbi Shlomo Yitzchaki of France, of whom you will read more in Chapter 11, consulted with the academy of Rome on a question of Jewish law, and records the opinion of Rabbi Klonimos of Rome in his Talmud commentary.

Torah study in Italy advanced in later centuries thanks to expulsions of Jews living elsewhere. In the fifteenth century, an influx of German Jews led to the establishment of a full Ashkenazic community there, as well as at least one school of Torah. Don Yitzchak Abarbanel helped lead the exodus from Spain in 1492, and with other Spanish Jews brought Italy again to the fore among centers for Torah study.

Spain, Portugal, and Northern Africa

The Jewish communities of Kairouan (Tunisia), Egypt, Morocco, and Spain developed with strong ties to the academies in Babylonia. The early Rabbis in Kairouan, in particular, had active correspondence with the later Gaonim heading the Babylonian schools.

The Four Captives

In the latter half of the tenth century, four great Torah scholars from southern Italy set out to raise money for the Torah academies of their country. They were captured at sea by a pirate, Ibn Rumahis, who ransomed them to four different Jewish communities along the coast of the Mediterranean Sea. While we don't know the identity or destination of one of the captives, the other three quickly attained recognition as the outstanding scholars in their new homes, and led academies there.

Rav Moshe ben Chanoch and his son, named Chanoch after his grandfather, were ransomed by the Jews of Cordova, and soon created a new academy there. Rav Chushiel was ransomed in Kairouan, where his son Rabbeinu Chananel wrote a Talmud commentary that is commonly studied today. Egyptian Jews ransomed Rav Shemaryah ben Elchanan, who helped to establish Cairo as an important center for Torah study.

Over time, Spain became the most important of the Sephardic nations in the development of Torah scholarship.

Shmuel HaNagid

Shmuel ben Yosef HaLevi HaNagid (993–1056 C.E.) was born in Cordova, Spain. He learned Talmud from Rabbi Chanoch ben Moshe, was taught Hebrew grammar by Rabbi Yehudah ibn Chayug, and was a student of the sciences, mathematics, and languages as well. Though he started off as a simple shopkeeper, he rose in Muslim society to become the vizier (prime minister) of Granada and commander of the Granadan army.

According to legend, the vizier's chambermaid asked Rabbi Shmuel, whose shop was nearby, to help compose some letters to the vizier. When the vizier saw the caliber of the writing, he immediately hired the Rabbi to be his secretary. Rabbi Shmuel proved so wise and capable that the vizier entrusted more and more of his duties to him, until—when the vizier fell seriously ill—he spoke about Rabbi Shmuel to King Chabus. When the vizier succumbed to his illness, Rabbi Shmuel was appointed his successor, and for this reason was called *HaNaggid*, "the Prince," by the Jews of Granada, and *ibn Nagdela* by the Arabs.

In that position, Rabbi Shmuel was able to build a prominent synagogue and Talmudic academy in Granada, in which he delivered the daily class himself. He was also the author of several scholarly works and books of religious poetry.

Upheaval and Persecution

This advancement occurred in a relatively peaceful and secure environment until the middle of the eleventh century C.E. After this time, areas of Spain were conquered by Berber rebels, the Almoravids (a Berber dynasty centered in Morocco), and the Almohads (fanatical Muslims), and then by Christian rulers. Persecution increased until finally, in 1492, the Jews of Spain were forced to choose between conversion to Christianity or expulsion. Jews discovered after that time were tortured and murdered during the infamous Spanish Inquisition.

Those Jews who adopted Christianity under duress during the Inquisition were called *Marranos,* and usually professed Christian beliefs on the outside while observing Judaism at home. Many were discovered and put to death.

The Jewish population of Portugal grew dramatically as refugees swarmed across the Spanish border. Their refuge, however, soon turned hostile—in late 1496, King Manuel expelled the Jews from his country as well. Navarre, a small kingdom crossing the Pyrenees from modern-day France to Spain, was the last holdout on the Iberian peninsula, before expelling its Jews as well in 1498.

France and Germany

While Jewish settlement in Northern Europe dates back at least as far as the Roman Empire, it truly began to flourish under another emperor: Charlemagne, who ruled in the late eighth through early ninth centuries C.E., encouraged Jews to migrate into his empire from Italy, Babylonia, and elsewhere—as he strove to make his empire the center of knowledge and progress. The Carolingian dynasty of Charlemagne and his descendants—notably his great-grandson, Charles the Fat (839–888)—was friendly to Jews and Jewish scholars.

A Quick Turn to Persecution

In the tenth century C.E., however, persecution of French Jewry began. The Crusades, from the eleventh through thirteenth centuries, brought death and devastation to Jewish communities across Europe—the Jewish communities of Mainz, Regensburg, Worms, Cologne, and Rouen are only a few of those that were entirely destroyed, their populations massacred. While many noblemen and churches attempted to protect local Jewry, the general effect of the pogroms and atrocities was devastating.

Rabbeinu Gershom Me'or HaGolah

In the midst of this upheaval, a shining giant of Torah learning was born in Metz, France, in 960 C.E. Rabbi Gershom became one of the first great Rabbis of the Ashkenazic community. He established a Talmudic academy in Mainz, Germany, that attracted students from as far away as Provence and Spain. Rabbi Gershom assembled many reliable manuscripts of the Talmud, and by comparing them was able to correct scribal errors and clarify many otherwise difficult passages. He also composed a Talmud commentary, of which some fragments have survived the centuries. He was so respected for his piety and brilliance that he was called *Me'or HaGolah*, "Light of the Exile."

In about the year 1000 C.E., Rabbeinu Gershom called a conference of Rabbis to enact several decrees, which were given weight by pronouncing a ban—a *cherem*—against anyone who transgressed them. The laws still known today as the Cherem D'Rabbeinu Gershom include proscriptions against polygamy and reading other people's mail, and required the active consent of a wife whose husband wanted to give her a Get, a writ of divorce. It also called for the immediate acceptance into the Jewish community of anyone who had been forced to adopt Christianity under duress, and was now returning to Judaism.

Blood Libels

Beginning in the twelfth century, blood libels were propagated in many communities. In 1171, the entire Jewish community of Blois was murdered following a blood libel. King Philip II (1180–1223) himself believed in this myth, and confiscated the property of all Jews in Paris and evicted them in 1182. In the thirteenth century, the Jewish communities of Frankfurt, Munich, and across Bavaria were wiped out on the basis of this cruel fiction.

FACT

The "blood libel" was the story that the blood of a non-Jew was required for the Matzah eaten by Jews on the Passover holiday. The tale usually involved a Christian boy kidnapped and tortured so as to bleed slowly to death. In actuality, Matzah is nothing more than a flat bread, and may contain only flour and water, but in an environment of ignorant fanaticism few were prepared to accept that.

Burning the Talmud

In 1240, a Jewish apostate named Donin accused the Talmud of blasphemy against Christianity. Though multiple Rabbis were called to defend it, twenty-four cartloads of Talmud manuscripts were burned in Paris in 1242. In those days, before the printing press, this tragedy was sufficient to cause a decline in scholarship throughout France.

In 1306, Philip IV "the Fair" ordered the first expulsion of the Jews from France. Louis X permitted them to return in 1315, but another edict of expulsion followed in 1322. In 1359 the Kingdom permitted Jews to return after receipt of a large bribe, but expelled them once again in 1394—this time, for nearly 300 years.

Jewish scholarship in Germany continued until the Black Death (bubonic plague) devastated Europe from 1348 through 1351. Jews were accused of causing this plague by poisoning the wells. No matter how absurd the allegation (the Jewish communities, of course, used the same wells), as many as 200 Jewish communities in Germany were attacked, pillaged, and murdered. Jewish scholarship in Germany essentially came to an end at this point, as the Jews migrated East to Poland or escaped elsewhere. Even centuries later, the best students of Torah would go east to Poland to study, while the German communities would import scholars from Poland and other countries to fill rabbinical positions.

The Provence Jewish Community

Today, the Provence region is best known for the Côte d'Azur, the famous French Riviera, and for the French Alps. But over 1,000 years ago, it too became a center for Jewish scholarship after the decline of the Babylonian academies. Jewish tradition records that a Jewish knight saved the life of King Charlemagne (or one of several other kings named Charles) during a siege of Narbonne, resulting in special privileges for the local Jews.

While this region was part of the French kingdom, the great distance between Provence and Paris meant that local counts had essentially complete control of the area. In 1113, the Count of Barcelona annexed Provence under his jurisdiction. This resulted in an influx of Spanish Jews fleeing from the Almohad fanatics, thus exposing the Provence schools to the flourishing scholarship of their southern neighbors.

In the early thirteenth century C.E., parts of Languedoc were reclaimed by France. The Jewish communities in these areas were thus expelled with the rest of French Jewry in 1306 and 1394. The Jews of Provence and the rest of Languedoc escaped expulsion, only to become the convenient scapegoats when the Black Plague swept across Europe in 1348. The Jews of this region were finally expelled in 1501, on the order of Louis XII.

A New Era

Although Italy was the center of the Catholic Church, it never had an Inquisition or nationwide expulsion of local Jewry. Various cities did expel their Jews, especially in the late 1400s. In Venice, however, they invented a new method of dealing with the Jewish population in 1516—the ghetto, into which all Jews were forced to move. The ghetto concept spread across Europe, and soon replaced outright expulsion as the preferred method of permitting Jewish commerce while preventing too much contact.

Despite the ghettoes, Italy was a major beneficiary when riots and expulsions in other countries drove Jews there to emigrate. By the early 1500s, Jews in Italy could be found worshiping in the old Italian manner, following the German Ashkenazic practice, and using the Sephardic style found in Spain.

The differences in style masked a convergence when it came to Torah learning. In the earlier centuries, the schools in each country were disparate, and communication was difficult. Now travel was becoming less difficult and, as a result, more common. A new invention, though, had an even greater impact than travel itself: movable type.

The Printing Press

While the written recording of the Oral Law ensured its preservation, its transmission relied for hundreds of years upon handwritten copies of the Talmud and other works. It is amazing that earlier writers demonstrate as much access to the writings of predecessors and contemporaries as they obviously had, considering that this meant countless hours on the part of many scribes throughout the centuries.

In the latter half of the fifteenth century, however, the invention of the printing press forever changed access to the written word. Jewish publishers were quick to take advantage, and the first things they printed were prayer and Torah books. The "People of the Book" soon had unparalleled access to its books—tens of thousands of Jewish books were printed in just the first fifty years.

FACT

Rabbis and non-Jewish printers often worked together to publish works for the Jewish community. After a dispute between printers in the mid-sixteenth century, however, one printer reported to the Church that the Jewish books contained unfavorable references to Christianity. A wave of book-burnings swept across Italy. After that time, the Jewish community reached an agreement with the Italian Church that ensured Jewish self-censorship, and publication of Jewish texts continued.

The Code of Jewish Law

Another major development sparking the convergence in Jewish thought and discussion was the acceptance of Rabbi Yosef Karo's *Shulchan Aruch*—with the glosses of Rabbi Moshe Isserles—as "the" definitive Code of Jewish

Law (these two Torah giants and their works will be discussed at greater length in the next chapter). The printing and dissemination of their joint work meant that scholars in all countries enjoyed a common point of reference. While difference in practice remained, the scholarship of great Rabbis all across Europe was less likely to differ profoundly based upon where they lived.

Turkey, Greece, and Israel

Jews fleeing riots in Germany and the Spanish Inquisition moved further east as well. The Turks captured Constantinople in 1453, and by the time the Jews were expelled from Spain and Portugal at the end of the fifteenth century, Sultan Bayezid II made it clear that the Ottoman Empire would welcome them. Constantinople, Salonica, and Smyrna soon hosted large Jewish communities and leading schools of Torah thought.

When Selim I conquered the Land of Israel in 1517, many Turkish Jews moved there. The close relationship between the Jews of Turkey and Israel that these migrants established was to continue for several centuries. Jews rose to prominent positions in the courts of the sultans of the sixteenth century, helping to ensure that the Jewish communities were relatively tranquil and free of persecution.

While Turkish Jewry continued to enjoy such freedom through the seventeenth century, the region surrounding Jerusalem was a separate territory under its own administration, only loosely controlled by the empire. A succession of greedy local rulers imposed very high taxes upon the Jews, and by the time the last of them was removed in 1626, the community was impoverished and many had fled. Over the next century the community recovered, only to be struck by a plague in 1720. The Jewish community in Jerusalem only began to grow and flourish again at the end of the nineteenth century.

Poland and Lithuania

The country or region called "Poland" has meant different things in different eras. Before 1772, the Ukraine and other parts of the Soviet Union were part of Poland, and the duchy of Lithuania was a subdivision as well. It was to all of these areas that Jews moved in the fourteenth and fifteenth centuries, escaping persecution in other Ashkenazic countries.

Centuries of Quiet

Compared to those in other nations across Europe, the Jews in Poland had an extraordinarily favorable relationship with the local rulers, and were able to enjoy relative peace. The kings asked the Jewish leaders to form an organization to represent Jewish interests across Poland, resulting in the *Vaad Arba Aratzos*, "Council of Four Lands." A Jewish writer wrote during the 1640s that "there was scarcely a house in all the kingdom of Poland where its members did not occupy themselves with the study of Torah . . . there were many scholars in every community."

The Chmielnicki Massacres

The Cossack revolt in 1648 brought a horrific end to years of quiet. Under the direction of Bogdan Chmielnicki, the Cossacks and Ukrainian peasants swept westward, Russian Orthodox Christians rebelling against the Catholics of Poland. But although Catholic priests were beheaded, nuns raped, and Polish nobles tortured to death, the Jews were singled out for the worst of Cossack cruelty. During one day in 1649, 6,000 Jews were murdered in Nemirov, and the waters of the river ran red with their blood. And when the Poles succeeded in putting down the Cossack rebellion, it was common for them to vent their rage upon the remaining Jews, accusing them of collaboration with the murderous Cossacks!

Rebuilding

Following these massacres, many Jews and Rabbis moved to Austria, Moravia (in central Czechoslovakia), and elsewhere. Nonetheless, the communities of Poland and Lithuania gradually rebuilt themselves, and by the late eighteenth century were to an even greater extent the preeminent center for Torah learning, and the birthplace of both *Chassidus* and the Yeshiva movement of formalized Torah academies.

Chapter 11

Commentators and Codifiers

Thanks to all of the ongoing scholarship of the last millennium, a person sitting down to learn Torah today isn't left on his own to figure out what a passage means. Today, to study the Five Books of the Torah means to access a wide range of commentaries. Studying the Talmud invites one to access a different set of commentaries, along with multiple legal codes that make it easier to understand how to apply the Talmud's teaching in daily life.

Rabbi Shlomo Yitzchaki—Rashi

Rabbi Shlomo was born in Troyes, France, in 1040 C.E. His father, Rabbi Yitzchak, was a poor Jewish scholar who traced his line back to Rebbe Yochanan HaSandler, one of the Tannaim of the Mishnah and a student of Rebbe Akiva, and from there back to King David. Rabbi Shlomo studied in Mainz and Worms under the tutelage of students of Rabbeinu Gershom *Me'or HaGolah*, and then spent the rest of his life writing and teaching. Many have pointed out that the acronym of Rabbi Shlomo Yitzchaki, or "Rashi," is also that of *Rabban shel Yisrael*, Teacher of Israel. Indeed, Rashi is known to this day as one of the most outstanding Rabbis and teachers in Jewish history, and is routinely termed the "Father of Commentators."

Rashi's Commentary on the Talmud

Rabbi Shlomo's primary work was his commentary on the Babylonian Talmud. It is simultaneously concise yet illuminating, demonstrating incredible mastery of the entire breadth of the Torah, Bible, and Talmud. He worked on this commentary for years, and what we have today is the third edition. He also discovered what he considered to be scribal errors and he suggested emendations; today, the printed "Vilna" edition of the Talmud incorporates many of these changes in the text. His notes proved so popular and famous that later commentators refer to Rashi's work as simply the "*kuntres*," or notebook.

FACT

The third edition of Rashi's commentary does not cover all of the tractates of the Talmud. Whether they were never written or were lost during the Crusades is unknown; his sons-in-law, grandsons, and students attempted to fill in the missing parts.

Rashi's style was to briefly explain the text phrase by phrase, rather than launching into an elaborate discussion of the topics presented. This made the Talmud much more comprehensible for a layperson, who otherwise would have required many years with a teacher in order to learn how to break up and understand the elements of a Talmudic passage.

Frequently Rashi refers to the opinions of his teachers, who were great scholars as well. Though he treated them and their words with the greatest respect, he would often offer a differing opinion based upon his own understanding, be it on a legal issue or the understanding of a passage in Talmud or Torah. At the same time, he would write without hesitation "I don't know" when he felt uncertain about an answer.

The Tosafos Commentary on the Talmud

Scholarship remained very much a part of Rashi's family line; though he had no sons, the best of his disciples became his sons-in-law. One of these, Rabbi Meir ben Shmuel, had three sons who, together with Rashi's other great students, founded the *Tosafist* (like the *Tosefta* in Chapter 8, this word comes from the Aramaic for "adding on") school of Talmudic study, responsible for the other great commentary—found opposite Rashi's own—on most every page of the Babylonian Talmud.

FACT

The most famous of the grandchildren is almost never referred to by his name, Rabbi Yaakov ben Meir. Genesis 25:27 says that "Yaakov was a *Tam* [pure man], a dweller in tents," and the Medrash explains that he studied in tents of Torah. Rabbi Yaakov ben Meir, who was incredibly dedicated to Torah study, is known as Rabbeinu Tam.

The Tosafos is a commentary developed by a group of scholars, not unlike the Talmud itself—at one point, eighty of the most prominent Tosafists studied in Rabbeinu Tam's yeshiva. They compare and contrast various Talmudic discussions of a topic, to understand the similarities and differences. All were fluent with Rashi's analysis of each passage, and when they argued with him, they would routinely first quote his opinion and then explain why they disagreed.

Rashi's Commentary on the Torah

Rashi is at least as well known for his commentary on the Torah. It is considered the single most fundamental commentary for students of all ages and at all levels of scholarship, and is found in most traditional printed editions of the Five Books of Moshe. He presents a basic explanation of the text, relevant concepts in the Oral Law, and Midrashic and Aggadic interpretations, all in a commentary written in his singularly concise style.

One indicator of his commentary's greatness and popularity is the fact that more than 200 works have been written that discuss and comment upon it. Other major Biblical commentaries use his words as a starting point, and demur, elaborate, or digress from there. He also composed a similar commentary on the other books of the Bible, which, though given less attention than his own Talmud and Torah commentaries, is also a work of both genius and comprehensive knowledge.

The Rambam—Maimonides

Rabbi Moshe ben Maimon is surely the best known of the great Rabbis of this era. His works on philosophy and law are valued by all varieties of Jewish and non-Jewish scholars, and on his tomb you will find the words: "From [the original] Moshe to Moshe [Maimonides], there was none like Moshe."

The Rambam was born in 1135 C.E. in Cordova, Spain, where his father was a scholar and judge on the local religious court. His illustrious parentage reached back to Rebbi Yehudah HaNasi, who compiled the Mishnah, and from there to King David.

FACT

When signing the end of his commentary to the Mishnah, Maimonides lists his paternal line back seven generations—five of whom are called Dayan (Judge) and one each called Chacham (Sage) and Rav (teacher and scholar of Torah).

During his early years, the family of Rabbi Maimon was forced to lead a nomadic life. The Almohad Muslims conquered the Cordova region when Moshe was but a child of thirteen, and they forced Jews to choose between conversion or exile. The family left, only to wander through Christian Spain for almost twelve years before moving to Fez, Morocco. There, too, religious persecution was the order of the day (observing Jewish rituals was an offense deemed worthy of the death penalty), and the family left for Israel—only to find themselves in the path of the Crusades. Finally they settled in Cairo, Egypt, in 1165.

While initially supported by his father and then by his brother, David, Moshe was forced to assume responsibility for both his own and his brother's family when David perished at sea, taking much of the family fortune with him. Rather than support himself through the Rabbinate, Rabbi Moshe became a physician—an excellent one, by all accounts—and he was soon appointed royal doctor to Sultan Saladin of Cairo.

This led to Saladin appointing the Rambam as the Naggid ("prince") of Egyptian Jewry, a position to be held by five generations of his descendants. By the time the Rambam passed away in 1204, he was so highly esteemed that even the non-Jews of Cairo mourned for him, and a day of fasting was declared in Jerusalem. He was buried in Tiberias, Israel, and to this day thousands visit his tomb every year.

Maimonides on the Mishnah

The Rambam's commentary on the Mishnah was written under difficult circumstances, as the family moved from country to country to escape persecution. In his own afterword, he refers to "some of it written while traveling over land, some on board ship." Yet a work of such scholarship would be a stunning accomplishment had it been written in the calm of the family study.

First of all, Maimonides clearly explains and analyzes each Mishnah. But in addition, he provides introductions to important fundamentals of Judaism. In his introduction to the Mishnah, he discusses the "chain of transmission" of the Oral Law, one of the sources for Chapter 8 of this book. His introduction to Avos, called "The Eight Chapters," discusses the soul, man's purpose, and philosophical issues such as the apparent contradiction between human beings having free will on the one hand, and God being

All-Knowing and knowing our future choices, on the other. And his introduction to the tenth chapter of Sanhedrin includes his Thirteen Principles of the Jewish Faith, the topic of Chapter 5 of this book.

The Mishnah Torah

The most frequently studied of all Maimonides' works is his fourteen-volume compendium on the full breadth of the Halachah, Jewish law. It is written in concise Hebrew, clearly delineating the law as he understood it in a well-organized fashion, while consciously not including the minority opinions in the Talmud that are not followed as law. He tried to make it easy for any layperson to look up any matter and quickly understand what to do. To this end, he reorganized the totality of Jewish law into fourteen volumes, not following the order of the Talmud. He called his work *Mishnah Torah*, Thorough Teaching of Torah; it is also called the *Yad HaChazakah* (Strong Hand), because the numerical value of *Yad* is fourteen.

ALERT!

The Talmud contains many minority opinions not followed as law. It was important to record them both in order to understand and learn from the reasoning process employed by the two scholars in the debate—and also to know and be able to correct someone who was erroneously following one of these minority opinions.

Maimonides' introduction was controversial, for he wrote that his work was designed "so that a person should not need any other work in order to know a law from the Laws of Israel, but that this work should collect the Oral Torah in its entirety . . . so that a person should read the Written Torah first, and then read this, and one should know from it the entire Oral Torah, and not need to read any other book besides these." In reality, he meant only that the reader should feel comfortable that he knows the law. He did not mean to imply that a scholar should no longer study Talmud—but his words were open to misinterpretation. In addition, he did not provide sources for his decisions, making it difficult to trace his statements back to their Talmudic origins. It is reported that he wanted to provide these footnotes in a separate volume, but did not have time to write it. Rabbi Yosef Karo—concerning whom you will read more below—wrote a commentary upon the Mishnah Torah, called *Kesef Mishnah*, in which he identifies Maimonides' Talmudic sources.

The Arguments of the Ra'avad

Rabbi Avraham ben David (Ra'avad) of Pasqueres lived in Provence from roughly 1120 until 1197 C.E. While a young man, he directed a Talmudic academy in N'imes, which achieved recognition as the leading such school in the Provence region. Later he opened a similar academy in Pasquieres, where he supported numerous needy students—he was independently wealthy, yet avoided lavish expenses in favor of a simple life of piety and scholarship.

He wrote many different works, but is best known for his *Hasagos HaRa'avad*, "Critiques of the Ra'avad," often sharply worded differences with Maimonides' Mishnah Torah that are published alongside it in all the standard texts. He disliked the fact that the Rambam did not quote or list the sources that led him to each decision, yet held Maimonides' work in the highest esteem. His love-hate relationship with the Mishnah Torah is apparent in the following quote:

> All that he has written here has no root in the Talmud or *Tosefta*, nor is it a logical deduction . . . by the life of my head, were it not that he did great work gathering the words of the Talmud, the Jerusalem Talmud, and the *Tosefta*, I would gather against him a gathering of the nation, its elders and wise men . . ." (Laws of Forbidden Mixtures 6:2)

The Guide for the Perplexed

Maimonides' most controversial work is his Guide for the Perplexed, finished in approximately 1190 C.E. As he wrote in his introduction, this work was not designed for beginners to philosophy, or for those who devoted the entirety of their days to Torah study. Rather, it was written in Arabic for the student of secular or Greek philosophy who was confused by apparent contradictions between philosophy and the Torah. In the Guide, Maimonides explains the anthropomorphisms of God used in the Torah—the descriptions of God's "hand," "arm," "eyes," et cetera, as well as God's existence, prophecy, revelation, and free will. In his view, it was important for a person to develop a rational understanding of God and His Creation.

Not all scholars shared this approach, however. Rabbi Shlomo of Montpelier and many other scholars condemned the study of philosophy as an exercise in confusion, and thus condemned study of Maimonides' Guide. Some even suspected that due to his rationalist approach, the Rambam did not believe in the concept of a coming Resurrection of the Dead. Maimonides responded to these critics with his Letter on the Resurrection, explaining (as he had previously in his Thirteen Principles) that this is indeed a fundamental concept in Torah.

The Ramban—Nachmanides

Rabbi Moshe ben Nachman, the *Ramban*, was born in Gerona, Spain, in 1194, and by the age of fifteen was already writing Halachic (Jewish legal) commentaries to the Talmud. For much of his life he was considered the foremost authority in Halachah in all of Spain, and was both a respected teacher and prolific writer. He helped to quell much of the controversy surrounding the works of the Rambam, Maimonides, while also showing great respect to the Rambam's leading detractor, Rabbi Shlomo of Montpelier.

Many of the Ramban's works are still studied today—two of his Jewish legal works are commentaries to the works of the early legal writer Rabbi Yitzchak al-Fasi, concerning whom you'll read more in a moment. Nachmanides' most popular work, however, is his Torah commentary, which is found in the standard study edition. He discusses many topics in detail, provides Medrashic and Kabbalistic interpretations of the verses, and frequently disagrees with Rashi, the Rambam, and others. He completed this work after he arrived in the Land of Israel, where he passed away in 1270 C.E.

The Halachists

Academic researchers will sometimes claim that Halachah was constantly developing and changing over time, before it suddenly became static—

or less charitably, "fossilized"—when an authoritative code was written in 1565 C.E. A careful examination of Halachic works, however, shows that they disagreed only concerning the details that the Talmud itself did not clarify. Whether or not one accepts the transmission of the Oral Law, Jewish law itself has not changed since the Talmud was written—but each new circumstance requires a new application of the law. This process continues into our day, as fax machines and in-vitro fertilization present questions that were certainly never addressed in the sixteenth century.

The *Shulchan Aruch* (Set Table), the code followed today, hardly arose in a vacuum. Besides Maimonides' fourteen-volume encyclopedia of Jewish Law, other Halachic commentaries on the Talmud were studied by Torah scholars in all communities, and laid the foundation for the writing of the Shulchan Aruch. All of them remain important resources to this day, for all who want to understand how Halachic decision-making works and how to apply the law to new circumstances.

The Rif—Rabbi Yitzchak al-Fasi

Born in Algeria at the turn of the eleventh century C.E., Rabbi Yitzchak, the *Rif*, studied Talmud and rose to prominence in Morocco (al-Fasi means "of Fez"). His greatest work was a summary of Jewish law called *Sefer HaHalachos*, Book of the Laws. In it, he assembled and abridged Talmudic passages, omitting the long discussions and providing the practical law alone. While he followed the general order of the Talmud, he included laws found in other places that were relevant to the subject at hand, so the reader could acquire a broad understanding without searching throughout the Talmud for pertinent material.

The commentaries upon the Sefer HaHalachos provide some of the most interesting—not to mention acerbic—rebuttals found in all Torah literature. The Ra'avad, Rabbi Avraham ben David of Pasqueres, wrote a commentary questioning the Rif, though he spoke of the Rif's great stature and apologized for his own inability to understand him. Nachmanides' *Sefer HaZechus*, Book of Merit, replies to the Ra'avad's questions.

Rabbi Zecharyah HeLevi of Lunel, Provence, wrote a critical commentary of the Rif while still a young man of nineteen. The Ra'avad, who was but five years older and living in the same city, wrote his own comments, which attacked Rabbi Zecharyah's disagreements with the Rif, defending the Rif in sharply worded retorts. Nachmanides then wrote *Milchamos HaShem*, "Wars for God," in which he defended Rabbi Zecharyah and often argued that it was the Ra'avad who was in error. All of these works are printed together in standard editions of the Talmud, making it easy to follow the debate from one topic to the next.

The brotherhood of Torah scholars did not prevent vigorous debate—on the contrary, their mutual search to understand and teach the true interpretation led them to argue their positions vociferously. Yet the loudest and most protracted debates were conducted in an environment of love and respect—as they are in Houses of Study to this day.

The Rosh—Rabbeinu Asher

Rabbeinu Asher, known as the *Rosh*, was born in Germany in approximately 1250 C.E., and became the outstanding disciple and successor of Rabbi Meir of Rothenburg, as spiritual leader and legal authority of German Jewry. Rabbi Meir was held for ransom when he became well known, so Rabbi Asher, when his fame spread, left Germany. He arrived in Spain in 1306, and was invited to become Rabbi of Toledo shortly thereafter.

His most famous work is his Halachic review of the Talmud, which is found today in all full editions. Unlike Maimonides, he followed the order of the Talmud rather than reorganizing the topics, and also carefully listed the major opinions on each question, showing how he arrived at his final conclusion.

The Baal HaTurim

When the Rosh passed away in 1327 C.E., two of his sons succeeded him: Yehudah, the younger of the two, served as the Rabbi of Toledo, while Yaakov became the chief judge on the city's Bais Din, the Rabbinical Court. Rabbi Yaakov wrote the *Arbah Turim* (Four Rows), an encyclopedic work of Halachah focusing upon those laws applicable today, when there is no Temple, no Temple offerings, no tithes, and no laws of spiritual purity related to them. As it was written in Spain, Rabbi Yaakov also omitted reference to the agricultural laws that apply only in the Land of Israel.

He thus reorganized the laws as Maimonides did, but in his own order, dividing the remainder of Jewish law into four volumes:

- **Orach Chayim** (Path of Life)—Daily practices from morning to night, including prayers, blessings on foods, the Sabbath and holidays
- **Yoreh Deyah** (Teacher of Wisdom)—Dietary laws, usury, idolatry, ritual purity, death and mourning
- **Choshen Mishpat** (Breastplate of Judgment)—Financial laws, damages, and the court system
- **Even HaEzer** (The Helping Rock)—Marriage, divorce and domestic relations

Rabbi Yaakov is more frequently known as the *Ba'al HaTurim*, Master of the Rows, a play upon the name of his magnum opus. He also authored two commentaries on the Torah, the shorter of which appears in the standard study editions as the Ba'al HaTurim commentary.

The Code of Jewish Law

One of the most profound developments in the history of Torah was the writing and universal adoption of the Shulchan Aruch. This encyclopedic work brought together all of the major legal opinions, and rendered decisions whose authority was respected worldwide from the day it was published. Ever since then, no work on Jewish law has failed to consider the opinions of Rabbi Yosef Karo of Tsfas, and the critical glosses of Rabbi Moshe Isserles of Cracow.

Rabbi Yosef Karo

Rabbi Yosef Karo was born in Toledo in 1488, but his family moved to Turkey following the expulsion from Spain just four years later. There, he learned Torah with his father, Rabbi Ephraim, and his uncle, Rabbi Yitzchak Karo. He moved to the city of Tsfas (Safed), Israel, in 1536, where he was immediately given a seat on the Bais Din, the religious court, of Rabbi

Yaakov bei Rav. Questions flowed into this court from around the globe, because of its famed expertise in Jewish law. He later succeeded Rabbi Yaakov as the *Rosh Bais Din*, Chief Justice.

The Bais Yosef

He began writing a commentary to the Arbah Turim while still in Turkey, which he completed and revised over the next twenty years, until long after his arrival in Tsfas. His work, the *Bais Yosef*, explains the Talmudic sources behind each decision. He also cites other Halachic works and commentaries—over thirty in all. But in arriving at a definitive conclusion, he refused to rely upon his own opinion, as we see from his introduction:

> There are three pillars of teaching upon which the House of Israel depends in their decisions, namely the *Rif*, the *Rambam*, and the *Rosh*, of blessed memory. Therefore I decided that whenever two of them agree, we should rule the Halachah in accordance with their opinion. The exception is in those few instances where all the Sages of Israel (or a majority) differ with that opinion, and therefore the prevailing custom is to do the opposite.

The Bais Yosef was published in Italy during the 1550s to much acclaim; by 1564, it was already necessary to reprint it.

The Shulchan Aruch

Rabbi Karo then created a concise summary of the decisions reached in the Bais Yosef. He called it the Shulchan Aruch, the Set Table, because he intended to lay out the law for students in a simplified, easy-to-read format. Although he followed the four sections of the Arbah Turim, he also divided his work into thirty sections, so that students who reviewed one section daily would review the totality of practical Jewish law on a monthly basis.

There was some controversy about this approach—one scholar even dismissed it as a book "for children and ignoramuses"—but many critics themselves later realized that it was a valuable and necessary resource. The one remaining issue was that reliance upon the Rif, the Rambam, and the Rosh resulted in a work partial to Spanish scholarship and customs, for two of the three were from Sephardic lands. It was the additional work of Rabbi Moshe Isserles that ensured the universal acceptance of the Shulchan Aruch.

Rabbi Moshe Isserles and the "Tablecloth"

Rabbi Moshe (the *Rema*), son of Rabbi Yisrael Isser (thus the name *Isserles*), was born in Cracow in 1530 C.E., and learned from Rabbi Shalom Shachna of Lublin, considered the pre-eminent *rosh yeshiva* (dean) in Poland. An outstanding prodigy, Rabbi Moshe was appointed Rabbi of Cracow while still a young man, shortly after his marriage to Rabbi Shalom's daughter.

The Rema had tremendous respect and admiration for Rabbi Yosef Karo, whom he once called "a prince of God in our midst," and the Bais Din of Rabbi Karo in Tsfas. At the same time, he was living and learning in Ashkenazic Poland, and recognized that Rabbi Karo's decisions often did not reflect his community's opinions or practices.

The Rema's Commentaries

Rabbi Isserles was busy writing his own commentary on the Arbah Turim when the first section of Rabbi Karo's Bais Yosef was published. Incredibly, Rabbi Moshe went back and abridged his own work, presenting it as merely a commentary on both the Arbah Turim and the Bais Yosef. Today, the standard edition of the Arbah Turim includes both commentaries, the Rema's in a further-abbreviated form.

Then he turned to Rabbi Karo's Shulchan Aruch, again humbly providing a commentary rather than creating a work of his own. He called his work *HaMapah*, the Tablecloth, "covering" the set table of Rabbi Karo. Today, the two are universally published together, with the comments by Rabbi Isserles interspersed in the text of Rabbi Karo—in a different font, so that you can easily tell them apart. Sometimes he elaborates upon or clarifies a point, while elsewhere he expresses a different opinion, showing where the accepted opinion in Ashkenazic circles is different.

Unified Development

Ever since the publication of the Shulchan Aruch with HaMapah, the two have served as the universal legal code of all Israel. It's not true that Sephardic Jews *always* follow one, while Ashkenazic Jews *always* follow the other—later authorities provided further detail, and sometimes expressed opinions contrary to both. But together, the two serve as the basis upon which further study rested.

The following chart displays six of the most popularly studied commentaries on the Shulchan Aruch and HaMapah—the ones that are printed to either side of the unified text in the standard editions. None of the commentaries covers more than two of the four volumes. All six of these commentaries, though, were written in either Poland or Lithuania, the dominant region for Torah scholarship until the middle of the twentieth century.

Author	Lived	Commentary	Covering
Rabbi Yehoshua Falk	1550–1614	*Sefer Me'iras Einayim*	Volume Three
Rabbi David ben Shmuel HaLevi	1586–1667	*Turei Zahav*	Volumes One and Two
Rabbi Moshe Lima	1605–1658	*Chelkas Mechokek*	Volume Four
Rabbi Shabse ben Meir HaKohen	1622–1663	*Sifsei Kohen*	Volumes Two and Three
Rabbi Avraham Abeli Gombiner	1637–1683	*Magen Avraham*	Volume One
Rabbi Shmuel Phoebus	1650–1700	*Bais Shmuel*	Volume Four

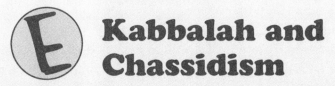

Chapter 12

Kabbalah and Chassidism

You probably turned to Chapter 4 first, and this one second, because Kabbalah is much in the news. But while the current interest may be a passing fad, the inherent holiness of the Kabbalah will not fade tomorrow. The Chassidic masters, in particular, incorporated Kabbalistic teachings into their philosophy, and they developed customs and practices based on them. They simplified their teachings so that any student of Torah could benefit from their words, making the spark of Kabbalistic inspiration available to all.

Kabbalah and the Inner Light

Despite all the interest in Kabbalah and mysticism in our day, it isn't a New Age religion or a collection of superstitions. Kabbalah, Qabalah, Cabala— however you spell it in English, it is ancient and holy Jewish mysticism. It provides an understanding of the essence of God, the Purpose of Creation, and our purpose and role in the world.

While the current hype about Kabbalah is likely to prove a passing fad, Kabbalah is part of the Torah itself. Torah is designed to teach and guide a person through life, rather than to give out five-minute solutions to life's major issues. Please don't be fooled by people who set themselves up as modern-day Jewish gurus, suggest that you say a few incantations, and call this "Kabbalah."

ALERT!

At one point, the same "Kabbalah" group that was selling red strings online "to protect you from the influences of the Evil Eye" for $26 was also selling a book, with red string included, for just $14. Clearly, an informed consumer isn't *their* best customer. From an elderly woman at Jerusalem's Western Wall, the same string is about $1.25.

True Kabbalah is entirely integrated into Torah and Judaism. People think of mysticism and spirituality as ethereal matters, divorced from the pragmatic issues of day-to-day life. In the secular world, you would hardly expect to find a Supreme Court Justice who was also a famous teacher of meditation and "guiding the inner spirit." Yet many of the great Talmudists and Halachists—such as Rashi, the Ramban, and Rabbi Yosef Karo—were also experts in the mystical secrets of the Kabbalah. This has been true since the earliest days; the Zohar, the great Kabbalistic work, was written by Rabbi Shimon bar Yochai, disciple of Rebbe Akiva and an oft-quoted Sage of the Mishnah.

The Inner Secrets of Torah

The word Kabbalah stems from the word *l'kabel*, which means "to receive." The Kabbalah is received wisdom. Like everything else in Torah, Moshe received it on Mt. Sinai. Moshe was, in fact, the ultimate Kabbalist, because he was able to receive God's wisdom as no one else could. In other words, he was the ultimate Kabbalist because he was the ultimate Prophet.

The Kabbalah is the concealed dimension of Torah—it is also called *Sisrei Torah*, the Hidden Torah, and/or *Sodos HaTorah*, Secrets of the Torah. Through the Kabbalah, one can access the inner dimension of reality and experience God in this world. At its essence, Kabbalah is the study of God, the Creator. In the Torah's eyes, the purpose of human existence is to draw close to God and become more Godlike ourselves—the Kabbalah takes this to the highest levels.

Torah and Kabbalah—Knowledge of God

The Kabbalah, then, is the highest, innermost level of Torah. Now if God wants the Jewish people to have the Torah, in order that they should know Him and be able to achieve Godliness in their own lives—why would He keep part of it "secret"? The only logical reason to keep it secret from most people is because it would not help them to achieve that goal, and could even be counterproductive.

The Kabbalah brings a person into contact with Torah at the highest, mystical level. Only through Kabbalah is it possible to achieve the deepest understanding of the entire Torah. But at the same time, its true benefits are not available to the beginning student. The Torah ideal is *not* to ascend into mystical realms and to lose touch with reality; you can achieve spiritual heights in the hidden Kabbalah only in accordance with your achievements in the revealed learning of Torah and pious day-to-day behavior. First achieve a level of learning in the revealed Torah, and only then will the secrets of the hidden Torah be comprehensible.

The Hidden Kabbalah

The Mishnah in Chapters of the Fathers, when discussing the Chain of Transmission, says that Moshe received the Torah on Sinai, and transmitted it to Yehoshua, Joshua his disciple. According to the Medrash, Moshe gave to Yehoshua the methods and spiritual preparations necessary to experience prophecy. This was, Kabbalistic sources say, the Kabbalah itself, which was then handed down by the Prophets as a central component of the Oral Torah. When the First Temple was about to be destroyed, the Prophet Yechezkel, Ezekiel, had a vision of the *Ma'aseh Merkavah*, the "Workings of the Chariot." This was a vision of the totality of the Kabbalah.

Dangers of the Hidden Kabbalah

At many times in history, Rabbis said that one should not learn the Kabbalah before a given age, in order to avoid misunderstandings or abuse of the secret knowledge. The Talmud in Tractate Chagiga says that the secrets of Kabbalah may only be taught to one student at a time, in accordance with his understanding. A story from that tractate, from Chagiga 14b, illustrates the risks of premature exposure to the mystical secrets of Torah.

To understand this story, you need to first know a teaching of the Kabbalah. It says that every line of the Torah can be understood on four levels:

- **Pshat**: The simple, straightforward meaning
- **Remez**: Hints of things not stated explicitly
- **Drush**: Homiletic interpretations
- **Sod**: Secret

Obviously, the level of *Sod*, the secret understanding, corresponds to the highest level of wisdom that is found in the Kabbalah. The Hebrew acronym for the four words, representing the four levels of Torah knowledge, is *Pardes*, which means garden, or vineyard. The original Pardes was the Garden of Eden—this is probably the source of the English word "Paradise."

This, then, is the cautionary tale in the Talmud. In Tractate Chagiga, it says that four Rabbis "entered into the Pardes," ascending into the spiritual realms to understand the Kabbalistic secrets. Of the four, one died, one went insane, and one became a heretic.

Only one, Rebbe Akiva, emerged safely. The ministering angels also wished to cast down Rabbi Akiva, but the Holy One said, "Leave this elder alone, for he is worthy of making use of My glory." One of the lessons from this is that the hidden Kabbalah could be used on practical levels—a great Sage could "make use of" it. One knowledgeable in the hidden Kabbalah could make things happen—and this was one very good reason that only the most qualified could touch it.

Early Kabbalistic Works

When Torah was in danger of being forgotten, the Mishnah was not the only written work that resulted. In addition to the Tosefta and other legal texts, four major Kabbalistic works were written then:

- The *Sefer HaBahir*—The Book of Illumination, by Rebbe Nechunyah ben Hakanah and his student, the High Priest Rebbe Yishmael ben Elisha
- The *Pirkei Hechalos Rabatai*—The Greater Chapters of the Divine Halls, also by Rebbe Nechunyah and Rebbe Yishmael
- The *Sefer Yetzirah*—The Book of Formation, by Rebbe Akiva
- The *Zohar*—The Book of Splendor, by Rabbi Shimon bar Yochai

Rebbe Nechunyah ben Hakanah was a teacher of Rebbe Akiva, while Rabbi Shimon bar Yochai was one of Rebbe Akiva's great students—so all of these works come from Sages of the Mishnah, and from the same small and direct line of scholarship. According to some, though, the origin of the Sefer Yetzirah goes all the way back to the patriarch Avraham, who received it through prophecy, and it was then revealed a second time to Rebbe Akiva. Concerning the Zohar, it is obvious that Rabbi Shimon bar Yochai and his disciples could only have written the nucleus of it, because later generations are mentioned therein. The later portions appear to date to the post-Talmudic Babylonian Gaonim.

What is clear from the caution in Tractate Chagiga, though, is that only certain individuals—even among the great scholars of Torah—were able to safely study the Kabbalah. They were required to possess great knowledge of the revealed Torah, and also the wisdom to know what they did *not* know and were not yet ready to learn and understand. The written Kabbalistic works were deliberately written in an extremely cryptic style, making them impossible to understand without help. No one knows which of the Gaonim actually possessed Kabbalistic knowledge, and after that time, the Zohar was in very limited circulation for centuries, until Rabbi Moshe de Leon of Spain, having come into a copy of the book, made many copies and distributed them.

The Revealed Kabbalah

The city of *Tsfas* (Safed) in Israel became a major Torah center for Spanish refugees following the expulsion of 1492. As already mentioned, Rav Yosef Karo wrote his Shulchan Aruch, the standard Code of Jewish Law, while in that city—and Rav Karo was also a Kabbalistic scholar. One of his students, Rabbi Moshe Cordovero (known as the *Ramak*) was an outstanding Kabbalist and the dean of a Kabbalistic Yeshiva in Tsfas. But it was an orphan from Jerusalem who became known as the greatest Kabbalist since Rabbi Shimon bar Yochai: the saintly Rabbi Yitzchak Luria.

The Ari HaKadosh

Rabbi Yitzchak lost his father at a young age, and his mother took him to live with her brother, Rabbi Mordechai Frances, in Egypt. There he studied under Rabbi David ibn Avi Zimra (the *Radvaz*) and his student Rabbi Betzalel Ashkenazi, both of whom were outstanding legal scholars—the Radvaz was the chief religious judge of all Egyptian Jewry—as well as Kabbalists. After six years of study with Rabbi Betzalel, Rabbi Yitzchak spent six years studying and praying alone, completely immersed in the study of Kabbalah, returning home only on the Sabbath.

The acronym of Eloki Rabbi Yitzchak, the godly Rabbi Yitzchak, is *Ari*, which means "lion." Rabbi Yitzchak became known as Ari HaKadosh, "the Holy Lion."

It is said that *Eliyahu HaNavi*, Elijah the Prophet, appeared to the Ari regularly. In 1570 C.E., Eliyahu told him that since he would soon pass from this world, he should move to the Land of Israel, where he would rise even further in holiness and transmit his Kabbalistic teachings to Rabbi Chaim Vital, who would become his dedicated disciple. Rabbi Chaim was studying under Rabbi Moshe Cordovero when Rabbi Yitzchak arrived, but Rabbi Moshe passed away shortly thereafter. The Ari absorbed Rabbi Moshe's approach to Kabbalah even during this brief period, and referred to him as "our teacher."

Contemporary Kabbalah

When the Ari began to lecture on a topic, be it Talmud or Kabbalah, the wisdom flowed so quickly that it was not possible for him to commit it all to writing. Most of his teachings come to us via Rabbi Chaim Vital. They spread around the globe, and Ari HaKadosh became known as "the Father of Contemporary Kabbalah."

Although Tsfas was a great center for Kabbalistic studies, this does not mean that there was no mysticism practiced elsewhere. A contemporary of the Ari, Rabbi Yehudah ben Betzalel Loew (called the *Maharal*) of Prague, was famed for using the hidden Kabbalah to create a *golem*, a man of clay, to protect the community from harm.

The Ari's teaching was "revealed Kabbalah," which one could access even without being on a saintly level and expert in the entire Talmud. Indeed, Lurianic Kabbalah answers practical philosophical questions, and explains concepts—using the wisdom found in the mystical tradition of Judaism—that are valuable to every follower of Torah. Among the concepts explained are:

- The physical world as but a covering over the true, metaphysical world
- The existence of the world in order for God to do good
- The *sod haTzimtzum*, the secret of God's self-limitation, which allows for both God's omniscience and our own free will to choose good and evil
- The collection and redemption of sparks of holiness, spread around the world from the "broken holy vessels" of Creation
- The exile as an opportunity to collect and restore these Divine sparks

Chassidism

The Chassidic (or Hasidic) movement was created by Rabbi Yisrael *Ba'al Shem Tov* ("Master of the Good Name") in the early eighteenth century. Two great disasters had come and gone in the preceding century: the Chmielnicki Massacres of 1648–1649 and the end of the episode of *Shabtai Tzvi*, the false Messiah, in 1666. Many believed that Shabtai Tzvi was the promised Moshiach who would end the exile, rendering pogroms and persecution nothing more than a memory until the end of time.

When the believers learned that he was an imposter, and, worse, converted to Islam when threatened by the local Sultan, many despaired. Were it not for the Chassidic movement and its emphasis upon joy and excitement in the service of God, many more would undoubtedly have abandoned Jewish practices when the Enlightenment swept across Europe.

Rabbi Yisrael Ba'al Shem Tov

Little is known about the early years of Rabbi Yisrael ben Eliezer. He was born in 1698 in Okopy, Poland, to an elderly father and was orphaned at a young age. He wandered from village to village, taking odd jobs and—as we know now—studying Torah and Kabbalah in seclusion. Rabbi Gershon Kitover, a renowned scholar, was embarrassed when his sister married a common day laborer like Yisrael.

At the age of thirty-six, however, Reb Yisrael turned to the public and began to teach, rapidly gaining a large following. He taught that attachment to God was attained not through fasting and asceticism, but through rejoicing in the Mitzvos, in prayer, even in singing and dancing. He taught that you should never consider yourself unimportant or a condemned sinner; on the contrary, every person is important in God's eyes, and can always begin anew.

Chassidic Philosophy

This was the seed of the Chassidic movement. Chassidism teaches that even a commoner, one who is not a scholar, can attain great spiritual heights through sincere and joyful prayer and performance of Mitzvos. Serving God with joy is the key—sadness and despair prevent a person from serving Him properly.

These teachings found a ready audience in the Jewish masses of Eastern Europe, who were both unlearned and depressed by the recent tragedies. The teachings of the Ba'al Shem Tov, or the *Besht*, brought them renewed faith and an infusion of joy—because if you are told that being happy is a priority, and work on being happy every day, you will certainly be happier as a result.

Many of the teachings of Chassidus were drawn from Kabbalistic sources, and Lurianic Kabbalah in particular. Chassidus teaches that God is everywhere, and hidden sparks of holiness are waiting to be freed. Even in evil, there is hidden goodness. Once all of these holy sparks are released, the world will be ready for its ultimate restoration—or *tikkun*, fixing—with the coming of Moshiach.

Role of the Rebbe

Chassidus also elevated the role of the *Tzaddik*, or Holy Man. The Tzaddik, one whose days (and nights) are spent in study and prayer, divests himself of earthly attachments and reaches great spiritual heights. He is able to advise others on how to grow in their service of God, and to guide them in responses to practical issues as well.

Even more than this, the Rebbe binds the Jewish people together, and serves as a link between God and the masses, who cannot achieve such exalted spiritual levels on their own. They all turn to him for blessings, because "the will of those who fear Him, He will do" (Ps. 145:19).

Opposition to Chassidism

Chassidism was hardly without its detractors. Many Chassidic innovations in both belief and practice were initially regarded with great suspicion. As the greatest center of Jewish learning at the time was Vilna, in Lithuania, it is unsurprising that this was the first city to act against a movement perceived as minimizing the importance of Torah learning.

In April of 1772, the leadership of the Jewish community of Vilna—including the famed "Genius of Vilna," Rabbi Eliyahu Kramer, whom you will meet in the next chapter—signed a ban against Chassidus. Rabbi Kramer's name was of particular significance because not only was his Torah scholarship unparalleled, but he was a master of the Kabbalah as well.

Reducing the Centrality of Torah Learning

While some of the charges were more important than others, the primary complaint was certainly the accusation that Chassidism placed insufficient emphasis upon Torah study, the lifeblood of the Jewish People. The Chassidic leader, Rabbi Yaakov Yosef of Polnoa, wrote concerning the Ba'al Shem Tov that "his soul told the Rabbi [the Besht himself] that he achieved communication with the heavenly realms not because he studied Torah, Talmud and the commentators, but because of sincere prayer." This sort of statement—that anything brought a person closer to God other than the study of Torah itself—was sure to draw a strong response. Indeed, as you will see in the next chapter, Reb Chayim Volozhner wrote in his book *Nefesh HaChayim* that learning is more important than prayer, and used Talmudic sources to prove it.

Chassidism also taught that it was almost impossible to achieve the best form of Torah learning—learning "for its own sake." The Chassidic masters taught that this meant learning uniquely for the sake of attachment to the Divine, requiring a high state of purity and an exalted soul. Here, too, the Nefesh HaChayim disagreed, saying that "for its own sake" merely means in order to understand Torah, without ulterior motives such as showing off, winning an argument, or financial incentives.

Other Complaints

While Torah study was the main issue, there were many others as well. The *Misnagdim*, those in the Opposition, complained that Chassidim were separating themselves from the main synagogues of their communities, praying in their own small groups.

The Chassidim also adopted what their opponents considered a lax attitude toward the time prayers were to be said. They also changed the accepted order of the services, replacing the Ashkenazic order of prayer with one inspired by the Kabbalistic teachings of the Ari. While this version of the prayers is not that used by the Spanish/North African community, it was influenced by them nonetheless.

Today the Chassidic order is called *Nusach Sefard*, the Sephardic style of prayers, as compared to the *Nusach Ashkenaz* used by those who did not adopt Chassidism.

There were other complaints as well—such as that Chassidim were advocating tobacco and alcohol use to acquire "happiness." Some Chassidim said that by concentrating on the ethereal mysteries, they were immune to earthly limitations such as, for example, not wearing holy objects such as *Tefillin*, phylacteries, into a bathhouse or other dirty place.

Reconciliation

It is reported that the third Rebbe of the Lubavitcher Chassidim, Rebbe Menachem Mendel of Lubavitch (1789–1866), said that the ban against Chassidism had a positive impact—it reduced the excesses of the Chassidim. While it is true that the Nefesh HaChayim accentuated the differences with Chassidic thought, it is a work of *Mussar*, of Jewish ethics, in its own right, and also makes it obvious that the Chassidim and non-Chassidim have far more in common than not.

By the early nineteenth century, barely fifty years after the first ban in Vilna, opposition to Chassidism had all but faded. Many Chassidic groups place a great emphasis upon Torah learning, and in any case, everyone acknowledged that it was strengthening the Jewish people. With the Enlightenment sweeping across Europe, there were groups of Jews adopting beliefs far more troublesome than whether it was okay to say the morning prayers after 11 A.M.!

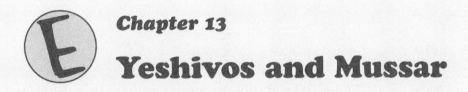

According to Jewish tradition, the idea of a yeshiva, a house of study, reaches back before the Torah was given to Moshe. The modern-day yeshiva, however, is a more recent innovation, dating back "merely" 200 years. Today yeshivos exist around the world, and they have revolutionized organized Torah learning. Throughout the Yeshiva system, the critical study of Torah is augmented by the study of Mussar, Jewish ethical development.

A New System of Study

Throughout earlier eras, the system of study for young men was very informal. While there was often a hired *melamed*, or educator, for young boys, by the age of ten or thirteen adolescent youths were already joining the labor force as apprentices or simple workers. It was unusual for a child to continue his studies full-time until age sixteen, much less to continue on into adulthood. This was the province of the truly elite young men, who demonstrated exceptional abilities in their studies.

In general, the Rabbi of each town would educate the young men who lived there. They would gather in the local synagogue, study individually or in pairs, and then meet around a table with the Rabbi. Occasionally, a truly notable Rabbi would attract students from other towns, but it was unusual for a student to leave his family—again, only the elite young scholars would even contemplate such a move.

Now the Enlightenment was sweeping across Europe, encouraging many of the less privileged to abandon the Talmud and its dictates entirely. The Chassidic answer to this threat to Torah was to encourage the common man to serve God with rapture and joy, developing an enthusiasm for Judaism. The great scholar known as the "Genius of Vilna" gave a different answer: unsurprisingly, he called for a newfound dedication to the study of Torah and Talmud—but in an entirely new environment.

The Vilna Gaon

Against all the other great Torah teachers of the last several centuries, the name of Rabbi Eliyahu Kramer, the Vilna *Gaon* (Genius), still towers above them all. It is extremely rare for a person to be known for either brilliance or piety—and all the more rare for one individual to be known for both. Rabbi Kramer was such a person.

Brilliance and Diligence

Born in 1720 to Rabbi Shlomo Zalman Kramer, who was descended from a long line of Rabbis, and his wife, Treyna, Eliyahu demonstrated his brilliance at a very early age. It is reported that he knew the *Chumash* (the

Five Books of Moshe) by heart before he was four. And at the same time, he demonstrated amazing dedication to his studies. When he was a boy of eleven, he sat up an entire night to learn two large and difficult tractates of Talmud by a self-imposed deadline. By morning he had not only completed both, but was able to answer challenging questions about them from a scholar visiting with the Kramer family.

As an adult, he managed to sleep only two hours each day (as reported by multiple witnesses, including his son), studying Torah constantly. He even studied alone in a hut after his marriage—only his wife knew the location of his study, and she brought him food each day.

FACT

Rabbi Kramer's great knowledge of Torah was supplemented by a deep understanding of mathematics, astronomy, biology, and medicine—surprising for a person always found delving in holy books. He saw the natural sciences merely as necessary tools for comprehension of Torah, however, and never encouraged their study while attaining basic fluency with Torah and Talmud.

The Rabbi's penchant for solitary study remained with him throughout his life. Despite his acknowledged greatness, Rabbi Kramer never held a formal, official position of any kind. He was never a synagogue Rabbi or dean of a school. Instead, he simply studied Torah—all day, and all night—and was recognized as the de facto leader of Vilna's thriving Jewish community.

New Texts, New Systems

Given his avoidance of any leadership position, the revolutions sparked by the Vilna Gaon are all the more surprising. Besides his writings and works of scholarly commentary, he changed the world of Torah learning for all following generations.

First of all, Rabbi Kramer standardized accurate texts of both Mishnah and Talmud. During the preceding centuries, hundreds of scribes had created thousands of copies of the Talmud, and errors were simply an inevitable part of that process. Of course, everyone trusted the texts they had received—so only a person with a great reputation for both piety and scholarship could have made emendations that would be accepted by all. The Vilna Gaon was such a person. Thanks to his corrections, many apparent difficulties in the text simply vanished, and today his version is universally accepted as authentic.

In addition, his dedication to straightforward and careful study of the Talmud, to elevating the level of Torah scholarship, gave birth to a revolution in Torah study itself. For it was on his directive and with his encouragement that his most famous student, Rabbi Chayim Itzkowitz, established the first modern-day yeshiva in Volozhin, Lithuania, just a few years after Rabbi Kramer passed away.

The Mother of All Yeshivos

Rabbi Itzkowitz, known throughout the Jewish world as Reb Chayim *Volozhner*, was born in 1749. He acquired from the Vilna Gaon not only great knowledge of Torah, but also the lesson that—above all else—Torah study was the key to the Jewish future. A new methodology was required to build up Torah study, so that more young men could grow into accomplished scholars and spread Torah back into their home communities.

Before opening his yeshiva, he wrote a letter to the Rabbis of all the Lithuanian Jewish communities. In it, he explained his opinion that a national house of learning was needed—to attract and immerse the finest students in an environment of intensive Torah studies, and thus to develop Torah scholars of the highest caliber.

Both for those without the financial means to hire their teachers, and those unable to find teachers, the Etz Chayim Yeshiva was a tremendous opportunity. Outstanding students applied, hoping to secure a place (eventually the yeshiva established a quota for each geographic region, to ensure fairness). Once accepted, they faced a demanding schedule of learning, six days a week. Some students rose as early as 3 A.M., while others stayed in the study hall until midnight, with brief interruptions for prayer and meals.

Rabbi Itzkowitz's major written work is called *Nefesh HaChayim*, "The Living Soul" (following a frequent custom of writers over the last several centuries, the name of his work is also taken from his own name, *Chayim*).

In it, he both analyzes our existence based upon Talmudic and Kabbalistic sources and speaks of Torah study as the most important effort of the Jewish People—with even prayer taking a secondary role. As you saw in the last chapter, this was designed in part to counterbalance Chassidic sayings to the contrary.

> The Sages call prayer "temporal life," and Torah study "eternal life," as found in the first chapter of Tractate Shabbos: "Rava saw Rav Hamnuna extending his prayers. He said, 'They are forsaking eternal life, and engaging in temporal life!'" (Shabbos 10a) This is because prayer . . . adds holiness and blessing in its appropriate time, but if the time has passed, it offers no further benefit . . . whereas involvement with study of the Holy Torah reaches to the core of life and the establishment of the worlds . . . therefore a person is obligated to involve himself and think about it at every hour, always. (Nefesh HaChayim 4:26)

The Mussar Movement

While the modern-day yeshiva unquestionably transformed Torah learning, this alone was not enough to withstand the winds of change that would soon blow across Europe. In order to counterbalance the influences that would tug a young student toward assimilation, Torah *life* also needed to be revitalized. The Chassidic movement offered one answer; Mussar, a devotion to Jewish ethics developed by outstanding students of the yeshiva, provided another.

The Philosophy of Mussar

Mussar is the study of ethics, but it is much more than that. It demands a personal commitment to moral values and to improving your behavior to meet that commitment. The goal of Mussar is to effect a self-transformation, by helping you to focus upon the type of person you want to be and the things standing in your way as you try to get there. Mussar is not about self-denial, but rather about something considerably more difficult: self-control.

As compared to conventional Torah study in Mishnah or Talmud, the point of Mussar is not to reach an advanced intellectual understanding of why a Rabbi might have expressed an ethical point as he did. Rather, the idea is to drive the Rabbi's message deep within your subconscious, to the point that when your values are tested, you react almost instinctively to choose to do that which is honest and appropriate, even when your personal desires reach out for you to do the opposite.

The study of Mussar sometimes involves repeating the same passage over and over. This is not, however, at all similar to chanting a mantra or some sort of nonsense sound. On the contrary, the student attempts to drive a short, powerful statement into his memory by studying it repeatedly.

All Torah scholars recognized that this sort of self-improvement is a requirement—as discussed earlier, the goal of the entire Torah is to help an individual to become more godly in thought, word, and deed. Nonetheless, as Rabbi Moshe Chaim Luzzato observed 100 years before the Mussar movement, it seemed that the intelligent scholars devoted all of their energy to the study of Talmud, without thinking about how they themselves should change as a result. Only those with lesser talents were spending time thinking about self-improvement, to the point that "when you observe a person becoming pious, you cannot hold back from suspecting him of being somewhat thick!"

Reb Yisrael Salanter

Born to Rabbi Zev Wolf Lipkin in 1810, Yisrael Lipkin was a child prodigy, recognized immediately for his brilliance and photographic memory. When he was but ten years old, his father sent him from his home town, Zaager, to learn with Rabbi Tzvi Hirsch Broida, Rabbi of Salant, also in Lithuania. There, Rabbi Yosef Zundel—an outstanding student of Rabbi Chayim Volozhner—became Yisrael's mentor.

It was Reb Zundel who taught Reb Yisrael to be devoted to the study of Mussar. But while Rabbi Zundel hid his greatness and worked on himself in secret—letting everyone think that he was a simple merchant—Rabbi Yisrael saw it as his calling to spread the study of Mussar throughout the Jewish community. After moving to Vilna, in 1845 Rabbi Yisrael Salanter produced a four-part plan to do just that:

1. Print and disseminate Mussar works.
2. Deliver regular Mussar lectures in synagogues and houses of study.
3. Create special "Mussar houses" for teaching and studying Mussar.
4. Teach disciples who will further spread and reinforce the study of Mussar.

His plan succeeded, for the study of Mussar soon became popular not only with scholars, but among laypeople as well. In short order, many of the finest Lithuanian yeshivos had adopted the study of Mussar into their curriculum. These became the prototype of yeshivos today, nearly all of which study Mussar late in the afternoon, after a full day of Torah study.

Great Mussar Works

When Reb Yisrael Salanter started to promote the study of Mussar, there were several major works already available for people to study. Since that time, more have been added, so that there are a wide variety of texts available for those interested in self-improvement. One of these is the aforementioned Nefesh HaChayim, by Rabbi Chayim Itzkowitz of Volozhin. The following are a few more of the classics.

Chovos HaLevavos

Chovos HaLevavos, "Duties of the Heart," preceded Reb Yisrael by 800 years—Rav Bachya (or Bechaye) ibn Pakudah of Saragossa, Spain, who was one of the early European Sages, wrote it in the eleventh century. He wrote this book in order to explain the ethical teachings of the Torah—as well as its fundamental beliefs—in a systematic way. He proceeds through a series of ten "gates," ten areas upon which a person should focus, such as

God's Unity, observing God's actions in the world, service of God, trust in God, etc.

Shaarei Teshuvah

The *Shaarei Teshuvah*, "Gates of Repentance" (or "Gates of Return"), was also written by an early Spanish scholar, namely Rabbi Yonah of Gerona. An early opponent of Maimonides' Guide for the Perplexed, he later decided he was wrong, and set out for *Teveria*, Tiberius in Israel, where he planned to beg the Rambam's forgiveness at his gravesite. He was kept back in Barcelona for three years, and spent those years teaching, always quoting from Maimonides. He set out again, only to be asked by the community of Toledo to stay a while and teach them as well. He passed away there, never having completed his journey.

His most well-known work is the Shaarei Teshuvah, Gates of Repentance. It is written as if he were speaking heart-to-heart with someone who has done various misdeeds but now wants to turn back to the path of Torah. Rabbi Yonah methodically outlines the basic steps that this person must undertake, and then moves forward into more advanced questions about how to behave from now on and how to avoid pitfalls.

Mesillas Yesharim

Rabbi Moshe Chayim Luzzato (1707–1747) was an outstanding student of both religious and secular subjects; he became fluent in six languages. Born in Padua, Italy, he later moved to Amsterdam and then Acco, Israel, where he passed away during an epidemic. A scholar of both the revealed Torah and the Kabbalah, he wrote several works. One of these, *Derech HaShem*, "The Way of God," is a systematic outline of basic Torah beliefs regarding the nature of God and the purpose of human beings in this world, and an explanation of how these principles lead logically to many other important teachings of the Torah.

Mesillas Yesharim, "Path of the Just," takes a step-by-step approach to self-improvement, looking at good character traits—such as caution (to avoid bad deeds), enthusiasm (to do good deeds), et cetera—explaining how to acquire each one and also what pitfalls might prevent you from acquiring it. Rabbi Yosef Zundel told Rabbi Yisrael Salanter that he once had asked Rabbi Chayim Volozhner what Mussar works to study. Reb Chayim had responded that all Mussar works are good, but "let the *Mesillas Yesharim* be your guide." It is the pre-eminent, most commonly studied work of Mussar.

Cheshbon HaNefesh

Cheshbon HaNefesh, or "Accounting of the Soul," was written by Rabbi Menachem Mendel Lefin of Satanow (1749–1826). This book is a very practical, hands-on guide to self-improvement. He presents thirteen traits for a person to improve: (1) tranquility, (2) patience, (3) order, (4) diligence, (5) cleanliness, (6) modesty, (7) justice, (8) thriftiness, (9) productivity, (10) silence, (11) gentleness, (12) truth, and (13) self-restraint. By working on these, one per week, you come back to each trait four times a year.

For every trait, your first task is to come up with a short saying that helps you to concentrate upon the trait, improving in a specific area where you think you are missing the boat. Then, you make a chart, and day by day you record how you have progressed in that area.

Growth of the Yeshivos

With the spiritual fire of Mussar added to the intellectual fervor of the yeshivos, this new model for Torah study soon became the norm across Poland and Lithuania. New yeshivos opened their doors up until the First World War, and while it is impractical to mention all of them, several are highlighted here.

Continuing Study in Volozhin

When Reb Chayim *Volozhner* passed away in 1821, his son Rabbi Yitzchak became dean of the yeshiva. He was succeeded by his son-in-law and assistant, Rabbi Elazar Yitzchak Fried, in 1849—but by this time Rabbi Fried himself was very ill. He passed away in 1853, at which point the governing board appointed a second son-in-law, Rabbi Naftali Tzvi Yehudah Berlin (known by the acronym of his name, *Netziv*), and a grandson of Reb Chayim Volozhner, Rabbi Yosef Dov Soloveitchik, to head the yeshiva.

The Bais HaLevi and Reb Chayim Brisker

Though the Netziv took the leading role in the Volozhin Yeshiva, Rabbi Yosef's brilliance and incisive style of Talmudic analysis have had even a greater impact on yeshiva learning in the ensuing centuries. Rav Soloveitchik left Volozhin in 1865 to become Rabbi of Slutzk, and then later was invited to become Rabbi of Brisk. Rabbi Soloveitchik wrote a series of works called *Bais HaLevi*, and thus is often referred to as "the Bais HaLevi of Brisk."

His son, Rabbi Chayim, entered the Volozhin Yeshiva in 1873, and in 1880 was appointed as assistant dean to the Netziv. The learning methodology of Rabbi Chayim Brisker became that of the yeshiva movement overall—careful analysis, penetrating logic, understanding of the underlying principles of each law—all joined with intellectual honesty and personal humility in the search for ultimate truth.

The Mirrer Yeshiva

In 1815, a second yeshiva was opened by Shmuel Tikitinsky in the small town of Mir. For eight years Mr. Tikitinsky—a layman—was the sole support of the yeshiva, but his son Rabbi Avraham Tikitinsky soon joined the yeshiva as its dean. By 1840, the Mirrer Yeshiva had over 100 students.

FACT

Rabbi Kamai was succeeded by his son-in-law, Rabbi Eliezer Yehudah Finkel, and to this day the leadership of the Mirrer Yeshiva—now located in Jerusalem—is associated with the Finkel Rabbinic family. Rabbi Avraham Kalmanowitz established a second branch of the Mirrer Yeshiva in Brooklyn, New York, after the yeshiva's escape during the Holocaust—which you will read more about in Chapter 15.

In 1835, however, both Tikitinskys passed away, and the Rabbi of the town, Rabbi Yosef David Mirrer, led the yeshiva. Shmuel's grandson Rabbi Chayim Leib Tikitinsky took the reins in 1850, and thanks to his talents as an educator, Mir and its reputation continued to grow. When his son Rabbi Avraham became dean in 1899, he sought out another outstanding person like his father, and soon Rabbi Eliyahu Baruch Kamai came to Mir to become both the Rabbi of the town and, with Rabbi Avraham Tikitinsky, dean of the yeshiva. When the yeshiva in Volozhin was eventually disbanded due to Czarist persecution, Mir became the leading institution for Torah learning.

Slabodka

While the yeshiva in Slabodka opened its doors in 1863 it was toward the end of the nineteenth century—as Volozhin was forced to close its doors—that this yeshiva attained prominence. While many great Rabbis taught in its hall, the greatest teacher among them was Rabbi Nosson Tzvi Finkel, known as the *Alter*, or Elder, of Slabodka. With Rabbi Moshe Mordechai Epstein, Rabbi Finkel made the study of Mussar a core element of the yeshiva's curriculum. Most of the leading Torah educators in the United States, following the Holocaust, were students of the Alter.

A second yeshiva in Slabodka opened in 1897, and this one eschewed the study of Mussar. Under the direction of Rabbi Baruch Ber Leibowitz, a student of Reb Chayim Brisker and a leading Talmud scholar, the yeshiva—despite interruptions during the First World War—reestablished itself in post-war Kaminetz, Poland, as Yeshivas Kaminetz. Following the Holocaust this yeshiva was reestablished once again, both in Jerusalem and in Brooklyn, New York.

Chapter 14

The Enlightenment and Modern Jewish Movements

While the Yeshivos and Chassidism were carrying Torah education forward, dramatic changes were happening in the larger Jewish world. The Enlightenment swept through Europe, accompanied by reduced religious fervor. Kingdoms formerly hostile to Jewish residents re-examined their relationships with Jewry from a more humane perspective.

These two changes in the larger population—rejection of orthodox religious views and new openness—influenced many Jews, causing them to dismiss or minimize the value of the distinct Torah practices that had held the Jewish nation together through over 1,600 years of exile. Today, the majority of Jews worldwide do not observe Jewish law as codified in earlier eras.

Winds of Change

The European Renaissance of the fifteenth and sixteenth centuries gave new prominence to philosophy and "the dignity of man," but the flames of religious warfare still burned across the continent. When peace finally reigned in Europe, the Age of Reason and the Enlightenment dawned; philosophers began to turn away from mysticism and traditional religious views and toward logic and skepticism.

Born in Amsterdam in 1632 to a family of Spanish-Portuguese Jews, Baruch Spinoza helped lay the groundwork for the Enlightenment. He developed a pantheistic/monistic philosophy, saying that God is "the mechanism of nature and the universe," that God and Nature are one. In his view, the Bible was merely a metaphor developed to teach the nature of God—but there is no God who intervenes in the affairs of our world. Traditional Rabbinic authorities took an unsurprisingly dim view of his theories, and in July of 1656 Spinoza was excommunicated—but non-Jewish philosophers welcomed his new philosophy.

The Enlightenment

During the eighteenth century, a group of intellectuals attempted to develop a set of ethics and knowledge based upon "enlightened rationality." The "Enlightenment" was an attempt to move out of the Dark Ages in Europe, and brought with it many new developments in art, science, politics, and philosophy.

Great scientific and political advances, such as Newton's discovery of the law of gravity and the development of democracy, were accompanied by changing views of God along the lines of Spinoza and others. Enlightenment philosophy, like its science, focused upon the development of universal laws, governing a comprehensible universe. A philosophy called Deism described "God the watchmaker," who created an orderly universe that then ran without His intervention. Belief in a supernatural Being who affects our world in ways beyond our comprehension was dismissed as "immature." Immanuel Kant, in his 1784 essay "What Is Enlightenment," wrote:

> Enlightenment is man's leaving his self-caused immaturity. Immaturity is the incapacity to use one's own understanding without the guidance of another. Such immaturity is self-caused if its cause is not lack of intelligence, but lack of determination and courage to use one's intelligence without being guided by another.

The relegation of religion to a matter of personal faith, rather than state dogma, was from one perspective a great benefit to persecuted Jews. The walls of the ghetto came down, and Jews were able to become full citizens with the same rights as the Christian populace, or at least nearly so. At the same time, however, this exerted unprecedented pressure upon the newly liberated Jews. In order to properly blend in with their new neighbors, Jews had to stop dressing and behaving in a distinctively Jewish fashion. Furthermore, the Deist philosophy of the Enlightenment was starkly at odds with the Torah's "immature" vision of God.

Moshe Mendelssohn

Moshe Mendelssohn was born in Dessau, Germany, in 1729, to a poor scribe named Mendel (from whom he took his surname, which means "son of Mendel"). Possessed of a brilliant intellect and tremendous diligence, young Moshe studied Torah under Rabbi David Fraenkel, both in Dessau and then in Berlin. He also took up mathematics, logic, and philosophy, and befriended Immanuel Kant and also Gotthold Lessing, a non-Jew who pushed for tolerance of Jews in Germany. Lessing considered Mendelssohn living proof of his belief that a Jew could have a noble, refined character. Lessing sponsored the publication of Mendelssohn's early works and collaborated with him on others, helping Mendelssohn to gain acceptance as one of Germany's leading scholars and philosophers.

Although he is known today as a father of the Jewish Enlightenment, Mendelssohn himself never attempted to move Jews away from Torah observance. On the contrary, he defended Judaism and its unique, Divinely Revealed code of legal, ritual, and moral law. All he did was attempt to make the Jews themselves more "cosmopolitan," not realizing where this might lead. His translation of the Torah into German was not designed to make German-speaking Jews more fluent with Torah, but, just the opposite, to help Torah-observant Jews to become more fluent with German.

Mendelssohn, with his intellectual dedication to Torah and observance, perhaps failed to recognize that while he was able to sit in the courts of German high society while remaining an observant Jew, the same would not be true of his co-religionists. He did not understand why Rabbis opposed his efforts, but the succeeding years proved that the Rabbis' concerns were well-founded.

Even on a personal level, his campaign for Jewish emancipation, closer relationships with non-Jewish governments, and integration of the Jews into secular society bore bitter fruit. All of his descendants—including his grandson Felix Mendelssohn, the well-known German composer—converted to Christianity.

The Haskalah—The Jewish Enlightenment

As the eighteenth century came to a close, laws placing restrictions upon Jews were nullified. Beginning in 1781, Emperor Joseph II of Austria eliminated restrictions on Jewish commerce and attendance at universities. Liberal "Edicts of Toleration" spread across Prussia, Germany, and Italy. In 1791, following the French Revolution, the new National Assembly emancipated all French Jewry.

Though the gates of opportunity were flung open for all Jews, integration required the Jews to be, well, less Jewish. The motto of the "Enlightened" Jew became "Be a man in the street, and a Jew in the home." The *maskilim*, or "enlighteners," devalued the Talmud in the educational system, in favor of secular knowledge, modern languages, and vocational training. For many, this rapidly developed into a complete abandonment of Torah and Jewish traditions. A number of famous figures of the nineteenth century were Jews who had entirely rejected their own Jewish heritage, such as

British Prime Minister Benjamin Disraeli, Communist philosopher Karl Marx, and the composer Gustav Mahler.

The Reform Movement

Other Jews were unwilling to abandon Judaism entirely in favor of Christianity, yet were swayed by the Enlightenment and its belief that human intelligence and reason were capable of both ensuring and advancing ethics and morality. These "enlightened Jews" also considered the informal nature of Jewish prayer to be "unseemly" by comparison with the orderly services of the European churches.

Changes in the Service

Reform synagogues, or Temples, revised the prayer service "in the direction of beautifying it and rendering it more orderly." The first Reform Temple was built in 1810 in Seesen, Germany, and featured German-language songs and prayers, ecclesiastical robes, a mixed choir, and an organ, all of which were previously foreign to Jewish congregations.

Abraham Geiger and Samuel Holdheim

Abraham Geiger received a traditional Jewish education, but became an active Reformer and a leader in Breslau. He believed that the way to keep bright, intellectual Jews from leaving Judaism entirely was to update Judaism by following the Enlightenment model of modern, rationalist views. Indeed, he viewed Judaism as an evolutionary process, and believed its traditions to be simply outdated.

Samuel Holdheim studied in a traditional yeshiva as a young man, but became still more radical than Geiger. He argued against the wearing of traditional Jewish prayer articles such as the *Tallis* (prayer shawl) and the *Kipah* (skullcap), the blowing of the Shofar (ram's horn) on the Jewish New Year, circumcision, and prayers for a return to the Land of Israel or to Jerusalem in the services. In his congregation, he also moved the Sabbath to Sunday.

FACT

The name *Temple* for a center of Reform worship is no coincidence. Historically the Jews have prayed toward a single Temple in Jerusalem, which was destroyed twice and, according to Jewish tradition, will be rebuilt yet again. The Reformers rejected the idea of a return to the Land of Israel or rebuilding of the Temple, and declared Germany to be their permanent home.

The Reform Society of Frankfurt

The Society of Reformers was organized in Frankfurt, Germany, in 1842. Its goal was to codify the new vision of Judaism toward which the Reformers would strive. In 1843 it issued a "Declaration of Principles" that stated:

1. We recognize the possibility of unlimited development in the Mosaic religion.
2. The collection of controversies, dissertations, and prescriptions commonly designated by the name Talmud possesses for us no authority, from either the dogmatic or the practical standpoint.
3. A Messiah who is to lead back the Israelites to the land of Palestine is neither expected nor desired by us; we know no fatherland except that to which we belong by birth or citizenship.

The Reform Movement in the United States

Several European Reformers moved to America, helping to create a new movement that quickly became dominant. The early American movement toward Reform, however, was led by Americans and was concurrent with, but not led by, German Reform.

Beth Elohim—The first American Reform Congregation

In December, 1824, Isaac Harby led a group of forty-six members of Kahal Kadosh Beth Elohim (Holy Congregation House of God) of Charleston, South Carolina, who petitioned the board for changes in the Sabbath service. Beth Elohim was founded in 1749 as a traditional congregation following the Spanish-Portuguese *minhag*, or custom. The innovations requested by the petitioners were, in fact, very modest, and none involved a clear violation of traditional Jewish law—that the Hebrew prayers be followed by English translations, that new prayers regarding life in America be added, and that the Rabbi offer a sermon in English.

When the board rejected the petition, though, Harby's group departed radically—from both the congregation and the tradition. They created a "Reformed Society of Israelites" that wrote its own prayer book, introduced music into the service, and worshiped without head coverings.

After the famous Charleston fire of 1838, the Reformers petitioned for the inclusion of an organ in the rebuilt house of worship, "to assist in the vocal part of the service." This new proposal again fractured the congregation, but this time a two-thirds majority of the congregants approved the decision (the traditionalists left to create Congregation Shearith Israel, "the Remnant of Israel"). In 1841, Beth Elohim officially became the first Reform congregation in the United States.

Isaac M. Wise

Isaac Wise was born in Steingrub, Bohemia, in 1819, and was educated there by his father, a schoolteacher named Leo Weiss, before continuing his studies in Prague. Ordained as a Rabbi, he served for two years in Radnitz before moving to the United States in 1846 and changing his last name to Wise. He was appointed Rabbi of Congregation Beth-El (House of God) of Albany, New York, where he soon instituted reforms in the service, such as mixed seating, a mixed choir, and a confirmation service.

In 1850, on the eve of Rosh HaShanah, the Jewish New Year, the board of directors of Beth-El reacted to these reforms by firing Rabbi Wise. This caused a split in the congregation; his supporters created a new Reform Temple called Anshe Emet, where he served until 1854. Then, however, he moved to Cincinnati, Ohio, where he again took the helm of an Orthodox congregation and led its conversion to Reform. He would serve there until his death in 1900.

Hebrew Union College

The unification of American Jewry in a single national mold was to be Isaac Wise's lifelong goal. In 1847, he wrote a prayer book and called it *Minhag America*, intending it to be used by all congregations nationwide.

Unity was so important to Wise that when the Central Conference of American Rabbis published the Union Prayer Book in 1894, he removed his *Minhag America* prayer book from his own congregation.

His efforts to unify American congregations led to the founding of the Union of American Hebrew Congregations (UAHC) in 1873, in Cincinnati, in order to establish a Hebrew Theological Institute. Two years later, the Union created the Hebrew Union College (HUC) to train American Rabbis to serve American congregations, speaking in English. It was another eight years before the College would ordain its first Rabbis, in 1883.

It must be emphasized that the name *Union of American Hebrew Congregations* represented no arrogance on the part of Wise and the other Reformers—they considered the small number of traditional congregations a dying vestige. In November of 2003, the UAHC was renamed the Union for Reform Judaism.

It was then that Wise's dream, of an American Judaism united under the Reform banner, shattered at the moment of its culmination. At the first graduation banquet, the College served clams, crabs, shrimp, and frog's legs, plus beef and ice cream. A number of Rabbis, appalled by this Epicurean feast of *Treifah* (non-Kosher) foods, fled the room, never to return. The "Treifah Banquet" led directly to the establishment of the Jewish Theological Seminary three years later, and the development of the Conservative movement.

Out . . . and Back

Following the creation of the UAHC and Hebrew Union College, Reform Rabbis assembled in Pittsburgh in 1885 and agreed upon a joint Declaration of Principles, similar to those adopted in Frankfurt forty years earlier. The Pittsburgh Platform, as it came to be known, declared the Bible the product of "the primitive ideas of its own age," and said, "We accept as binding only its moral laws." It rejected "all such Mosaic and rabbinical laws as regulate diet, priestly purity, and dress . . . their observance in our days is apt rather to obstruct than to further modern spiritual elevation." The assembled stated that they considered themselves "no longer a nation, but a religious community," and no longer desired a return to Palestine. In 1889, the Central Conference of American Rabbis (CCAR) was formed as the organized Rabbinate of Reform Judaism, and they continued to meet periodically.

By 1937, however, the passionate rejection of a unique Jewish people, a Jewish country, and unique Jewish practices had all been re-evaluated. The Columbus Platform, produced by the CCAR in convention there in Ohio, recognized a "Jewish People," as well as "the group loyalty of Jews [including those] who have become estranged from our religious tradition." Concerning "the rehabilitation of Palestine," they affirmed "the obligation of all Jewry to aid in its upbuilding as a Jewish homeland."

One reason for the 1937 reversals was a change in Jewish American demographics. Whereas the early immigrants were German Jews influenced by the early, fiery Reformers, by the twentieth century they were overwhelmed by new waves of immigrants from Eastern Europe. The Eastern European Jews were far more attached to, rather than dismissive of, Torah beliefs and practices.

Most profound of all was the rapid change in attitude toward Jewish ritual. "Judaism as a way of life requires in addition to its moral and spiritual demands," they wrote, "the preservation of the Sabbath, festivals and Holy Days, the retention and development of such customs, symbols and ceremonies as possess inspirational value, the cultivation of distinctive forms of religious art and music and the use of Hebrew, together with the vernacular, in our worship and instruction."

FACT

An earlier bit of history reveals how dramatic this reversal was. In 1845, Rabbi Zecharias Frankel—considered the ideological father of Conservative Judaism, as you will read below—left the Reform conference in Frankfort. He published a journal article detailing his reason: that the Rabbis had insisted upon declaring the Hebrew language unnecessary for public worship. Just ninety years later, Reform Rabbis adopted the very position that they had previously scorned over Frankel's objection.

By 1976, the original Pittsburgh Platform had been reduced to history. Meeting in San Francisco in commemoration of the centenaries of the UAHC and HUC, the Rabbis designated "the People Israel," "the State of Israel," and "Religious Practice" central elements of the platform itself. "Born as Hebrews in the ancient Near East, we are bound together like all ethnic groups by language, land, history, culture, and institutions," they said. Concerning "the newly reborn State of Israel," they acknowledged that "we are bound to that land." And concerning the same rituals that the Pittsburgh Rabbis warned were likely "to obstruct . . . modern spiritual elevation," the group in San Francisco insisted that "Judaism emphasizes action rather than creed as the primary expression of a religious life."

Reform Today

Today, the Reform movement has a large presence in America and Europe, and a modest but active group in Israel. It believes that Judaism is a religion in constant flux, able to change based upon the demands of the laity—and as it subscribes to a doctrine of individual autonomy, change is the one constant.

Often, the movement rejects elements of Jewish tradition in compliance with changing Western values. Reform was the first to abolish the idea of separation between the genders, and ordained the first woman Rabbi in

1972. In 1983, Reform leaders announced that they would accept patrilineal descent—meaning children of a Jewish father—as sufficient for children to be Jewish. At its 1996 convention in Philadelphia, the Central Conference of American Rabbis announced its support for civil marriage between homosexual partners; the Conference fully supports those member Rabbis who conduct religious marriages for these couples as well.

Yet at the same time, the movement embraces tradition as never before. Today, it is common for Rabbis and congregants to wear the traditional Kipah and Tallis during services. In 1999, the Union adopted a new platform, this time back in Pittsburgh. It called for lifelong study of Hebrew and Torah, "renewed attention" to the "whole array of mitzvot," and emphasis of the Sabbath as a day of "*kedushah*, holiness, *menuchah*, rest and *oneg*, joy."

An earlier draft of the 1999 platform was even more emphatic. It said, "Standing at Sinai, the Jewish people heard God reveal the Torah"—and made many other statements indistinguishable from the beliefs of the Torah-observant. That draft was not adopted, following a backlash from those who favored Classical Reform.

The Conservative Movement

Conservative Judaism is essentially an American movement, created in the wake of what became known as the Treifah Banquet—the Hebrew Union College 1883 graduation, as recounted above. This, however, was not the first time that individuals enamored with the concept of Reform were, at the same time, unwilling to endorse what they perceived as the excesses of the Reformers.

Zecharias Frankel

Zecharias Frankel, descended from august Rabbinical families on both his father's and mother's sides, was born in Prague in September of 1801, trained in the yeshiva of Bezalel Ronsperg, and appointed the district Rabbi of Leitmeritz at the age of thirty. Five years later he was invited to become chief Rabbi of Dresden, where he served for eighteen years, developing and promoting a new philosophy that he called Positive-Historical Judaism.

Frankel's stated goal was to uphold the authority of traditional Jewish belief and practice, while still allowing for freedom in both thought and practice after careful research. His vision allowed for reforms instituted by Rabbinic scholars, but not at the direction of the laity.

While Frankel never intended to start a new movement, he attracted the ire of Reformers and traditionalists alike. His reaction to the new Reform prayer book published in Hamburg in 1842 satisfied no one. The liberals were upset because he pointed out historical and theological inconsistencies, while the Orthodox could not accept his assertion that other deviations from the tradition were permitted.

When Frankel was nominated president of the Jewish Theological Seminary of Breslau in 1854, Abraham Geiger—who had encouraged the founding of this institution—strongly opposed Frankel's selection. Geiger later reprinted the final examination given to the first graduating class in German translation, in order to ridicule Frankel's style of Talmudic analysis.

At the same time, the traditionalist Rabbi Samson Raphael Hirsch demanded of Frankel a statement of the religious principles upon which the Breslau seminary would stand: "What will revelation mean in the forthcoming Seminary? What will the Bible mean? What will tradition mean?" Frankel did not reply, for he knew that Hirsch and the traditional community would not agree to his belief that Rabbis could change and develop the Jewish religion.

Rejection of Reform—and Orthodox

In 1886, Rabbis Sabato Morais and Marcus Jastrow of Philadelphia, and Henry Pereira Mendes of New York, led a group that formed the Jewish Theological Seminary (the JTS) of New York. They were responding to what they considered the rationalist, anti-Halachic (Jewish legal) excesses of the Reformers in general, and of the Treifah Banquet in particular, which had caused several of the Rabbis present to contemplate formation of an alternative group.

Initially, they did not see themselves as a new movement at all, but merely as representing a more liberal Orthodox group—as did Zecharias Frankel himself. JTS was instrumental in the creation, in 1898, of the Orthodox Jewish Congregational Union of America in New York. It was Isaac Mayer Wise, founder of HUC, who decried JTS an "orthodox Rabbinical School" created by men "who are themselves *poshim* [sinners] in the eyes not only of the genuines of Poland and Hungary, but also of the leaders of that class in Germany and Italy." Rabbi J. D. Eisenstein, an Orthodox scholar, agreed: "In my opinion, the objective of Conservatism and the law of the Radicals lead to the same path, the only difference between them is time"—referring to how long it would take them to adopt the same changes as the Reformers. By 1902, the traditionalists took firm control of the Orthodox Union, and JTS pulled out.

Conservative Judaism

In 1902, Prof. Solomon Schechter assumed the presidency of the seminary; he would greatly strengthen the institution. In 1913 he took a leading role in the formation of the United Synagogue of America (which changed its name to the United Synagogue of Conservative Judaism in 1991), the Conservative movement's answer to the Orthodox Union.

In theory, the Conservative movement, unlike the Reform, maintains an allegiance to Halachah. In practice, however, the movement's own scholars agree that the movement has moved away. JTS Professor Rabbi Neil Gillman writes that "the Conservative Movement did redefine a good deal of traditional Jewish law. Today it permits men and women to sit together in the synagogue and worshipers to drive to the synagogue on the Sabbath. More recently, it permitted women to assume a totally equal role in synagogue rituals and to become rabbis and cantors" (*Conservative Judaism: The New Century*, Neil Gillman, Behrman House, 1993, Chapter 4).

To a great extent, Rabbi Eisenstein's prediction that Conservative would follow Reform is born out by history. Each of the changes documented by Professor Gillman was preceded by a similar move by Reform. As early as the 1980s, only half of Conservative Rabbinical students said that "living as a Halachic Jew" was "extremely important" to them. Today, only 29 percent of Conservative congregants keep strictly Kosher, while just 15 percent consider themselves Sabbath observant.

FACT

The move to ordain women as Rabbis was opposed by the JTS Talmud faculty and leading Conservative Halachists. Approval of the change resulted in the formation of a splinter group, the Union for Traditional Judaism, which claims that "today's Conservative Movement is, at best, selectively loyal to *Halakhah*."

Reconstructionism, Jewish Renewal, and Secular Humanism

Today, the move away from strict observance of Jewish law has resulted in a panoply of Jewish groups. Unlike the various groups of Torah-observant Jews who offer different means to the same end, each of these groups offers a different vision of how the ideal Jew should respond to Torah and Jewish law.

Reconstructionism

The Reconstructionist movement was founded by Conservative Rabbi and philosopher Mordecai Kaplan. His beliefs could be summarized by one of his favorite aphorisms: tradition has "a vote, but not a veto." Reconstructionism emphasizes "Judaism as a civilization," defined as "the integration of selected Jewish beliefs with the Jewish people's culture and folkways."

The Jewish Reconstructionist Federation (JRF) was founded in 1955, followed by the Reconstructionist Rabbinical College (RRC) in 1968, and the Reconstructionist Rabbinical Association (RRA) in 1974. Reconstructionists reject the authority of Jewish law, but "where Reform Judaism emphasizes individual autonomy, Reconstructionism emphasizes the importance of religious community in shaping individual patterns of observance." Today, there are over 100 Reconstructionist congregations and *havurot* (prayer groups) in North America.

Jewish Renewal

Jewish Renewal was inspired by the havurot, prayer groups that arose as part of the cultural rebellion of the late 1960s. Some groups, such as the Boston-area Havurat Shalom, functioned as Jewish rural communes, while others formed havurot within Jewish communities, operating outside the institutionalized models of Judaism.

The Jewish Renewal movement emphasizes meditation, dance, chant, and mysticism, borrowing from Buddhism, Sufism, Native American religion, and other faiths. One division emphasizes healing the earth and "eco-Kosher" practices, sponsoring activities such as a Tu B'Shvat, Seder in the Redwood Forest (Tu B'Shvat, the fifteenth of Shvat, is the new year for trees), and Sukkot on the banks of the Hudson River.

Humanistic Judaism

The Society for Humanistic Judaism was founded by Reform Rabbi Sherwin Wine, in 1969. Humanistic Judaism is entirely secular, denying the existence of God, and values the power of human reason as well as the creation of "a meaningful Jewish lifestyle free from supernatural authority." It celebrates Jewish holidays merely as "cultural expressions" of the natural cycle of the calendar.

The Unaffiliated

The silent majority of Jewry today are the unaffiliated—members of no congregation at all, of no movement or group. In most cases, their parents were or remain members of a congregation; "unaffiliated Judaism" is rarely a multigenerational allegiance, and the children either affiliate or (more often) no longer self-identify as Jews.

Sociologists have already observed a pattern in American Jewish life, in which Orthodox immigrants had children who wanted to see a variety of traditional observances, but not be told to observe the Sabbath—and who therefore affiliated Conservative. The Conservative movement remains the dominant choice of those over age 60, but, according to Jack Wertheimer, provost of JTS, it has been in steady decline for two generations.

The next generation preferred a less traditional style, and went Reform, which now represents the plurality of American Jewry. Yet it is unusual to find a Reform family with a history going back more than three generations; by and large, the next generation dropped all synagogue affiliation.

This is the choice of today's majority—only 46 percent of self-identified Jews today are synagogue members, according to the most recent survey of the U.S. Jewish population, and the story is little different worldwide. Even in Israel, secular Zionists still greatly outnumber the Torah-observant.

Chapter 15

Torah Survives the Holocaust

For 1,000 years, the centers of Torah were in Europe. Then, in less than a decade's time, every one of these centers for Torah learning was destroyed, each city rendered *Judenrein* (free of Jews) by the evil that was Nazi Germany. The incredible and ongoing rebirth of Torah today, in new lands, is a modern miracle.

New Yeshivos in the Early Twentieth Century

The study of Torah continued apace in the era preceding, during, and after the First World War. All of the pre-eminent Torah schools were in Europe, in cities such as Ponevezh, Slabodka, Telshe, and Vilna in Lithuania, and Kamenitz, Grodno, Mir, and Novardok in Poland. The United States was already known as a place to acquire material wealth, but the six-day workweek tempted all too many to abandon observance of the Sabbath and the Torah lifestyle overall. The Jewish communities in Palestine were small, and the Zionist aspiration for a new Jewish country caused relations with Arab residents to deteriorate.

Ponevezh

Ponevezh, also called Panevezys, is a Lithuanian city just over eighty miles north-northwest from the capital, Vilna. In addition to the main Bais Medrash, or house of study, Rabbi Yitzchak Yaakov Rabinovitz founded a yeshiva there in 1912. Though it existed for only seven years, many prominent scholars studied under Reb Itzele Ponevitcher. Rabbi Yosef Shlomo Kahaneman became the Rav of Ponevezh in 1919, and served there until the Holocaust. In 1940 he escaped to Palestine, where he founded the Ponevezh Yeshiva in Bnei Brak. In 1939, there were 6,000 Jews in Ponevezh, 22 percent of the population.

Slutzk

In the 1890s, Rabbi Yaakov David Willowski, Rabbi of Slutzk, founded the Etz Chaim Yeshiva. Rabbi Nosson Tzvi Finkel, of Slabodka, helped the new yeshiva by sending fourteen of his best students and teachers there in 1897. One of the teachers from Slabodka was Rabbi Isser Zalman Meltzer, who succeeded Rabbi Willowski as the Rabbi of Slutzk and *rosh yeshiva* when the latter emigrated to America.

The Bolshevik Revolution caused such upheaval that the yeshiva was forced to move to Kletzk, Poland, where it was headed by Rabbi Meltzer's son-in-law, Rabbi Aharon Kotler. Rabbi Meltzer was imprisoned by the

Communists before escaping Russia, rejoining the yeshiva in 1923. Soon thereafter, however, he moved to Israel.

Under Rabbi Kotler's direction, the yeshiva grew to 260 students by 1939. Rabbi Kotler escaped to America in 1941, and reopened his yeshiva as Beis Medrash Gavoha in Lakewood, New Jersey.

FACT

Rabbi Willowski (known by the acronym *Ridbaz*) authored one of the main commentaries on the Jerusalem Talmud. He left Slutzk in 1903 to become Chief Rabbi of Chicago, and then settled in Tzfas, Israel, where he is buried.

Radin, Home of Rabbi Yisrael Meyer Kagan

Radin, in modern-day Belarus, is a small village on the road from Cracow to Vilna. Its most famous resident, Rabbi Yisrael Meyer HaKohen Kagan, was the son of Rabbi Aryeh Zev Kagan, a student of the original yeshiva of Volozhin. Rabbi Yisrael Mayer moved to Radin in 1869, and he founded a yeshiva shortly thereafter. Rabbi Naftoli Tropp became the *rosh yeshiva* of the yeshiva in 1904, and it expanded dramatically, to over 300 students. When he passed away in 1929, Rabbis Baruch Faivelson and Menachem Mendel Zaks succeeded him (the latter escaped to America during the Holocaust, and joined the faculty of the Rabbi Isaac Elchonon Theological Seminary of Yeshiva University in New York).

Among the great Rabbis who studied there were Rabbi Yosef Kahaneman, who became the Rabbi of Ponevezh, and Rabbi Elchonon Wasserman, who later headed the yeshiva in Baronowitz and was martyred during the Holocaust. Rabbi David Leibowitz, another student, later founded Yeshivas Chofetz Chaim in Forest Hills, New York.

The Mishnah Berurah

Rabbi Kagan towered above them all, and indeed above most any Torah scholar of the twentieth (or twenty-first) century. His *Mishnah Berurah*, "Clear Teaching," is perhaps the definitive commentary on the section of the

Shulchan Aruch, the Code of Jewish Law, that deals with daily living. Most of the adopted practices of traditional Jews today are in accordance with Rabbi Kagan's opinions in the Mishnah Berurah.

The Chofetz Chaim

Rabbi Kagan is even more closely identified with his work, *Chofetz Chaim*, concerning the rules governing the avoidance of gossip. The words mean "one who desires life," and come from the words of Psalm 34:13–15: "Who is the man who desires life, loving days to see good? [Let him] guard his tongue from evil, and his lips from speaking guile, turn away from the bad and do the good, seek peace and pursue it."

Ask anyone, and they will tell you that gossiping is a bad and destructive habit. Yet everyone does it, and entire magazines are devoted to little more than gossip about celebrities and others. But thanks to the Chofetz Chaim, there are many different books today devoted to knowing when and how to avoid it.

But Did Rabbi Kagan Gossip, Himself?

Before endorsing the Chofetz Chaim, another scholar wanted to ensure that Rabbi Kagan "practiced what he preached." So he sent one of his students to engage the Rabbi in conversation for six hours, during which the student repeatedly attempted to get Rabbi Kagan to say even the most minor bit of negative gossip. The mission was a most successful "failure"—the student was amazed at how careful Rabbi Kagan was in this regard, although the Rabbi was friendly and engaging, not at all quiet or reticent about his opinions. As if in reward for observing the words of the Psalm, the Rabbi lived to age ninety-five.

The Bais Yaakov Movement

Who did the most to advance Torah learning in the last century? The person who did this didn't wear a hat or have a long beard. This individual wasn't even a Rabbi: she was Sarah Schneirer, the eldest child of a Chassidic family in Cracow, Poland. Originally trained as a dressmaker, she became a teacher—and revolutionized Torah education.

Until the twentieth century, women's education was done in the home. The idea of a school for boys and a yeshiva for men, to enable them to study difficult Talmudic concepts, dates back to King David. Women, on the other hand, historically absorbed the spirit of Torah—along with a "hands-on" education in practical Jewish observance—from their mothers.

"Frau Schneirer" recognized that a new age of intellectual life was dawning, and that young Jewish girls were drawn to the exciting ideas of the day—while their brothers were learning the timeless messages of Torah. She recognized the need for formal, Torah-based Jewish education for women.

First, she began to teach—and her classes grew to over eighty students in the first year. She then created a school for teachers, the first Bais Yaakov Seminary, in the 1920s. Her school and seminary, backed by many of the greatest Chassidic, Lithuanian, and German Torah leaders of the time, were the prototypes for a global network of schools and seminaries. By the time the Nazis came to power, Bais Yaakov schools were scattered all across Europe.

The Destruction of Europe

Once one understands that Europe was the true center of Torah learning before the Holocaust, it becomes possible to understand the magnitude of the blow that followed. Hitler and his minions did their very best to render the European continent Judenrein, and succeeded to an alarming degree. The organized Jewish communities—and the yeshivos they contained—essentially ceased to exist.

Assimilation Is Not an Option

The Nazi Holocaust laid to rest the idea that if Jews would forget their Torah, and instead join the other nations, that they would be accepted by all. There was no country considered as cultured and as civilized as Germany, and there was no country where the Jewish population was more assimilated into the larger society. Yet it was in Germany where the anti-Semitic portrayals of Jews took root, forming a worldview whose very mandate was their destruction.

ALERT!

Even the Christian descendents of the most assimilated Jews did not escape Nazi persecution. The Nazis defined anyone with even a single Jewish grandparent as a Jew, rather than focusing upon those who were ethnically or religiously Jewish.

Eliminating the Jews

Not satisfied with racist laws restricting Jews from many trades and professions, Hitler proposed his "Final Solution": the complete eradication of the Jewish population. This became a national goal second to none. The German war machine was hampered from the beginning by the diversion of men and materials to guarding, imprisoning, and murdering Jewish civilians.

When the war turned against the Germans, transportation was desperately needed for soldiers, arms, and equipment. Instead, the Germans sped up the deportations to the death camps, in a frantic effort to kill as many Jews as possible before their liberation.

Other Nations Closed Their Doors

At the same time that Germany was systematically denying the Jews their basic civil rights, and even after it had launched a program of organized, systematic murder unprecedented in world history, other nations of the world were turning a blind eye. Even when Jews escaped from the Nazis, there was no guarantee they would find safe haven elsewhere.

The Nations Met, with No Results

On July 5, 1938, just eleven days after the Nazi annexation of Austria, President Franklin Delano Roosevelt called an international conference to discuss the plight of Jewish refugees. The overwhelming response was to do nothing at all—as one nation put it, "We do not have a 'Jewish problem' and we do not wish to import one." The only countries willing to accept more refugees were the Dominican Republic and Costa Rica, and they expected generous financial support from other countries.

In May of 1939, the *St. Louis* sailed from Hamburg with 930 Jewish refugees on board. They carried American quota permits, as well as special permission to stay temporarily in Cuba. Yet the Cubans declared all but thirty of the permits worthless due to new regulations, and the United States not only refused to take in the refugees, but also sent the Coast Guard to prevent passengers from jumping overboard. Eventually, the *St. Louis* was forced to return to Europe. The Germans considered this all the proof they needed that extermination of the Jews would be met with indifference elsewhere.

FACT

In a tragic story, the *Sturma*—a coal barge—left Romania with 769 Jewish refugees in February of 1942. It reached the Turkish port at Istanbul, but Turkish authorities would not permit the passengers to disembark until the British agreed to accept the refugees into Palestine. After more than two months, the Turks towed the ship back out into the Black Sea—though by then its engine was beyond repair—where it sank, leaving but one survivor.

President Roosevelt and the Americans

President Franklin D. Roosevelt himself is considered by many historians to have been mildly anti-Semitic. He once referred to the "understandable complaints which the Germans bore towards the Jews in Germany," claiming that more than half of the doctors and lawyers in Germany were Jews. In actuality, Jews were merely 10.9 percent of the medical doctors and 16.3 percent of lawyers.

Yet he did make some steps, such as calling for the suspension of immigration laws and pointing out that troop ships returning from Europe could carry Jewish refugees. Neither of these ideas came to reality. According to a Gallup poll, 83 percent of Americans opposed the admission of a larger number of Jewish refugees before the war, and little changed throughout. According to Holocaust scholar David Wyman (the grandson of two Protestant ministers), the Allied countries had many tools in their arsenal that could have been used to save Jewish lives—from diplomatic efforts to publicizing what they had learned about the atrocities to bombing the death camps—but employed none of these.

The Blood of Their Brothers

Even Jewish leaders failed to prioritize the rescue of their brethren trapped in Europe. The American Jewish Joint Distribution Committee had the opportunity to bribe the Cuban government to take the refugees from the *St. Louis*, but in the words of their own historian, the Joint "had never agreed to pay ransom to unscrupulous operators for innocent human beings." Because they rested on this principle, 900 lives were lost.

Many Jews were convinced by the Allies that the best way to save Jewish lives was to simply win the war—despite the fact that the Allies were, as mentioned above, systematically failing to take advantage of their many opportunities to rescue persecuted Jews. Wyman points in particular to the adulation of Franklin D. Roosevelt by Stephen Wise, an American Reform and Zionist leader, as particularly harmful to Jewish interests:

> Wise's autobiography, completed shortly before he died, shows that Roosevelt remained his hero until the end. It also leaves the clear impression that after about 1935 Wise was unable to be critical of, or even objective about, the President. He was convinced that FDR was personally anxious to help the persecuted European Jews in the 1930s, that he wanted to do everything possible to rescue Jews during the Holocaust years, and that he fully, though quietly, supported the Zionist movement. These assessments were wide of the mark and should have been recognized as such at the time. In

retrospect, in view of Wise's position as the foremost Jewish leader, his total trust in Roosevelt was not an asset to American or European Jews. (*The Abandonment of the Jews*, p. 69)

The American Zionist movement set its sights upon the establishment of a Jewish State in Palestine, relegating the extermination of Jews in Europe to the back burner. Its call for an American Jewish Conference in 1943 focused upon "the rights and status of Jews in the post-war world," and "implementation of the rights of the Jewish people with respect to Palestine." Rescue of European Jewry wasn't even on the original program!

The Torah Scholars' Response

The response of Torah Scholars was immediate and unanimous: everything must be done to rescue the Jews of Europe. A *Vaad HaHatzala* (Rescue Council) was created to spearhead Orthodox efforts. Although the United States prohibited commerce with Germany, the Vaad sent care packages to Jews that usually reached their destinations, and, later in the war, even ransomed Jews from the Nazis.

Breaking the Law

In this effort, the Vaad was opposed by the U.S. War Refugee Board, which opposed any ransom because it might aid the German war machine. The Board was also concerned about how the American public would react if they learned that bribes were going to the enemy in order to ransom Jews.

The truth is that other Jewish groups, such as the Jewish Agency and World Jewish Congress, also opposed the WRB's ban on ransom, but the Vaad went ahead with its efforts in defiance of American law and that of other Allied and neutral countries.

The Sages teach that "one who saves a single life . . . is as if he saved an entire world." To those steeped in Torah values, this was their mandate. Isaac Sternbuch, a leading Orthodox rescue activist in Switzerland, admitted that "some activities necessary in our operations are punishable," but he regarded saving Jewish lives as a "sacred cause" that justified these efforts. Another agency commented that the Vaad was "prepared to disregard any consideration other than the rescue of the maximum possible number" of refugees.

Rabbi Michael Dov Weissmandl

Another hero of the rescue effort was Rabbi Michael Dov Weissmandl, born in Hungary, whose own ransom efforts helped save Jews in Slovakia. He and Gisi Fleischmann, a Zionist women's leader (and his distant relative), bribed an SS captain who was supervising the deportation of Slovakian Jewry in 1942. The deportations came to a halt, though historians have not established conclusively that the ransom payments were the cause. It seems clear, at least, that three forced-labor camps were opened for Jews thanks to the bribes, saving as many as 4,000 Slovak Jews from the death camps.

Rabbi Weissmandl was nonetheless distraught that his much larger plan, to raise over two million dollars to ransom one million European Jews, never came to fruition. This plan reached as far as Heinrich Himmler, head of the Gestapo and the Waffen-SS, but the funds were never made available to Weissmandl to carry out his plan. Not only did officials with the Joint Distribution Committee fail to fund his efforts, but some actually worked to prevent their success. Rabbi Weissmandl's own wife and family perished in Auschwitz; after the war, he remarried in the United States and rebuilt the yeshiva of Nitra, Slovakia. It is now located in Mt. Kisco, New York.

The Mirrer Yeshiva in Shanghai

The story of the Mirrer Yeshiva during the Holocaust years is so extraordinary, so bizarre, that were it not for hundreds of eyewitnesses, no one would believe it. And yet the story is entirely true, and was recounted by one who experienced it: Rabbi Yecheskel Leitner, who today resides in Brooklyn, New York.

Escape to Vilna

At the beginning of World War II, the small township of Mir, in Poland near the Russian border, hosted one of the world's great centers of Torah learning. Students came from Poland, Russia, and Lithuania, of course, but also from the United States, England, France, Germany, Sweden, and even South Africa. All were studying in Mir when the fury of the Nazi Blitzkrieg descended upon Poland.

In October 1939, Radio London reported that the city of Vilna—which, like Mir, was under Soviet occupation—was to be returned to the neutral country of Lithuania. One student heard this report, and it spread like wildfire through the yeshiva. Whoever managed to get to Vilna would automatically gain freedom when the transfer of power took place!

Within just two days, on the basis of this one rumor heard from a radio broadcast, the entire yeshiva started moving. Everyone packed their bags and secured whatever transportation they could find, in order to reach the nearest train station and buy tickets to Vilna.

The Impossible Transit Visas

Eight months later, in June of 1940, the Russian Army suddenly invaded and occupied the independent states of Estonia, Latvia, and Lithuania. Teachers and students were now trapped in Communist Russia, where the eradication of religion was a national goal and a clergyman was automatically an enemy of the state.

En masse, the students applied for exit visas from Russia—and the authorities were prepared to grant them, as long as the refugees could show the necessary transit and destination visas. This news was greeted with skepticism, for the Communists were already setting up their infamous Iron Curtain, and had even tricked hundreds of thousands of Polish Jews and others to indicate their desire to leave, and then exiled them to Siberia instead. To apply for an exit visa was suicide; to receive it, impossible. Yet the authorities in Lithuania behaved in uncharacteristic fashion, granting exit visas liberally—as long as the refugees had somewhere to go.

Even more incomprehensible was the behavior of the Japanese, who for years had neglected to send a consul to Lithuania—and now, when it was merely a province of the Soviet Union, sent a consul at the very time that other nations were closing theirs down. The new consul, Chiune (Sempo) Sugihara, then violated a standing Japanese policy to deny refuge or even transit visas through Japan, because a traveler might end up stranded there. As long as the refugees could find a final destination, Mr. Sugihara said that he would issue transit visas.

FACT

Sempo Sugihara asked permission from his government to issue transit visas to Jewish refugees on three separate occasions, and all three times his requests were denied. Yet he violated orders and risked his career, in order to save more than 6,000 lives. Indeed, the Japanese diplomatic service dismissed him after the war.

So now only one piece of the puzzle remained—a destination. Where would the refugees go? A Dutch student of the Telshe Yeshiva went to the Dutch consul, and discovered that the island of Curacao, in the Dutch West Indies, required no visas. The Russians would not be satisfied without a stamp of some kind, but the Dutch consul agreed to put a stamp in each passport that said: "Entry to Curacao permitted without a visa." Now, the refugees had all the visas necessary to leave—although no one ever planned to go to Curacao.

Leaving for Japan

To reach Japanese territory required a trip across Russia on the Trans-Siberian Railroad, the same one that many other Jews were forced to travel as slave laborers. Instead they traveled as paying passengers, and the price seemed to go up each time a train left the station. During this time, observant Rabbis in America drove on the Sabbath in order to raise funds—recognizing that this was truly a matter of life and death, when the laws of the Sabbath are pushed aside.

After a relatively peaceful journey to Vladivostok, the refugees then boarded a steamship that docked in Tsuruga, on the Japanese main island, Honshu. Although the governor of Curacao contested the alleged final destination on the refugees' visas, the Japanese nonetheless repeatedly extended the "transit" visas well beyond the original two-week limit. The students lived in the city of Kobe until, just three months before Pearl Harbor, they were deported to Shanghai in occupied China.

Torah in Shanghai

Ten years before the refugees arrived, a wealthy Jew, Silas Hardoon, had a dream. In his dream, he was told to build a synagogue. And Mr. Hardoon, estranged from Judaism, married to a non-Jewish woman, built the Beis Aharon synagogue, on Museum Road in Shanghai. The synagogue was in the business district rather than a residential neighborhood, and it was barely used; its 250 seats were never filled.

Then, the Mirrer Yeshiva arrived—and found a home. All 250 students had a place to sit, in this synagogue seemingly prepared just for them. It even had a kitchen facility, dining rooms, and a mikveh (ritual bath) in the building next door. On the basis of a dream, Mr. Hardoon provided a place for the yeshiva to survive and flourish for five years, until the war was over.

Most of the refugees moved to the United States after the war, where Rabbi Abraham Kalmanowitz founded the Mirrer Yeshiva in Brooklyn, New York. Others joined Rabbi Chaim Shmuelevitz, the rosh yeshiva, as he traveled to France and then to the Land of Israel, to rebuild the Mirrer Yeshiva on holy ground, in Jerusalem.

Chapter 16

Modern Challenges and Torah

Many people imagine that the Torah is somehow outdated—that modern scientific discoveries contradict Torah, or that progress in modern Western ethics supersedes it. Yet the interaction between Torah and modern thought is hardly a matter of simple denial. There are many people today who understand Torah philosophy well and carefully observe its tenets, and who also make great contributions to modern science and medicine.

Do Modern Discoveries Contradict Torah?

It is said that many professors of the liberal arts are agnostic or atheist, and that when you ask them why, they say that science proves the Bible is outdated and inaccurate. Yet at the same time, the saying continues, most professors of the hard sciences believe in God. While this may be the result of a survey or merely armchair analysis, it certainly seems true that scientists are, for whatever reason, more likely to believe in God than professors of the liberal arts. Those involved in the sciences are apparently more likely to recognize the hand of God in their work.

In addition, the apparent contradictions between Torah and modern science can be reconciled in a number of different ways, all of which are intellectually honest and consistent with the most recent discoveries and analyses of our world. Professor Gerald Schroeder, a nuclear physicist at MIT and now an author and lecturer on religious topics, says that whenever one finds a contradiction between Torah and science, the cause is one of two things: bad science or bad Torah.

The Torah Describes Our World

At no point do we find Jewish thought willing to "live with" a contradiction. Theologians from other religions may be comfortable distinguishing between "scientific truths" open to analysis and research, and "theological truths" that come from the Bible and are not open to examination. In Torah thought, however, the Torah is the blueprint of Creation—and must accurately describe the world in which we find ourselves. There is nothing that is "not open to examination" according to traditional Torah thought.

Every word of the Torah, according to Torah thought, is the Word of God. As such, it is perfect and eternal. If there were something in the world that flatly and absolutely contradicted the Torah, this would create significant theological problems not only for traditional Jewish scholars, but possibly for Christians and Muslims as well. Reconciling Torah and the modern world is therefore of great importance.

Science and The Talmud

The Talmud demonstrates a remarkable level of scientific knowledge. To give but one example, the Talmudic Sages knew the number of days in a lunar month down to six decimal places—beyond what anyone else knew until NASA timed it against an atomic clock.

At the same time, you will find suggestions, especially in medical matters, which would never be recommended today. Later authorities cautioned long before the modern era that many of these suggestions in the Talmud should no longer be followed. This seems to imply that the recommendations were not necessarily mistakes, but rather rendered obsolete by changes in our habits, diet, and other factors. You will find other suggestions about medicine that are startling for their accuracy, so it is worth keeping an open mind even when confronting a passage that seems to reflect outmoded or "primitive" thinking.

When Talmud (Appears to) Contradict Science

In almost every case, statements about the natural world contained in the Talmud are not relevant to Jewish law. Instead, they are observations or Midrashim, intended to teach ethical lessons. So how one chooses to resolve apparent errors in the Talmud has little practical impact; the lesson in ethics is valid nonetheless.

These difficulties most often fall into one of four categories:

1. Statements that are entirely correct, but sometimes misunderstood
2. Statements intended to be allegorical rather than factual
3. Things said based upon the science or medicine of the day, which we would no longer utilize
4. Things that we believe to be inaccurate, but that we then discover upon closer examination to be correct

You would be surprised to learn how many Talmudic statements have fallen into the fourth category. Nonetheless, apparent inaccuracies in the Talmud do not create a theological problem, and are in fact to be expected. It is only the statements of the Torah itself that must be reconciled with current scientific knowledge.

The Age of the Universe

If you would ask someone for a statement in the Bible that contradicts science, the given age of the universe would surely be Exhibit A. The Bible says that God created the world in less than a single week, culminating with the creation of humankind on the sixth day and God resting on the seventh. This was no more than about 6,000 years ago, and according to commonly accepted Jewish thought, was slightly less than 5,766 years before the publication of the Bible. Meanwhile, the latest estimate from astrophysicists is approximately 15 billion years. Even if we manage to deal with 14.999 billion of those years, that leaves nearly a million awaiting an answer. So clearly there is a lot of ground—or time—to cover.

How Do We Define a Day?

The first problem with an overly literal reading of Genesis is that our definition of a "day" is based upon the rotation of the earth around the sun. As the Torah itself says, "and it was evening and it was morning, one day" (and the second, third, and so on). There was no sun until the fourth day—so why assume that the first three were merely twenty-four hours long? In reality, while some commentaries say that the days of Creation were twenty-four hours long in any case, others view the days as units of time, as eras. The first days of Creation are viewed from God's perspective rather than a human one, and to God, as King David says in Psalm 90, 1,000 years are like a day.

FACT

Einstein was asked, near the end of his life, what he would have done differently if he could do his life over. He answered that given the opportunity, he would have studied Talmud.

Gerald Schroeder took note of this, performed a few calculations, and made an astonishing discovery. Schroeder compared the perspective of one outside the entire mass of the universe to the perspective of one within it. He did this based upon Einstein's theory of relativity, which relates mass to time. Schroeder determined that while someone inside the mass of the universe would experience fifteen billion years, this same period of time would appear to one outside that mass as merely five and one-half days—and man was created halfway through the sixth day.

It Only Looks Natural

There is another, completely different way to look at the story of Creation, which even allows for the possibility that its days were merely twenty-four hours long. To understand this, let's look first at Adam and Eve (or, in Hebrew, Chava). As we know from the story, God has adult-level conversations with Adam immediately after creating him. No baby is able to speak fluently the day he or she is born, so it must be that Adam was created not as a baby, but as an adult, able to think and talk intelligently. In other words, Adam's biological age was far greater than a day, on the day he came into existence. The Midrash puts a number on it, and tells us that a doctor's examination would have shown him to be twenty years old.

The Midrash says that this same general rule is true of all Creation—that each created thing looked as if it had grown into its current state naturally, at the moment it was created. This means that the fully grown trees in the Garden of Eden had rings inside their trunks, indicating years of growth that never actually happened.

If so, it should be no surprise that the world and the entire universe appear to be very old—for they too should appear as if they grew into their current states naturally, and according to our best scientific understanding of the universe, that takes a very, very long time. The Torah and Talmud explained, many years before modern astrophysicists were able to examine the world, that God hides his presence within it, giving us the ability to choose not to follow Him. In fact, if the world appeared to be only 6,000 years old, it would be all too obvious that it was the product of God's Creation, and that would deny the very purpose of Creation itself in Jewish thought.

And God Created the Big Bang

Long before scientists developed the big bang theory, the concept that the universe came into existence in a single blinding flash of pure energy, philosophers such as Aristotle believed that the universe was without beginning or end—that it, in fact, was eternal. Obviously this was further from what the Torah says than is the big bang. Yet Maimonides wrote that the Aristotelian theory of an eternal universe would not contradict the Torah, even were it demonstrated to be true. Nothing in the Torah is wrong—only our limited understanding of it is.

Compared to the theory of an eternal universe, the big bang is far more consonant with the literal words of the Torah. Many in the scientific community found themselves psychologically resistant to adopting the big bang theory, precisely because it sounds exactly like "Creation ex nihilo." One even described the experience using the metaphor of struggling to climb a high mountain, only to find a group of theologians relaxing comfortably at the top. Dr. Arno Penzias, who shared the 1978 Nobel Prize in Physics (with Robert W. Wilson) for discovering evidence of the big bang, adopted observance of the Torah after making his discovery! In 1984, he explained his position to the *New York Times Magazine.*

What we find when we look at the universe is order. We also find direction. The universe has a very well marked beginning. It starts with a creation—a big bang, if you will—and has a directionality to it. We have a result for which there ought to have been a cause. And although there's no picture of an old man with a white beard standing there, what we see of the world from a physical point of view is consistent with what Maimonides observed from a metaphysical point of view—without a large telescope or watching the flight of galaxies. ("American Jews Rediscover Orthodoxy," *New York Times Magazine,* Sept. 30, 1984)

Does the age of the universe contradict the Torah? Few are better qualified to answer than Professor Arno Penzias, and his answer is somewhat obvious.

The Theory of Evolution

Concerning the theory of evolution, you may have heard that impartial scientists have firmly proven that evolution happened, and also that if it did, this contradicts the Torah. Neither of these is actually true. The topic of this book is Torah, not evolutionary theory—we needn't enter the debate about the evidence pro or con. For our purposes, it is enough to understand that physical evidence for evolution can be reconciled in similar ways as the Age of the Universe.

The Documentary Hypothesis

Several centuries ago, a French scholar, Dr. Jean Astruc, postulated that there were multiple source documents for the Five Books of Moshe, the Torah. Over time, this developed into the Graf-Wellhausen Hypothesis, after the names of the two nineteenth-century scholars who put it in its classic form. It is also called "JEPD," named for four groups of early Israelites:

J: A group of believers who referred to God by the four-letter name often shown in English as YHWH, also called "the Tetragrammaton"

E: A group of believers who referred to God by the name *Elohim*, at least until the Tetragrammaton is revealed to Moshe in Exodus 3:6

P: The Priests, who concerned themselves primarily with Temple laws, and were the most recent of the four groups

D: The Deuteronomists, who, not surprisingly, wrote Deuteronomy, and also Joshua, and probably Samuel and Kings as well

These four groups, according to the Hypothesis, produced four texts that were then assembled by a Redactor. This Redactor did some editing, but left the basic flavor of each text intact—so that modern analysts could distinguish them later.

The general concept of multiple authors quickly became the dominant view among Bible critics, even though later scholars rejected Wellhausen's view of the specifics, such as the times that the various source documents came into existence. Today one can find schools of thought claiming that the Torah as we know it came into existence in Solomon's time (more than 800 years before the Common Era), or in Ezra's time (roughly 400 years later). They all reject the idea that the Torah came into existence at the hand of Moshe—but they have not agreed upon any single alternative theory.

The Chicken or the Egg?

The research of impartial analysts is more credible than that of individuals with a preconceived agenda. For that reason, it's worth knowing something about the people who designed this theory. Did they conclude that single authorship of the Torah was untenable based upon detailed research, or did they come to the task with a bias toward "disproving" it?

Dr. Jean Astruc published his work anonymously, because he was living under a repressive French Catholic regime, and his work, "Conjectures on the original documents that Moshe appears to have used in composing the Book of Genesis," claimed to have been published in Brussels to protect him from retribution. Both the title of his work and the time in which it was published are instructive. Further, his essay was part of an encyclopedia devoted to "destroying superstitions and providing access to human knowledge." Astruc took it "as axiomatic that scriptural documents could be analyzed in the same manner as secular ones and… that the varying use of terms indicated different writers." Therefore he made an assumption and then set out to prove it—rather than discovering problems with the concept of single authorship that *necessitated* an alternative.

Julius Wellhausen's bias was even clearer. In his *Israelitische und Juedische Geschichte*, he ridicules the account of the miracles that occurred at Sinai, saying "Who can seriously believe all that?" As R. K. Harrison wrote in "Introduction to the Old Testament": "The underlying premise, that there can be no such thing as supernatural revelation, resulted in the conclusion that the Bible is not a supernaturally revealed document."

So Where Are the Texts?

The first problem with the Graf-Wellhausen Hypothesis is that none of the alleged source texts—or even a fragment of one—has ever been found. No historical figure has ever referred to any of these texts.

Furthermore, the Samaritans, a group who broke off from the mainstream of the Jewish People very early in Jewish history, have a Torah scroll remarkably similar to the standard Jewish one. They, too, endorse the idea that the Torah was given by God to Moshe during forty years in the desert. If the Torah was assembled from source texts provided by different groups, why is there no group that accepts only some of these sources, or even refers to them? Why is there no shred of evidence that these distinct groups ever existed?

Professor Yechezkel Kaufman writes in his book *History of the Jewish Faith* that while people once imagined that critics had disproved the Bible, history has proven them wrong:

> Biblical Criticism finds itself today in a unique situation. There is a dominant theory, yet no one knows why it dominates. Wellhausen . . . based his theories on an interlocking system of proofs that seemed to complement each other, forming layers of solid intellectual foundations upon which he erected the definitive edifice of his ideas. In the meantime, however, these foundations disintegrated one by one. The proofs were refuted outright or at least seriously questioned. The scholars of Wellhausen school were forced to admit that most of the proofs do not hold up under scrutiny. Nonetheless, they did not abandon the conclusions.

Does Literary Analysis Work?

The determination of the origin of a document from analysis of its text is, of necessity, a subjective field. The researcher must look at two sentences and offer his or her opinion as to whether the sentences came from the same source, or two different ones, as well as which other sentences might have come from the same source.

In the early 1980s, Professor Yehuda Ruskay of the Weizmann Institute attempted to resolve this problem by performing a computer study of the Book of Genesis. Dr. Ruskay and his colleagues enabled a computer to perform its own analysis of the text and determine if the texts attributed to different source documents actually had distinct styles and language uses. The computer determined that it was roughly 82 percent likely that "J" and "E" were not separate at all, but came from the same source.

The literary analysis used in the field of Biblical Criticism was also once used as evidence in court, and in front of an impartial panel of judges it was not a great success. In 1931, Florence Deeks sued H. G. Wells for plagiarism. She claimed that Wells had copied a book of hers, and she used Rev. W. A. Irwin, MA, BD, PhD, associate professor of Ancient and Old Testament Languages and Literature at Toronto University, as her expert witness.

Prof. Irwin's job was to prove that Wells had duplicated Deeks's language and style, not merely her content. In accepting the task, Prof. Irwin said, "I consented in considerable measure because this is the sort of task with which my study of ancient literature repeatedly confronts me, and I was interested to test out in modern works the methods commonly applied to those of the ancient world." He concluded, based upon his study of both texts, that H. G. Wells had used Deeks's style of writing rather than his own, and on this basis it was obvious that Wells had plagiarized her work.

Deeks lost in court. She lost again on appeal. Then she ended up in the Court of Appeal for Toronto, where Ontario Justice William Riddell examined Irwin's testimony, and in his opinion called it "fantastic hypotheses," "solemn nonsense," "comparisons without significance," and "arguments and conclusions alike puerile."

In other words, neither a computer nor an impartial judge was able to substantiate the methods used in the field of Biblical Criticism. And, unlike the critics, these sources had no other agenda than arrival at the truth.

Why Are There Two Words for God?

The Torah is filled with references to both YHWH, usually translated as "the Lord," and Elohim, usually translated as "God"—and often you'll find the two together. In reality, the word *Elohim* means a leader. When building the Golden Calf, the Israelites said they wanted to make an Elohim to replace Moshe—and Aharon responded that they would make a holiday "to YHWH" on the next day, and no one saw that as a contradiction. In the Book of Shmuel (Samuel) a woman saw a vision of Shmuel after his death, and said that she saw Elohim.

The word *Elohim* is related to YHWH in the same way that "the first President of the United States" is related to "George Washington." YHWH is God's Name, and was only said in the Temple. In prayers, people will pronounce the word *Adonai* instead, which means "Our Lord," but the printed word itself is not translated—nor, in fact, do we know how to pronounce it today.

ALERT!

According to most readings of the text, the Israelites did not intend to worship the Golden Calf, but to replace Moshe with it. Only a few stooped to actual worship of the Calf.

It's Old News

There really isn't an alleged anachronism or misused term that was not already addressed by Jewish sources centuries ago. Every turn of phrase was analyzed by earlier and later religious authorities, and used to derive important information and theological instruction from the text. So when all of these same terms are used as proof that the Torah was actually a hodge-podge of previously composed materials, it should be fair to ask why the Rabbis' explanations were deemed insufficient.

This was the thinking of a young man studying at Yale, who ended up in a yeshiva in Israel over summer vacation. When he returned to Yale he decided to enroll in a course in Biblical Criticism so that he could compare both sides. After studying the alleged signs of multiple authorship, he went to a Rabbi who sat with him and showed him the traditional commentaries and their explanations of those same passages.

Toward the end of the course, the professor invited comment, and the student asked how they should address the existence of ancient account-ings for those same problematic words and phrases. The professor's answer should remind you of the discussion of preconceived agendas. "That's the most ridiculous thing I've ever heard," he said. "*Everyone knows* that the Torah was composed by multiple authors!"

Modern Technology and Judaism

Modern technologies give rise to all sorts of new questions that never con-fronted earlier generations. Can you use electricity on the Sabbath? What about a microphone? If you live in the United States, can you send a fax to Europe on Friday afternoon, where it will emerge from the destination printer on the Sabbath?

The questions have only grown more serious in recent years: issues such as definition of life's beginning and end, stem cell research, organ donation, and even cloning are being explored by scholars. Articles discussing religious observance in space, as well as discussions of artificial intelligence and human identity, have appeared in journals of Jewish studies.

None of these, however, are studied in a vacuum. The principles of Jewish law, as studied for thousands of years, can be applied to these new situations in a fairly consistent manner. There is actually relatively little disagreement among Jewish legal scholars about any of these issues, despite their overwhelming complexity—because the groundwork for these topics has been laid out so well in discussions of earlier issues.

Women's Rights

Anything written by a man on the topic of women in Judaism is automatically suspect. This is especially true because traditionally, Rabbis are men, and Rabbis officially determine Jewish law. Nonetheless, a chapter discussing Torah and modern issues would hardly be complete without a discussion of women, feminism, and Judaism. You have probably heard something about women having inferior status in Torah, expected to live unfulfilled lives of child-rearing and cooking for their husbands. A few comments about this perception are therefore in order.

Women Are Different

In recent years, feminists have begun to acknowledge and explore more thoroughly the feminine side of women. Men and women are not the same, and what is good for the gander may not, in fact, be good for the goose. Give men and women the same math problem, monitor their brain waves, and you will see that the male and female brain respond differently to reach the same solution. Men and women respond differently intellectually, emotionally, and, yes, even spiritually, to the same influences.

In Judaism, women are considered inherently more spiritual, and closer to God. According to the Talmud, women have *binah yeseirah*, "extra understanding." Many husbands come to realize that their wives have more common sense than they do; the Talmud agrees that this is true!

ALERT!

This may be contrary to what you've heard, so it bears repeating: Judaism considers women to be inherently *more* spiritual than men. If you look at the statistics for violent crimes and other acts obviously contrary to spiritual life, you will quickly observe that men are much more likely to distance themselves from God in these ways.

Responding Differently

If a belief system is developed by human beings, then, just as humans are imperfect, that system will be imperfect. If it differentiates between men and women, but is developed by men, then it is likely to be biased toward men—the same way that "separate but equal" in the segregated South was anything but equal. This is the premise that has driven forward the movement for egalitarianism within Judaism, as it has within other religions.

But if God gives a system of behavior to human beings, and if God created men and women as unique and different beings, then we should expect God to respond to the unique, different nature of each.

Women and Prayer

When you think of Judaism or Jewish observance, you might naturally think of the synagogue. In reality, however, and in contrast with the Christian societies that dominate most of the Western world, Judaism is not centered around the synagogue, but around the home—where, if anything, a woman's influence in a married family is usually felt more than a man's.

Rabbis enacted all of the synagogue services, from the concept of group prayer to Torah readings several times a week, for men. Women are not obligated to perform these duties, because the Rabbis did not see that women would benefit spiritually from these activities. Even for men, religious services are hardly considered the most important of religious acts, from any legal or spiritual perspective.

In the Torah, only one who is obligated to perform a mitzvah is able to fulfill the obligations of others. This means that if you have already made a particular blessing, you can't repeat it merely for the benefit of others—they should say it themselves, or find someone who has not yet made that blessing to say it for them.

This is one of the major reasons why women do not lead prayer services and perform other synagogue functions according to Jewish tradition. At the very least, having someone who is not obligated performing a function implies that none present who *are* obligated are also competent to do it!

Chapter 17

Studies in Bereishis, the Book of Genesis

The First Book of the Bible is Genesis, called by its first word—*Bereishis*—in Hebrew. The Medrash says that if God merely intended to teach His Commandments to the Jewish People, He could have skipped right to the Book of Exodus—and "passed over" most of what happened in Egypt, as well. According to the Medrash, God wanted to teach humanity that He Created the world and He ultimately controls our destiny. You might want to have a Bible handy while reading this chapter, to see the quoted verses in context.

Part 1: Bereishis—Genesis 1:1–6:8

> And the woman saw that the tree was good to eat . . . and she took from its fruit and ate, and she also gave to her husband with her, and he ate. (3:6)

Rabbi Shlomo Yitzchaki (Rashi) explains why she gave her husband some of the fruit. She worried that she would die, Adam would live forever, and she would be replaced and forgotten. The author of the *Yalkut Lekach Tov* commentary wonders about this. Eve was seduced by the snake into believing that the fruit was not deadly—so what was she worried about? To explain, he gave a parable.

The Council of Governors

There was a certain land of many provinces, whose governors would meet annually. One time, the governor of a small province told the others about a "holy scholar" who lived in his region. He claimed that this righteous Sage was even able to reveal the future.

The governor of the largest province could not tolerate the idea that one of his juniors should have something to brag about that he did not, and insisted that the Sage himself be brought to the next meeting. So the frightened scholar was forced to travel to the meeting, praying constantly as he went.

The Confrontation

When they arrived, a podium had been set up, and the governor of the largest province called the Sage to join him upon it. And then he asked, to much laughter, "Tell me now, on what day will you die?" The governor had planned this question carefully, and had a dagger in his cloak. If the scholar would say he would die on any other day, the governor planned to kill him immediately, while if he claimed he would die that same day, then the governor would hold him until evening.

Instead, the Sage paused a moment from his prayers and responded, "I will die on the same day that you do."

The governor froze, and allowed the Sage to leave in peace. When others asked him afterward why he didn't go through with his plan, he said,

"You fools! Didn't you hear him predict that on the same day that he will die, I am going to die as well?"

The Bias of the Beholder

This, writes the Yalkut Lekach Tov, is the power of a personal bias. Initially, the governor wouldn't believe the claims about a Sage who could tell the future. But then, all of a sudden, his bias changed—he wanted to remain alive. In that instant his perspective changed, and he suddenly feared that this scholar could be a Prophet as well.

This explains why Eve fed her husband. When she saw the fruit as "desirable to the eyes," she was tempted by it, and seduced into believing the words of the snake. But as soon as she ate it, that temptation, that bias, immediately vanished. And just as quickly, she began to worry that the snake was wrong after all, and that now she would die, her husband would marry another, and he and his wife would live forever while she was forgotten.

Part 2: Noach—Genesis 6:9–11:32

> And God said, "Behold, they are one people with one language for all of them, and this is what they have begun to do; now will nothing be beyond them, to do anything they plan to do?" (11:6)

Even after the destruction caused by the Flood, there was no guarantee that people would devote their efforts to improving the world and to knowing their Creator. On the contrary, they were able to band together to do just the opposite—to rebel.

The verse quoted above seems to tell us that the source of their power was their unity, which was facilitated by their ability to communicate. Because they all spoke the same language, and were convinced by Nimrod to follow his leadership, there was no disagreement.

The Chofetz Chaim says that when you read this story, you should contemplate the great power of unity and *Shalom*, peace. Without Divine intervention, nothing could stop them from doing whatever they wanted to do—because they did it together. Because they were one nation with one language, nothing stopped their idolatry and their rebellion.

The Talmud teaches that any attribute used for good is more powerful than when used for evil. If so, says the Chofetz Chaim, it is impossible to imagine what it would be possible for us to achieve in the true service of God—were the world, or even the Jews alone, truly united and willing to serve God "with one mind." Just think what we could accomplish, if we would only do it together.

Part 3: Lech Lecha—Genesis 12:1–17:27

> And God said to Avraham, "Go out from your land, from your place of birth and the house of your fathers, to the land which I will show you." (12:1)

God didn't describe the land. He didn't even tell Avraham where he was supposed to go. He merely said "go out"—leave, and you'll get more information later about where you should go.

Rashi says that HaShem did not immediately reveal the location in order to increase Avraham's desire for it, and "to reward him for every word [spoken about it]." The Chassidic Rebbe of Modzhitz, Rav S. Y. Taub, asks why there would be further reward "for every word." After all, what greater reward is there, once God has spoken directly with Avraham about his move, and has told him to go?

Moving Day

To answer this question, think for a minute about what normally happens when someone leaves town and moves to a new place. When you find a moving van outside your neighbor's house, what's going to be your first question when you speak to your neighbor? "Where are you going?" It's obvious! And it's just as obvious that anyone who is moving already has an answer to give you. They already know where they're going to work, they have a new rental agreement or a down payment on their new house, and by the time the moving van pulls up, they've probably redone half the interior of their new home as well.

Of course, we know that this wasn't true many centuries ago. Back when journeys of several hundred miles were not simple day trips, people didn't go to scout things out in advance. But even so—actually, even more so—a person moved with a clear reason for leaving, a carefully selected destination, and a reason for going there.

Isn't Avraham Acting Strange?

Avraham's journey was different. God told him, "Go out from your land," and didn't reveal the destination to him.

Do you think people saw Avraham packing, and never asked, "Where are you going? Why? What do you intend to do there?" Of course they did—and Avraham had no answer to give them. He himself had no idea why he was leaving, didn't know where he was going, and didn't know why he was going there.

If someone responded "I don't know" to these questions, would you accept that answer? The Rebbe assures us that Avraham's contemporaries didn't accept it either. "Can it be that a person heads off on a long journey, and doesn't know his destination, and doesn't even know why he is traveling?"

So Avraham was forced to provide more detail, to explain to them that "God told me to go." And he, of course, told them that he honestly believed that he would find a new place to settle, wherever God told him to go.

The fact that Avraham did not know his destination caused him additional discomfort, and forced him to speak with other people about his travels—far more than would otherwise have been necessary. Says the Rebbe: Of course he should have been rewarded, for every word.

Acting like Avraham

Sometimes you do the right thing, and it looks funny. This is especially true if a person follows a Mitzvah in the Torah such as building a Sukkah in the back yard, and the neighbors can see. People don't want to look different or act strange. However well-meaning the questions, we can be embarrassed to answer someone's curiosity. So the Rebbe is saying that if you put yourself into this sort of situation because you're trying to follow God's will, it only makes sense that you should be rewarded for every word you have to say about it.

Part 4: Vayera—Genesis 18:1–22:24

And it came to pass, after all these things, that God tested Avraham . . . And He said to him, "Please take your son, your unique one whom you have loved, Yitzchak, and go forward to the land of Moriah, and bring him up as a sacrifice there, on one of the mountains which I will indicate." (22:1–2)

The Torah says that Avraham faced ten tests, and he passed them all. This one—sacrificing his son Isaac—was the greatest of them all. Many people are confused by his actions. Wouldn't it have been right, they say, to refuse?

Avraham Worked for God

If you are asking this question, though, you should think first about Avraham's relationship with and recognition of God. Unlike most of us, Avraham didn't *imagine* that God was talking to him—it really happened. And if God created us all, then He is certainly entitled to tell us what we should do with ourselves, and even with others.

What made this the supreme test, though, wasn't merely the fact that he would be sacrificing his only son with Sarah his wife. God had already promised Avraham that through Yitzchak, not any other child, he would become a great nation—yet even that wasn't the biggest problem. Avraham was going to publicly destroy everything he had worked for, on behalf of God.

Throughout his life, Avraham taught belief in the One God—and he also taught that God *abhorred* human sacrifice, a common idolatrous practice at the time. Avraham acquired an excellent reputation as a teacher, leader and generous Man of God. And with Yitzchak learning to follow his ways, Avraham was succeeding in his mission to bring knowledge of God into the world.

Avraham was asked to throw it all away—no son, no reputation, and going from leader to laughingstock all at the same time. The biggest problem for Avraham wasn't about him, or about his son. He thought about everyone *else* in the world, and their knowledge of God. His every instinct, from every angle, positively screamed out to him that this was the wrong thing to do.

A Human Being Is More Than Animal

How did Avraham respond? With a simple "I am here!" "And Avraham rose early in the morning to saddle his donkey . . ." (22:3). Though he had servants, he ran to perform God's will himself.

The greatness of human beings lies in our ability to do this type of thing—something that violates our instincts, requiring us to rise above the animal within. To use a term coined by the Chassidic Rebbe (and practicing psychiatrist) Rabbi Avraham Twersky, MD, a human being is not merely "homo sapiens," but "homo *spiritus*"—one capable of spiritual dominance over animal instinct.

The atheist says that we are creatures of instinct, higher animals who still act only in response to one or another of our desires—even charity is done because we cannot stand the sight of other people suffering, or because we want to feel beneficent. One who understands that God Created us recognizes we have both capabilities and responsibilities far greater than those of animals.

Part 5: Chayei Sarah—Genesis 23:1-25:18

Sometimes the Torah seems to be repetitive. You find yourself wondering why the Torah felt it necessary to tell us the same thing twice, and attempt to determine what changes and nuances can be learned from the retelling.

A good example is found here, when we read the story of Avraham's servant, Eliezer, going to find a wife for Yitzchak. The story of Eliezer's meeting with Rivka (Rebecca) is told in great detail. Then we are given a complete record of Eliezer's conversation with her brother and father, during which he *repeats* the story in great detail. One of the most crucial elements, the "test" that Eliezer devised in order to determine which woman was meant for Yitzchak, is found repeated *four* times.

Any editor would have hacked and slashed away at these paragraphs—so why is the Supreme Being being repetitive? The editing possibilities are so obvious that we clearly need to look deeper. To know *all* the answers, you might have to reach an advanced level of understanding of Talmud and Kabbalah. The Kanfei Nesharim elaborates: "When we concentrate and delve more deeply, we find within them [in the stories of the forebears, in Genesis] many other lessons, intentions, and hints toward holy and great things."

But here is one insight offered by the Bais HaLevi, Rabbi Yosef Dov Soloveitchik of Brisk. Eliezer tells Rivka's family that Avraham told him to "take a wife for my son" (24:38). But Avraham really told him to "Take a wife for my son, for Yitzchak" (24:4). Why did Eliezer omit his name?

The answer, says the Bais HaLevi, is pretty simple. To have their daughter marry the son of such a prestigious public figure as Avraham was a great honor. But having her marry a scholar such as Yitzchak . . . why, that's another matter! If he's studying all day, that means he won't be making money or going on vacations.

When Avraham instructed Eliezer to find a young woman, Avraham said she should be "for my son," meaning appropriate as a daughter-in-law "for Yitzchak," in accordance with Yitzchak's own great character and potential. But when Eliezer went to Rivka's family, he recognized immediately that discussing Yitzchak in any detail might blow the whole match. So instead, he merely discussed the fact that *Avraham* was seeking a wife for his son.

Part 6: Toldos—Genesis 25:19–28:9

> And he ate, and he drank, and he arose and he left; and Esav denigrated the right of the first-born. (25:34)

According to the Medrash, the right of the firstborn meant the ability to lead the service of God. Before the selection of the tribe of Levi, service was led by the firstborn. This is what Esav sold to Yaakov for a bowl of lentil soup!

The Sha'ar Bas Rabim commentary says that in the beginning of this story, you could look at Esav in a favorable light. You could say that he was extremely tired and hungry, and feared that he was near death—and that's why he agreed to Yaakov's deal.

But after eating and drinking, what should we have expected? Someone who *valued* serving God would be very upset. "I was forced to do it! And I regret what I did! I regret the entire sale!"

What actually happened? "And he ate, and he drank, and he arose and he left . . ."—he got up and went away satisfied, as if nothing had happened. Even more, "Esav denigrated the right of the first-born." This didn't happen just because he was hungry, but because he really didn't care. He *didn't* value the right of the firstborn.

Everyone has to aim to do the right thing, even if we sometimes don't do it—whether because of circumstances or just because we didn't behave. If you do the wrong thing, are you upset about it, or do you feel as if nothing went wrong? How you feel afterward will have a big effect on your drive to improve.

Part 7: Vayeitzei—Genesis 28:10–32:3

> And he (Jacob) dreamed, and behold, a ladder was implanted in the ground, and its top reached into the heavens, and behold Angels of God were ascending and descending upon it. (28:12)

Rav Avraham Zalmans was a leading figure in the Mussar movement for ethical development, which you read about in Chapter 13. He interprets this verse homiletically, using the ladder as a parable to describe people as they strive to perfect themselves and their natures. Rav Zalmans derives three special insights from the ladder.

FACT

As you might imagine, Rav Zalmans is hardly alone in using the ladder as a parable for our existence. The Talmud says that we must always work to go up—if a person merely tries to remain where he or she is, then like a man standing on a ladder, gravity is going to act to pull him or her down.

One Step at a Time

Just as a ladder has many rungs, and a person must proceed one rung at a time in order to safely reach up high, a person attempting to improve his or her character cannot simply leap blindly. Everything comes in steps, in stages. One must learn and use the rules of ethical behavior laid out in works of Mussar, and adopt specific practices in order to gradually improve.

These, say Rav Zalmans, are the rungs of the ladder. What fool would ignore the rungs, and attempt to drag himself up the left-hand pole of the ladder by his hands? And how far would he get?

Secure the Ladder

Second, a ladder cannot stand unless it is leaning against a high place. In order to climb spiritually, you need models, paragons of ethical conduct, who can guide and inspire you. You can't look down, or fear catcalls from people below who would rather you not try to improve your character. Instead, you need to look up toward the top, relying upon the ladder and the high place upon which it leans.

If You Slip, Keep Going

Finally, if you encounter difficulties, if you slip back or trip on a broken rung, all is not lost. Just catch hold of the next rung, and start moving again. This is normal. It is even the path of those who are like Angels of God—truly righteous people. They are not perfect, standing at the top of the ladder. Rather, they go upward, and then they even go down a bit . . . and then they resume. The Torah says, "Seven times a righteous person falls, and arises." Even a righteous person falls from time to time.

Too often, people try to achieve perfection overnight. It doesn't work that way. The trick is to not be discouraged, to not give up, to not slide back down. This is how we can rise above our current state, and reach our goals.

Part 8: Vayishlach—Genesis 32:4–36:43

> And Yaakov was left alone, and a man wrestled with him until the break of dawn. (32:25)

As you learned in Chapter 4, Jewish sources teach that two forces struggle within each of us: the Yetzer HaTov, the Good Inclination (what we might term our "conscience"), and the Yetzer HaRa, the Evil Inclination. Jewish Sages explain that the "man" locked in battle with Yaakov was the spiritual guardian of Esav—and just as Esav was Yaakov's physical adversary, his guardian is Yaakov's spiritual adversary, none other than the Evil Inclination.

In Tractate Chulin 91a, the Talmud presents two opinions concerning the physical form that was given to this spiritual force during the fight. One opinion is that the Yetzer HaRa looked like an idol worshiper, while the second is just the opposite—the Evil Inclination looked like a scholar.

The *Avnei Nezer* commentary justifies both opinions. Sometimes, he says, the Yetzer HaRa comes to you like an idolator, someone diametrically opposed to doing that which is morally correct. The idolator tells us to ignore Torah values, ignore our consciences, and to sin.

Sometimes, however, the same Yetzer HaRa comes to you dressed like a scholar. It tries to convince you that doing a particular transgression isn't merely okay—it's a Mitzvah, a Commandment. To give one possible example, someone who feels wronged by a particular businessman may feel that he or she has a "Mitzvah" to warn others not to get ripped off—thus leading to a violation of the laws of *Lashon HaRa*, evil speech. This is the Yetzer HaRa dressed in scholar's garb, offering great justifications for immoral acts.

At the beginning of the parsha, Yaakov prays: "Rescue me please from the hand of my brother, the hand of Esav" (32:12). Commentators such as the Bais HaLevi, Aznayim LaTorah, and others, explain that Yaakov's prayer dealt with two possibilities—he asked to be saved whether Esav came as his loving brother or as the wicked Esav. The same is true regarding the corresponding spiritual force: We need to beware of the Yetzer Hara, whether it comes to us looking like an idol worshiper or like a scholar.

Part 9: Vayeishev—Genesis 37:1–40:23

> They [the brothers] sat down to eat bread, and they lifted up their eyes, and they saw; and behold, a caravan of Yishmaelites was coming from Gilad, bearing various spices, going to descend to Egypt. (32:35)

Rashi asks a simple question: why does the verse describe the cargo? Does it make a difference? He explains that these caravans would normally carry kerosene and resin, which have bad odors. For Yoseph's sake, this one happened to be carrying pleasant spices.

In common language: Who cares? Yoseph (Joseph) went out to meet his brothers. They turned on him, stripped him of his coat, and threw him in a pit. Then they take him out, only in order to sell him into slavery!

And Rashi tells you that because Yoseph's a righteous person, the people carrying him into slavery are carrying spices. How is that helpful? In his mental state at that moment, would Yoseph even *notice* the smell?

God Delivers Exactly What's Needed

The answer offered by Rabbi Asher Rubenstein is that whether or not a person even recognizes it, God gives a person exactly, precisely what's needed. For whatever reason, Yoseph needed to go down to Egypt not as a prince, but as a slave—and to enjoy elevation, downfall, and then a rise to princehood while he was there. This was all part of the Divine plan.

But there was no need for Yoseph to experience a bad odor. He had no transgression that he might be moved to correct with this mild punishment. The odor would not better enable him to fulfill his destiny or elevate himself spirituality. So he was given only what he needed—and the same is true for every person. God also gives you the experiences you need in order to grow.

With You in the Darkest Moments

There's another angle here as well. It looked pretty bad for Yoseph, going down into slavery. When the situation was so terrible—perhaps that was exactly the time to recognize a small signal that God was still with him.

When everything looks bad, we often only need to look around us more carefully to see the good parts. Perhaps the best way to find the light at the end of the tunnel is to look for its reflection on the walls.

Part 10: Miketz—Genesis 41:1–44:17

> And Yosef was the ruler over the land . . . and Yosef's brothers came and bowed twice before him, down to the ground. And Yosef saw his brothers, and he recognized them, but he made himself a stranger to them . . . (42:6–7)

Many commentators explain why Yosef felt it necessary to display cruelty toward his brothers. The Kedushas Levi (from Rabbi Levi Yitzchak of Berditchev), though, tells us that this so-called cruelty was actually compassion—and a demonstration of great self-control.

When someone loses a battle or contest against another person, it's normal to be hurt and upset. When Yosef dreamed—many years earlier—that his brothers would bow before him, they had mocked him terribly. So right at this moment, if the brothers would have known that this was their brother Yosef, and the dreams were coming true—that would have been hard to bear.

The Torah is showing us Yosef's tremendous character. A normal person would have been delighted to take maximal advantage of a situation such as this, for revenge if nothing else—to let those who mocked him feel embarrassed about it. Yosef did precisely the opposite. Specifically at the moment when they were bowing before him, fulfilling his prophecy, he hid his identity from them in order to shield them from pain and embarrassment.

ALERT!

The Talmud says that publicly embarrassing a person—destroying his or her reputation—is comparable in some ways to murder, and is enough to ruin a person's share in the World to Come. So even if the average person cannot reach Yosef's level of avoiding even incidental embarrassment, it is important to keep the feelings of others always in mind.

Part 11: Vayigash—Genesis 44:18–47:27

> And [Yaakov] sent Yehudah before him to Yosef, to guide before
> him to Goshen, and they came into the land of Goshen. (46:28)

Why did Yaakov send Yehudah on ahead? The brothers had been down
to Egypt and back—twice. Yehudah didn't need to hail a camel driver for
directions. So what, then, did Yehudah need to accomplish in order to prepare the way for Yaakov?

The Midrash provides the answer: Yehudah went to prepare a House
of Study for the brothers and their families. The word *Torah* actually means
"guide" or "instruction"—from the same verb, *l'horos* ("to guide") found in
"to guide before him to Goshen."

Yehudah went down to Goshen to set up a House of Study, to ensure that
the brothers engaged in the lifelong pursuit of Jewish learning. Thanks to
his efforts, learning continued throughout the Egyptian exile. This was why
Yehudah had to go first.

The Iturei Torah writes: "The first thing which must accompany the
founding of a Jewish community is that there be a place for Torah study, for it
is impossible for it to stand even a moment without it. There cannot be a Jewish settlement without a House of Study, from which teaching emerges."

The Iturei Torah does not mean that the people will mysteriously die or
suddenly lose all vestige of Judaism. He does, however, say that a Jewish
community not founded upon Torah study cannot stand; it sows the seeds
of its eventual collapse. Without Jewish learning as a communal focus, without the House of Study at the center, the result is not really a Jewish community at all—rather, it could better be defined as a community of Jews who
are losing their attachment to the Jewish people.

The message you find again and again in the Torah: The Torah itself is
what ensures the survival of the Jewish people. Without Torah, a Jewish
community will wither.

Part 12: Vayechi—Genesis 47:28–50:26

In the blessing given to Yehudah (Judah), Yaakov says "His eyes will be red from wine, and his teeth white from milk" (49:12). The simple reading of this verse is, of course, a blessing for material wealth.

Rabbi Yochanon, in the Talmud (Tractate Kesubos 111b), teaches a lesson by changing one of the vowels in the text. With this change, the verse reads, "and to whiten his teeth from [meaning: better than] milk." He says: To whiten one's teeth to another—meaning to offer a warm smile—is better than giving him milk.

Too often, we think of charity as something to give to the poor, the sick, and the miserable—as if they were all the same. Is it necessary to be poor or sick in order to be miserable?

Certainly not—our generation may have material wealth by comparison to earlier eras, but we also have an abundance of therapists. Many people today are lonely, sad, and in need of a warm smile. Yes, it's possible to give to a less fortunate person without writing a check! And unlike money, you can never run out of smiles—in fact, the more you give away, the more you have left.

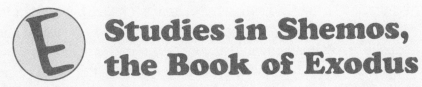

Chapter 18

Studies in Shemos, the Book of Exodus

The second book of the Torah is titled *Shemos*, "Names," because it begins with "And these are the names of the Children of Israel, who came to Egypt" with Jacob. Its content focuses primarily upon the slavery and liberation that followed, and the formation of the Jewish People into a distinct and new nation. The Latin title "Exodus" is thus an apt description.

Part 1: Shemos—Exodus 1:1–6:1

> And God said to him, "What is in your hand?" And he said, "A staff." And He said, "Cast it to the ground," and he cast it to the ground and it became a snake, and Moshe ran away from it. (4:2–3)

The Medrash tells the following story (Shemos Rabba 3): A Roman matron said to Rebbe Yossi, "My god is greater than your God." He asked her why. She explained, "At the moment that your God revealed Himself to Moshe in the bush, Moshe covered his face [but did not move]. But when he saw the snake, which is my god, immediately 'Moshe ran away from it'!"

Rebbe Yossi replied that she did not understand. "When our God was revealed in the bush, there was no place to run. Where would he run—to the heavens, the sea, or to dry land? What does it say concerning our God? 'Behold, I fill the heavens and the earth . . .' With the snake, which is your god, if a person merely runs two or three steps away he can escape and save himself, and this is why it says 'Moshe ran away from it'!"

A Tyrant Is like a Snake

Rabbi Tzvi Elimelech Hertzberg sees within this conversation a message about leadership. The Roman matron's god was a snake, because that was the type of leadership to which she was accustomed. Her leader was also a "snake." Snakes will strike without cause or benefit, and we still find leaders of this variety today: dictators, who punish their people without cause or personal benefit, but only in order to demonstrate how powerful they are.

Rav Hertzberg also compares those who spread gossip to snakes, because their only "benefit" is malicious—the sense of superiority that they get from putting down others. The dictator and gossip work together: the power of the dictator depends upon the gossip that people tell about one another, even that ministers tell. No one dares make a misstep, and thus the dictator rules from fear.

A Torah Leader

Moshe ran away from "leadership" of this nature. He wanted no part of it, for it runs completely contrary to the kindness and generosity demanded by the Torah. The Torah path toward leadership is built upon humility, mercy, and righteousness, not the methods of a snake. The Torah path is indicated only a few verses later, when God says, "in order that they will believe that the God of their forebears appeared to you, the God of Avraham, the God of Yitzchak, the God of Yaakov" (4:5).

This lesson applies to all of us: When we behave with kindness, consideration, and love for others, we inspire respect for ourselves, for our people, and for our God.

Part 2: Va'era—Exodus 6:2–9:35

God said to Moshe, "Come to Pharaoh and speak to him: 'So says HaShem, God of the Hebrews: Send out My people, that they may serve Me.'" (9:1)

In this reading, we find one of the most famous of Biblical quotations: "Let my people go!" But in actuality, it is one of the most infamous of half-quotes. It is a distortion of the truth—for the message God told Moshe to deliver to Pharaoh was "Let my people go—*that they may serve Me!*"

What Is Freedom?

The modern world's image of freedom is based upon our "inalienable right" to "life, liberty, and the pursuit of happiness"—and especially the latter. People seek as few boundaries upon individual behavior as possible. Or as Madison Avenue presents it, "No Limits."

Most of us realize that "total freedom" is impossible—it leads to anarchy and benefits no one. If we placed no limits on personal behavior, then it would be impossible for us to prevent one person's behavior from interfering with the liberty and pursuit of happiness of others.

So, in fact, limits are necessary. But are they merely a necessary evil, or are they a positive good?

Learning from Our Children

In recent decades, many parents have experimented with child rearing by permitting their kids to "discover their own boundaries"—in other words, by laying down no rules. Contrary to their expectations, the children turned out to be not only less well-behaved, but also less *happy* than their disciplined peers.

While overly harsh rules can hamper a loving relationship, some rules are not merely necessary, but demonstrate parental love and concern for the child's well-being. The happiest children are most likely to be found in families where the guidelines are clear, unmistakable, and fairly applied.

We Know Better . . . or Do We?

But, we say, we are different from children! We are adults, and capable of making our own decisions. We know what is right, and what is wrong.

Do we? Is there anyone who can say that he or she really knows how the world works, and what is good for us? Or is it not clear to us that guidelines would help us as well—if we only knew who we could trust? No person knows everything that the world has to offer—but the Creator of the world certainly does.

As you saw in Chapter 4, the Torah is a guide to life. This is why the Torah calls a person "free" while bound by its multitude of Commandments, decrees, Rabbinic enactments, and ancient customs—because all of these simply help a person to go in the right direction.

So it is not simply "let my people go" but "that they may serve me"—they have no human master, but rather the guidance of a loving father. This, says the Torah, is the greatest freedom of all.

Part 3: Bo—Exodus 10:1–13:16

Moshe and Aaron returned to Paro [Pharaoh], and he said to them, "Go and serve HaShem, your God—who, precisely, will be going?" And Moshe said, "We will be going with our children and our elders, with our sons and our daughters." And [Paro] said to them, "It will surely be that God will be with you, when I send you out along with your children—see that evil is before your faces. It will not be so; let the men go out and serve God, for that is what you request," and he threw them out from Paro's presence. (10:8–11)

The Sifrei Drush commentary notes that Paro agreed to send out the adults, as long as the children remained with him. Paro knew that as long as the children stayed behind the Nation of Israel would not survive. Moshe, of course, knew exactly the same thing, and this is why he insisted that the young people go out along with the elderly.

Why, on the other hand, did Moshe also insist that the *elderly* go along? Here is something that Moshe understood—and Paro did not. Moshe knew that one could not go without the other. Without the elders, who would impart wisdom to the children? Wisdom is acquired with age. "You shall rise in front of an old person, and honor the presence of a Sage, and you shall fear your God—I am HaShem" (Lev. 19:32). In fact, the word for "Sage" in this verse is *Zaken*, which literally means "elderly person." The Medrash says, based upon this verse, that we have the same obligation to stand when an elderly person approaches as in front of a scholar. Regardless of Torah knowledge, a person who has reached the age of seventy represents wisdom acquired with age, and deserves respect and honor.

The knowledge of older people is crucial to Torah. The Nation of Israel was led in the desert by Moshe, Aaron, and the seventy elders—Moshe and Aaron were themselves both over eighty. The Chapters of the Fathers opens with: "Moshe received the Torah on Sinai, and he transmitted it to Yehoshuah, and Yehoshuah to the Elders . . ."

As mentioned earlier, the Torah view is that each preceding generation is closer to Sinai, and even in our day Torah teachers admit that those of earlier generations knew more than they do today. But even without that, the Torah says that any person who has seen seventy years of world history can be a source of wisdom and guidance.

Part 4: Beshalach—Exodus 13:17–17:16

> And it was, that when Paro sent the nation out, that God did not lead them by way of the land of the Philistines, though it was close; for God said, "The people may change their minds when they see war, and return to Egypt." (13:17)

The nascent Jewish nation needed to break away entirely from their lives as slaves in Egypt. They were not ready for war, for confrontation and resistance. There was a spiritual component of this as well, given the Sages' teaching that the greatest war is the one within ourselves, between our Good and Evil Inclinations. The Philistines shared many of the same immoral practices as the Egyptians, and exposure to their society could have been a further negative influence. Instead, God effected a "clean break" from the degraded practices and enslavement of Egypt, taking the Jewish People out into the open desert.

Rabbi M. Miller of Gateshead, in his book *Sabbath Shiurim*, identifies this—the sudden break—as one of two competing models for how one should halt a bad habit or practice. The other, of course, is more gradual—and he finds a source for this in the Torah as well: Moshe says to Paro, "And now, let us go out three days' journey into the desert, and we will sacrifice to HaShem our God" (Exod. 3:18).

Why did Moshe imply that the people would return in three days, when they were never to return? Rabbi Miller says that this was designed to accustom the Jewish Nation to the idea of leaving. They could go out into the desert for a while, but still have the opportunity to return. This provides a paradigm for the idea of a slow, gradual transition.

So which method is best? When a person wants to improve his or her life, is it better to gradually modify previous habits or suddenly leap into a new pattern of behavior?

The answer, Rabbi Miller says, is that we need both. To make a sudden change has obvious risks—if one fails in the attempt, then he or she has accomplished nothing, and may be too bruised to try again. "To undertake more than one is really capable of, and then to regret one's action, is worse than never to have tried at all: the aftermath of failure can become a serious and permanent drawback to moral progress." At the same time, the advantage of sudden change over gradual shifts is that once a person successfully crosses a narrow bridge, he or she can "burn it"—and permanently close out the bad behavior.

What one should do, he says, is follow the model of the Israelites. First, think about making a "small" change—to go out on a three days' journey. Gradually build strength and confidence. Improve gradually. Then, when one is ready, make the leap forward that will firmly establish new practices and do away with the old.

Part 5: Yisro—Exodus 18:1–20:23

> I am HaShem your God, who brought you out of the land of Egypt. (20:2)

The existence of the One God is the first and most fundamental principle of Judaism. Maimonides begins his Halachic Encyclopedia, the Mishneh Torah, with "The foundation of foundations and pillar of all wisdom is to know that there exists a First Being, and He brought into existence all that exists." Maimonides also lists this as the first Positive Commandment in his Sefer HaMitzvos (Book of Commandments). The Sefer HaChinuch says that "the roots of this commandment need no explanation—it is known and revealed to all that this is the foundation of religious belief."

Can Belief in God Be a Commandment?

Countering the position of Maimonides, major commentators and legal works such as Nachmanides, the Ba'al Hilchos Gedolos, and the Kina'as Sofrim commentary all argue that knowing God is *not* a Commandment. The Kina'as Sofrim explains that the concept "was problematic to many writers—how can it be correct to count the belief in the existence of a

Commander among the Commandments? It is impossible to have commandments without first clarifying that a commander exists!" In their eyes, knowledge of God is not a Commandment, but the prerequisite upon which all Commandments depend.

This helps us to better understand why Maimonides calls belief in God's existence the "foundation" of all the Commandments, and not simply the first, greatest, or most important. To have Mitzvos, Commandments, we must have a *Metzaveh*, a Commander. The translation of Mitzvos as "good deeds" is figurative at best. It is true that Mitzvos are good deeds, but only because we know that God is good and His Commandments are good.

Now, I'm Not Aristotle!

Philosophers both ancient and modern have attempted to create systems of morality that depend upon human wisdom to determine what is correct and good, and to do those things. Judaism says "the inclinations of the heart of man are evil from his youth" (Gen. 8:21). We know that external compulsion is not always successful (have you never violated a local ordinance?)—but it is far more powerful than our own devices.

The Commandment to know of God's existence is thus not merely a religious value, but—in the Torah view—a moral obligation, that which compels moral behavior even when it is difficult. "These are the things which Hashem commanded you, that you shall do them . . ." (35:1)—even when it is not easy.

Part 6: Mishpatim—Exodus 21:1–24:18

The word *Mishpatim* means judgments. The Sages divide the Commandments into three categories: those that signify the special relationship between God and the Jewish Nation, those that are not understood by us ("statutes"), and judgments—laws that every nation realizes must exist in order for a group of people to function as a society. This last category includes prohibitions against murder, kidnapping, stealing, and cheating in business, and covers setting up a court system.

Why did God place the Torah portion of Mishpatim, which contains more laws than any other, immediately following the revelation at Sinai?

Answers Rashi: So that people will realize that just as the Ten Commandments were given at Sinai, so were all the others—even those that appear to be typical under a man-made system.

It is traditional in Torah schools for young boys—and has been for centuries—not to start at the beginning. They don't start learning Talmud by studying the first chapter of Brachos, the first tractate (as you learned in Chapter 9), but rather with the second chapter of Bava Metziah, part of the order concerning monetary damages.

That chapter is called *Elu Metzios*—"These found objects are yours, and these must be announced," it says. The Mishnah discusses whether various objects are identifiable enough to require the finder to attempt to return them to their owners.

Some educators came to one of the great Torah Sages of the last century, Rabbi Moshe Feinstein, and asked whether it might be appropriate to break this habit, and instead start with Brachos. After all, that tractate starts with "Reading the Shema," a declaration of faith that every boy in a Jewish school learns to do twice a day—certainly far more often than he finds scattered fruit on the ground.

Rabbi Feinstein replied that they must not change, but must continue to teach Elu Metzios first. A child, he said, must understand that "These found objects are yours, but these you must announce [and return to their owner]" is also Torah. The Torah is not just ritual. Furthermore, it is all-encompassing, requiring a truly rigorous standard of justice and ethics.

ALERT!

God demands a high standard in every area of life. Just consider the contrast between "These found objects are yours, but these you must announce [and return to their owner]" and what most people learn in school: "Finders keepers, losers weepers."

Part 7: Terumah—Exodus 25:1–27:19

The Bais HaLevi, Rabbi Yosef Soloveitchik of Brisk, discusses why this reading follows Parshas Mishpatim in the Torah. Mishpatim describes an abundance of interpersonal laws. Our parsha, Terumah, starts off with the collection of donations for construction of the Holy Tabernacle.

What's the Connection?

The Bais HaLevi explains that these two Torah readings are intimately related. Before you give charity with your money, he says, you must first ensure that you got that money honestly, and not through theft or dubious business practices. If not, the "charity" will be of no benefit, meaning that it will not be considered a Mitzvah at all.

This is a further demonstration of how the interpersonal laws and those between man and God are intertwined. Just as one cannot take a stolen *Lulav* (a palm frond used at Sukkos) and do a Mitzvah, one cannot take stolen money and give it to charity. The principle is the same—you can't do a Mitzvah with stolen goods.

Build the Temple, Honestly

The first Mitzvah in this reading is found in verse eight: "And they will make for me a Temple, and I will dwell among them." Before describing this Commandment, the Sefer HaChinuch, the Book of (Mitzvah) Education, explains the underlying reason for this and for all of God's Commandments: in order that we perfect and prepare ourselves to receive the great good that God wants to give us. We must make a dwelling place upon which the Divine Presence can rest. This principle can be applied within ourselves, within our homes, within our communities (synagogues and places for Torah study), and within all Israel in the building of the Holy Temple.

Whatever the Mitzvah, be it a ritual or matter of personal ethics, this underlying goal of self-improvement should always be present. Taking a Lulav should also make us better people, and remind us to be certain that it and the money used to purchase it were acquired honestly.

Part 8: Tetzaveh—Exodus 28:1–30:10

You shall make sanctified garments for Aaron your brother, for honor and splendor . . . these are the garments that they should make: a breastplate, an Ephod [a type of reversed apron, worn over the robe], a robe . . . (28:2, 4)

The Talmud says, in Tractate Erchin 16a, that the robe was designed to aid repentance for the sin of Lashon Hara, gossip. The robe was designed with gold bells hanging from the bottom hem—and God said, "Let this vocal garment cleanse that [sin] done with the voice." There are also several other "hints" in the design of the robe to aspects of gossip. So a person, knowing these things, would see (and hear) the robe of the High Priest, and would be inspired to no longer misuse his voice to speak badly of others.

The Chofetz Chaim notes, however, that there were not only bells hanging from the hem, there were also woven tassels. These tassels were shaped like pomegranates—round, closed balls. These did not make any noise. There were noisy bells, but there were silent adornments as well.

Psalm 58:2 asks, "Is there silence, when you should be speaking righteousness?" In Tractate Chulin 89a, the Sages explain: "What is the task of a person in this world? To make himself mute. [Knowing this] you might think that this applies to Torah discussion as well, but the Scripture says, 'You should be speaking righteousness.'" There are times when you need to clamp down upon yourself, and not speak—but there are also times when a person must speak. This, says the Chofetz Chaim, is what the robe teaches us with its noisy and silent decorations. And, the Talmud adds, one of the best things a person can do is to speak up when studying or discussing Torah.

Part 9: Ki Sisa—Exodus 30:11–34:35

Each person who passes to be numbered, from age twenty, shall give a half-shekel, from a shekel of the Temple . . . a donation to God. (30:13)

The shekel was a coin with a specific value. The Medrash says that God actually showed the half-shekel coin to Moshe. "Rebbe Meir said that the Holy One, Blessed be He, brought out from beneath his throne of Glory a coin of fire, and showed it to Moshe, and said to him, 'They shall give [a coin] like this.'"

Don't Get Burned . . .

The *Noam Elimelech* explains why God showed Moshe a coin of fire. When handling money, he says, you need to remember that a coin is much like fire. It has good sides, and bad sides. Fire can burn and destroy, but can also warm, cook, and help in other valuable ways; money can do the same. If you direct your money to good purposes, for charity and kindness, then it is very valuable and helpful—but if someone uses money improperly, then the same coin can "burn," and cause serious harm.

Manage Your Resources

Rabbi Moshe Feinstein also comments on this Medrash. He asks the following question: Why did God have to show Moshe a coin at all? Or, in effect, why was it so difficult for Moshe to understand what a half-shekel was? The verse says that a shekel was twenty *geirah*, a known sum, so it should have been easy to determine a half-shekel.

Rabbi Feinstein explains that Moshe could not understand how people living in a materialistic world could involve themselves with spiritual pursuits. God showed him a half-shekel to demonstrate that a person should divide his time: only half of a person's efforts can be devoted to material gain; the spiritual side must be cared for as well. The division also shows a middle ground—a person living in this world also cannot be so overwhelmed with spirituality that he ignores his material needs. It is crucial to find a balance.

Part 10: Vayakhel—Exodus 35:1–38:20

Moshe gathered all the congregation of the children of Israel, and he said to them, "These are the things which HaShem has commanded [us] to do." (35:1–2)

Moshe is about to tell Israel how to build the Mishkan, the Tabernacle. Instead, he takes a sudden detour to talk about Shabbos. Why repeat Sabbath observance before talking about building the Mishkan?

The King's Palace

The Medrash offers a parable: a king decides to build a new palace. He calls in leading architects and contractors to discuss how it should be built, and is involved with every detail.

The queen notices—that is, she notices that the King is so busy that he isn't noticing *her*. She complains to the King that she is being ignored. The King, realizing that she is right, holds a party to honor her, and from then on he is more careful to keep her in mind.

The Sabbath: A Basic Priority

Similarly, God cautioned the children of Israel not to forget the Sabbath, in their excitement over building the Mishkan. Although some might otherwise have "lost themselves" building the Mishkan, perhaps even arguing that building it was more meaningful in terms of their own contact with God, the Torah tells us what we must do—and not do—in the service of God.

In Torah, Shabbos is a "basic priority." It is a sign of the unique relationship between Israel and the Creator. Even the building of an earthly home for the Divine Presence cannot take precedence over the Sabbath.

Idealists versus Fanatics

What is the difference between an idealist and a fanatic? You've probably already heard that "an idealist is someone totally dedicated to ideas with which I agree, while a fanatic is totally dedicated to ideas with which I disagree." Among those who observe Jewish law carefully, there's a twist on that joke: "An idealist is someone who observes Judaism and Jewish law as meticulously as I do, while a fanatic is someone who observes Judaism *more* meticulously than I do."

The Torah gives us a better answer. Both types of people are dedicated to making the world a better place, and both believe that specific objectives must be achieved. But a fanatic loses sight of basic priorities. Without even thinking about it, he or she concludes that "the ends justify the means." The idealist realizes that preserving the forests is a good thing; the fanatic places metal pegs into trees in order to maim loggers.

Dedication to ideals doesn't make a fanatic—losing touch with more basic priorities makes a fanatic. You don't break the Sabbath, even to build a Mishkan!

Part 11: Pikudei—Exodus 38:21-40:38

> In accordance with all that God commanded Moshe, the children of Israel did all the work; and Moshe saw all the labor, and behold, they had done it as God commanded. And Moshe blessed them. (39:42–43)

Building the Mishkan, the Tabernacle, involved extraordinary attention to detail. In the Torah, each activity is described, with precise details of how items in the Tabernacle were built, and exactly where they were placed.

Each person had a precise job to perform. Some were doing this, some that, but each person had to do the job to his or her maximum potential. Every part was crucial—what would a Mishkan be without a Menorah, the candelabra to be lit each day? There were many different things to be done, so completion of this great structure required everyone's dedicated participation. But when everyone worked together, they built a structure of unparalleled holiness. Great things are achieved when everyone does their part and works together toward a common goal.

Chapter 19

Studies in Vayikra, the Book of Leviticus

The Third Book of the Torah was given the Greek title Leviticus, because much of its content concerns the Tabernacle, the Temple, and Priestly Ritual. While you might think that its message is not truly relevant today, when there is no Temple, its many lessons remain applicable to any time and place.

Part 1: Vayikra—Leviticus 1:1–5:26

> Speak to the Children of Israel, and you should say to them, "A person, when he will bring from you an offering to God, from the domesticated animals, from the cattle and the flock you shall bring your offerings." (1:2)

The book begins by detailing the laws of sacrifices. The Hebrew original uses the word *korban*, and Rabbi Samson Raphael Hirsch regrets the absence of a better translation of this term into German—a complaint equally applicable to English. He points out that a korban does not involve giving up something of value as implied by "sacrifice," nor is it a gift as implied by "offering."

The root of the word *korban* is *karov*, a Hebrew word meaning to approach, to come close. "The *MaKriv*" (the person bringing the *korban*), says Rabbi Hirsch, "desires that something of himself should come into closer relationship with God."

ALERT!

Many mistakenly believe that a korban or offering was for expiation of sin. In the Torah itself, however, most korbanos are not associated with transgressions, and the exceptions are mostly inadvertent acts. For the vast majority of deliberate violations, the Torah does not describe any offering to be used as part of an atonement process.

In actuality, there are many different types of offerings, involving every sort of property a person might have—not only animals, but flour, wine, water, and salt were all placed on the altar. One sanctified his or her first fruits, could donate property whether movable or land, and gave money as well. All of this is in addition to the foods destined for the Kohanim (priests), Levi'im, and the poor, and for the needs of the festivals in Jerusalem.

Never in Torah is there any notion of God "eating" a korban. The korbanos are called a *re'ach nikhoach*, which could be translated as "pleasing smell," but *re'ach* can mean a spiritual uplift as well. There is certainly no physical benefit or need fulfilled. The idea of a korban is that it is pleasing to God when we express a desire to make ourselves godly at the expense of our physicality. This can be expressed in our deeds, in our charity, and, yes, in the korbanos.

Part 2: Tzav—Leviticus 6:1–8:36

> A permanent fire shall be kindled upon the altar; it shall never be extinguished. (6:6)

Many commentators draw a connection between the Altar in the Temple, and the altar a person must build within him- or herself. The *Toras Moshe* interprets the verse above along these lines. Within every person, there is a holy spark. "The candle of God is the human soul" (Prov. 20:27). Even if it remains only a small spark, it is never extinguished. All that you need to do, in order to bring the spark to full blaze, is to feed the fire with words of inspiration every day.

If those able to fan the flames make the appropriate efforts, then the sparks that lie within others will come to light as well. Those who encourage and spark the flames of others, concludes the Toras Moshe, can rest assured that the eternal flame will never be extinguished.

Part 3: Shemini—Leviticus 9:1–11:47

This Torah portion begins nearly one year after the Exodus, with the consecration ceremonies for the Altar in the Holy Tabernacle. Aharon blessed the nation, Moshe and Aharon entered the Tent of Meeting, and then the Divine Presence rested on the Tabernacle.

The Death of Aharon's Sons

From the joy of this spiritual high, Aharon's heart descends as he faces a great tragedy: his two sons, Nadav and Avihu, are killed when they offered a "strange fire before God." One possible explanation of their error is found in the next command God gives to Aharon: "Wine or alcoholic beverages you shall not drink, you and your sons, when you come into the Tent of Meeting, and you shall not die, this is an eternal decree for your generations" (10:9). The implication, according to many commentators, is that Nadav and Avihu were drunk.

Nadav and Avihu were judged so harshly, says Rabbi Samson Raphael Hirsch, precisely because they were so close to God. "And Moshe said to Aaron, this is what God said: 'Through those that are close to me I will be sanctified, and so I will be honored before all the nation,' and Aaron was silent" (10:3).

Rabbi Hirsch points out a contrast between the Torah view and modern society. Today people are often willing to overlook the moral lapses of intellectual and political leaders. The Torah teaches that God, on the contrary, expects *more* of those who are closer to him. The Talmud (Yevamos 121b) says: "God is exacting to a hair's breadth with those closest around Him."

A footnote to this story tells us the level of Moshe's humility. Believing that Aaron and his remaining sons behaved improperly with regard to one of the offerings of the day, he criticized them—only to be reminded by Aaron that their behavior was appropriate, since they had buried his sons and their brothers that day. "And it was pleasing in his eyes," says the Torah regarding Moshe. The Talmud (Zevachim 101) comments: "He admitted and was not embarrassed to say, 'I did not hear.'"

Kosher Foods

The Torah goes on to specify Kosher animals, those that a person observing the Torah is permitted to eat. The Kosher members of the animal kingdom are:

- Land animals with a cloven hoof that chew their cud
- Fish that have both fins and scales
- All birds not specified in Leviticus 11:13–19
- Four varieties of grasshoppers or locusts

Several general observations may be made about the Kosher versus non-Kosher species. For example, with the exception of the grasshoppers and locusts, only vertebrate animals are Kosher. Carnivorous animals are not Kosher, and neither are predatory birds. As a general rule, any animal that would strike you as hostile or disgusting probably isn't Kosher.

FACT

The Torah uses the terms pure and impure to divide between what we call the Kosher and non-Kosher animals. By bringing God's Word into such a mundane behavior as eating, the Kosher consumer elevates purely physical sustenance to the level of a spiritual act.

Part 4: Tazria—Leviticus 12:1–13:59

The spiritual blemish called *Tzara'as*, which could afflict a person's body, clothing, or house, is a major topic of discussion in this reading. The cause of Tzara'as, says the Medrash, was the sin of gossiping about others. Because the individual secretly tried to make others look bad, his or her own blemish is displayed in public.

ALERT!

Some translations use the word "leprosy" to define Tzara'as, because both involve the skin of the victim turning white. However, leprosy does not affect clothing or houses, nor would a person whose entire body was afflicted with it be declared "clean"—as is true in the case of Tzara'as. And, of course, one would consult a doctor, not a priest, with a disease.

Tzara'as was an entirely spiritual ailment—just like gossip itself, which causes intangible rather than physical harm. The spiritual nature of gossip is actually what makes it such a great transgression, worthy of a special and unique punishment. Communication is the real-world expression of the intellect that God gave to humanity. So the person who gossips takes this, the most spiritual element of his or her physical existence, and uses it for evil, causing harm beyond what mere sticks and stones could ever do. Tzara'as no longer exists, the Sages say, because only a person on a very high spiritual level would be "blemished" so profoundly by the sin of gossip.

Part 5: Metzorah—Leviticus 14:1–15:33

A person who contracts Tzara'as is called a *Metzorah*, and this Torah portion is a logical continuation of the discussion of contracting Tzara'as found in the previous one. Indeed, these two portions are usually read together during non–leap years on the Jewish calendar.

The Purification Process

The reading begins with a discussion of the purification process that the Metzorah must undergo after the blemish or blemishes disappear. He or she must bring "two living pure birds, cedar wood, scarlet wool, and hyssop" (Lev. 14:3). One of the birds becomes an offering; the other is set free.

Rabbi Hirsch explains that the cedar and hyssop represent the highest and lowest forms of plant life. The wool, colored with a scarlet dye extracted from worms, represents the highest and lowest forms of animals. These things, taken together, remind the Metzorah that a person's mission is to master his or her animalistic nature, rather than succumbing to base materialism.

This is just the beginning of a seven-day period of purification, at the beginning and end of which the Metzorah shaves off *all* hair visible on his or her body. On the eighth, the Metzorah returns with a new offering, which is different for the wealthy and the poor. In all of these actions, the Metzorah engages in self-negation where previously his or her ego was paramount. Then, at the conclusion of this process, the individual is finally considered ready to return to normal life.

A Blemished House

The laws dealing with blemishes on a house are detailed next, and here we find the Torah demonstrating kindness even in the middle of punishment. The house becomes impure not when the blemish appears, but only once the priest examines it, determines that it is Tzara'as, and pronounces the house impure. Until the priest has *proclaimed* the house impure, it isn't. So when the priest is summoned to examine the house, the first thing that he does is order that the house be cleared out—in order that all the property found inside the house not become impure at the same time.

Part 6: Acharei Mos—Leviticus 16:1–18:30

> God spoke to Moshe following the death of two sons of Aaron, when they came close before God, and died. And God said to Moshe, "speak to Aaron your brother, that he not come to the Sanctuary whenever he wishes . . ." (16:1–2)

The death of Aharon's sons, Nadav and Avihu, is described several chapters earlier, in Lev. 10:2. This being the case, why does the Torah preface God's new instruction to Aaron by mentioning the death of his sons?

Rabbi Shlomo Yitzchaki (Rashi) quotes the Talmudic Rabbi Elazar ben Azariah, who explains that the Torah is explaining the warning given to Aaron, and in so doing is making it much more clear and meaningful. Rabbi Elazar demonstrates by offering a parable of two doctors coming to make a house call on a sick patient.

The first doctor comes in, examines the patient and his symptoms, and says, "Don't eat cold foods or sleep on a damp bed." The second doctor comes in, and says, "Don't eat cold foods or sleep on a damp bed, in order to avoid dying just like Mr. Smith."

Obviously, the latter doctor is providing a much stronger warning to his patient, telling him how important it is that he take care of himself. Without it, the patient might not realize the severity of the issue. So, similarly, the Torah warns Aaron about entering the Sanctuary "following the death of two sons of Aaron."

One of the lessons of this reading is that "those who ignore history are doomed to repeat it." Only if we look at errors made previously, and realize the severity of the consequences, can we avoid making the same mistakes. Otherwise, the value of the advice is all too easily lost.

The Torah is a guide to life and living. Its instructions are designed to help us live and grow, and its stories deliver lessons for all generations. When a Jewish community follows its dictates, that community survives and passes the Jewish spark on to the next generation. The Torah itself tells us later in the reading that it gives life: "And you shall guard My decrees and judgements, that a person shall do them and *live* in them, I am God" (18:5).

Part 7: Kedoshim—Leviticus 19:1–20:27

> You shall be holy, for I am holy, HaShem your God . . . You shall sanctify yourselves, and you shall be holy, for I am HaShem your God. (19:2, 20:7)

Immediately after telling us to "be holy," the Torah instructs the reader to fear his or her parents, guard the Sabbath, avoid idolatry, and more. The implied lesson is then made explicit: "Sanctify yourselves, and you shall be holy." Holiness doesn't happen by accident. You *make* it happen through study and action.

Holiness isn't easy, either. Moral behavior requires restraint when a person wants to fulfill his or her desires. Some would prefer to avoid the necessary study and effort—and some will even attempt to convince you that trying is a waste of time.

First, they trot out examples of supposedly moral individuals who, despite their studies, engaged in immoral behavior. Then, extrapolating wildly, they tell you that this proves that the attempt at self-improvement is of no benefit.

Imagine if top athletes never practiced their sport. It's obvious that before long, they would fade from the scene, replaced by those with less innate talent who were willing to work. Does this mean that anyone who plays basketball on a regular basis will become a Michael Jordan? Of course not. But it would be ridiculous to conclude that it is all a matter of natural ability, and practice causes no improvement. Not every physicist becomes Albert Einstein, and not every pre-med student becomes a capable surgeon, but only after years of study and practice is it even possible.

So if a scholar of the moral harms of gossip should ever stumble in this area, it's silly to conclude that this scholar is just as likely to gossip as anyone else—or, more to the point, as likely to gossip as he would be if he *didn't* try to improve. To say that is to imagine that moral behavior is somehow different and distinct from every other area of life.

The Torah tells us otherwise. It is no different: We must study and practice in order to grow. "Sanctify yourselves, and you shall be holy!"

Part 8: Emor—Leviticus 21:1–24:23

> They shall be holy before their Lord, and they shall not desecrate the name of their Lord, for the sacrifices of God, the bread of their Lord do they bring, and they shall be holy. (21:6)

Given only a shallow understanding of the laws of Kohanim, the priests, we might consider them a higher class, "creatures of privilege." When the Jewish Nation had its Land and its Temple, all gave the Kohanim a portion of their crops. Even the children of Levi, who were also given special portions, gave the Kohanim part of what *they* received. Only Kohanim could enter many parts of the Temple, only they could offer sacrifices, and only they could aspire to the position of High Priest.

Penalties of the Priesthood

A closer examination reveals a far more complex distinction than simple privilege. The Kohanim received their designated presents, but they did *not* receive a portion of land. Perhaps they were assured that they would have a basic income, but the opportunity to amass individual wealth was greatly reduced. They were prohibited from numerous actions permitted to others. To be a Kohen is not simply to enjoy privileges the rest of us do not.

The verse describes the holiness of the Kohanim as not simply a fact, but a command: "they shall be holy," similar to "you shall be holy" found in the previous reading of Kedoshim. Rashi takes note of the difference—"they" rather than "you" shall be holy, as if there were a commandment upon others to *make* them holy. And yes, he says, there is indeed such a command. "They shall be holy—by force, the *Bais Din* [Jewish court] shall make them holy."

ALERT!

The limitations placed upon Kohanim cast into doubt the idea that they themselves could have authored some portion of the Torah, as modern critics say. Kohanim face restrictions limiting whom they may marry and preventing them from performing funeral services and burial rites, which apply even to this day.

The Grass Is Always Greener . . .

We may look at other people and feel jealousy. We wonder why this person was born wealthy, that one with a brilliant mind, that one with great beauty. Others may also look at the Torah and wonder why one group is different from another, such as men and women, or Kohanim and plain old Israelites.

The restrictions upon the Kohanim teach a valuable lesson. The Torah doesn't tell you to seek fame, power, or privilege. The Torah says that you were placed on earth to grow, become Godly, and to perform those Commandments that apply to you.

So it's counterproductive to wonder why God couldn't have made you something other than the person you are. God determined that what will help one person to grow could be harmful to another. And when you do what you're supposed to do, that's what determines who is considered truly worthy: "An ill-begotten scholar is preferable to an ignoramus priest." It is not how we were born that makes us great—it is how we die.

Part 9: Behar—Leviticus 25:1–26:2

Six years shall you sow your field, and six years shall you prune your vineyards, and gather its produce. But in the seventh year, it will be a Holy Sabbath, a Sabbath to God; you shall not sow your field, and you will not prune your vineyards. (25:3–4)

The commentary of the *Kli Yakar* teaches a powerful lesson from this verse. A person could think that the land is his and he can do as he wishes with it. If he is intelligent and uses good strategic planning, then his fields will flourish—and he will deserve credit in accordance with his intelligence and expertise.

With the Commandment of *Shmittah*, the Sabbath of the land in the seventh year, God delivers the message that the land is His, and all success is His. "Six years shall you sow your field"—the Kli Yakar says that this is a guarantee. You can plant your field for six years, and it will not become weak. You don't need to employ the standard strategy—at least, before fertilizers—of planting the field for two years and then letting it rest in the third.

Not only this, but your field will flourish precisely at the point where it should be *weakest*. "And if you will say, 'What will we eat in the seventh year, when we will not sow nor will we gather our grain?' I have commanded my Blessing to you in the sixth year, and you will produce grain for three years" (25:20–21).

So if the field is at its *best* after six years of constant use, it doesn't help the field to rest in the seventh. Shmittah is not for the good of the land, but for the farmer—to realize that he doesn't really have control, and in the end it is not his own efforts that bring success.

Part 10: Bechukosai—Leviticus 26:3–27:34

> If you will follow My statutes and observe My laws and you will do them; then I have given your rains in their time and the land will give its produce, and the tree of the field will give its fruit. (26:3–4)

Rashi asks: If the Torah says, "Observe My laws," then what does it mean when it also says "Follow My statutes"? And he answers: "That you will toil in Torah."

The two portions of *Behar* and *Bechukosai* are often read together. One possible connection is that in the last portion, the Torah tells a person not to invest too much effort in material success—that God is the one who provides, even when a person abandons his farm for a year. Where, then, should you invest your efforts? "Toil in Torah," and "the land will give its produce"—do what you're supposed to do, and God will help with the rest.

Most of this reading, however, is not so optimistic. The *Tochachah*, the Rebuke, is a lengthy description of the terrible punishments awaiting the nation if they do not follow the Torah. It is customary for the reader to hurry through this reading in a lowered voice, as if to indicate a desire never to see this portion actualized.

Unfortunately, of course, the tragedies of the Tochachah are very much a part of Jewish history today. Yet the Torah also promises that "for all that, even when they are in the lands of their enemies, I will not despise or reject them . . . and I will remember for them the Covenant with their ancestors" (26:44–45).

The Kedushas Levi asks why the Covenant made with the early ancestors is so important. He answers that, as you read earlier, the Jews in Egypt were in a very lowly spiritual state. This is what King David said in Psalm 74:2: "Remember Your congregation, which You acquired at the beginning, You redeemed the tribe of Your inheritance." God already demonstrated that He would still redeem the Jewish Nation even in a bad state—there is no permanent rejection.

Chapter 20

Studies in Bamidbar, the Book of Numbers

The fourth book, *Bamidbar*, tells the story of the Jewish People "in the desert"—from shortly after Sinai to the last months preceding their entrance into the Land of Israel. While the English name "Numbers" alludes to the two times the Israelites conduct a census during this period, this is but one minor part of the story.

Part 1: Bamidbar—Numbers 1:1–4:20

> Take the sum of all the congregation of the Children of Israel, by their families . . . (1:2)

Moshe conducts a census of all males over the age of twenty, and registers them according to their paternal ancestry. He also arranges and counts the Kohanim and the Levites.

Why does God command a count at this point in the Torah? Rabbi Samson Raphael Hirsch comments that a count done in the wilderness serves no political or economic purpose. It was an exclusively religious function, and had religious meaning not just for God, but for Israel as well.

Rabbi Hirsch explains as follows. The Book of Vayikra, Leviticus, discusses the many obligations that the Nation of Israel had to the Mishkan, the Tabernacle. It also describes the sacrifices that each individual can offer, as a voluntary commitment. In other words, it talks about national obligations, but when it comes to individuals, it speaks primarily about voluntary donations.

Upon reading that, you could imagine that the nation could do what it needed to do without you and your unique contribution. You can sit on the sideline. From the discussions in Vayikra, the reader does not see that every individual is important on his or her own.

The census contradicts this mistaken impression. Every person counts. You are unique, different from every other, with a unique function and unique contribution to make. Although this count included only the Israelite soldiers, males over age twenty, they served as public representatives for the larger nation. The count itself indicated how each individual was part of a family unit, part of a larger tribe, and a crucial building block in the larger whole. This count sends a message for all generations: Every person has something to contribute.

Part 2: Naso—Numbers 4:21–7:89

This portion begins with a conclusion—finishing the process of counting the Levites, and assigning them different areas of responsibility when it came time for the Israelites to decamp and move on. Then, however, it goes on to discuss a series of interesting and challenging topics for those wanting to understand the Torah, each of which involves a bit of insight.

The Sotah

A Sotah is a woman suspected of adultery. Her husband warned her previously that he was worried about her contact with a particular man, and that she should not seclude herself with him. She then did so anyway—and many a jealous husband would already assume the worst.

The Sotah procedure was not a way of punishing an unfaithful wife—any woman could admit guilt and accept a divorce, avoiding the Sotah water and its potential consequences. On the contrary, this process was a method of complete exoneration for the innocent, and the Torah blesses them.

God provides a method of saving that marriage before the husband lost his head, which only worked in the Holy Temple (or the Tabernacle in the desert). The Holy Name of God is written on a parchment, and is then erased in a drink of water. In Jewish tradition, erasure of the Name of God is strictly avoided—but the Talmud teaches that God considered it better to erase His Name than to break up a marriage. If she is guilty, however, she should confess and accept a divorce—for this otherwise harmless vessel of water will prove deadly to a guilty party.

Some people have the misconception that there were other, toxic ingredients in the Sotah water. All sources in Torah and Talmud make clear, however, that this was simply water with a bit of harmless ink.

The Nazir

In Chapter 6, the Torah discusses a Nazir, a person making a special vow. The Nazir withdrew from drinking wine, eating meat, or cutting his or her hair, until the end of their vow.

The Talmud asks, Why does this portion follow that of the Sotah? The answer is that if one sees a woman accused of adultery, and realizes that things such as intoxication can lead a person to such debased behavior, then he or she should be inspired to make special efforts to avoid problems—and this means avoiding wine!

The Priestly Blessings

This Torah portion also includes the Priestly Blessings, which are a regular part of the morning service in synagogues. You may recognize them from a song or reading:

May the Lord bless you and guard you,
May the Lord cause his countenance to shine upon you,
May the Lord lift his countenance toward you, and give you peace.
(6:24–26)

The Princes' Offerings

Finally, this Torah portion describes the offerings brought by the princes of each tribe at the inauguration of the Altar. Each offering is described in detail, which is perplexing for one simple reason: they were all precisely the same. Since every tribal prince offered exactly the same gifts as every other, one should wonder why the Torah found it necessary to be repetitive.

Many commentators resolve this puzzle. One particularly beautiful answer is that from their example, you can learn about true unity and mutual respect. The later princes saw what the earlier ones brought, and could have chosen to engage in spiritual one-upmanship. They could each have tried to outdo the previous gifts with their own. Instead, they chose the sincerest form of flattery—imitation. They each endorsed and shared in what the others had done, rather than seeking greater glory for themselves.

Wouldn't the world be a better place if everyone tried to live that way?

Part 3: Behaaloscha—Numbers 8:1–12:16

> And the man Moshe was extremely humble, more than any person on the face of the earth. (12:3)

Rabbi Yisrael Meyer Kagan asks a straightforward question. How could the person who led the Jewish people out of Egypt, who split the sea for them, and who received the Torah from God Himself—how could he possibly be so humble?

True Greatness

The answer is: True greatness is measured not in the eyes of other people, but in the eyes of God. We cannot judge people by absolute standards of measure. Precisely because Moshe had ascended to Heaven, he believed that he had not fulfilled what he, having witnessed what he saw, should accomplish. He could not judge himself against the people "on the face of the earth," for he alone had spoken with angels.

The Torah doesn't judge everyone by the same standard. Everything depends upon what you accomplish with the tools you were given. Moshe had such lofty experiences that, in his eyes, he failed to accomplish what was expected of him. He made no such judgment of others—and thus was truly the most humble person on earth.

FACT

Two verses in this Torah reading (10:35–36) describe what Moshe would say when the Ark was lifted or placed back down. These verses are surrounded on both sides by a single letter, Nun, written facing backward. According to one Talmudic opinion, these Nuns are intended to designate these two verses as a "book" of the Torah unto themselves—meaning that the Book of Numbers is actually three separate books, and there are *seven* books in the Torah!

Part 4: Shlach—Numbers 13:1–15:41

This Torah reading relates the tragic story of the Spies, sent to travel through the Land of Canaan in advance of its conquest by the People of Israel. Although God promised the Israelites that they would be able to enter and dominate the land, the Spies came back with a report that the inhabitants were giants, whom they could never defeat by natural means. The people thought that due to their sins, God would not work miracles for them—and they were doomed.

Who Were the Spies?

The Torah tells us that Moshe himself appointed the men who would tour secretly through the Land of Canaan, so that the Israelites would know what lay ahead as they entered. God told Moshe, "Send men for yourself"— you, Moshe, should personally select the Spies. And he did, choosing people of exceptional quality, "leaders among the Children of Israel." Even in the company of the Holy Generation that stood at Mount Sinai, these twelve were exceptional.

This makes their failure all the more bizarre. They stood before Moshe, handpicked representatives of the Jewish People to go scout out their new homeland. Forty days later, only two returned to discuss how wonderful this land was and would be. The other ten Spies told the nation that the residents were unconquerable giants—and besides, the land was killing its inhabitants.

A Bad Report from an "Evil Congregation"

The nation believed this evil report, and sat down to mourn its fate. As a result, God decreed that this generation, which mourned unnecessarily, would not be privileged to enter the land. They would, instead, die in the desert.

These ten great men were recorded in the Torah not for their good deeds, but for becoming an "evil congregation" and inflicting forty years of desert wanderings upon the entire nation. Obviously they fell before a destructive force of massive potential, yet one so devious in its influence that they failed to see it.

Evil Eye and Evil Tongue

In reality, what struck them down was a toxic mixture of an evil eye and an evil tongue. One looks out for the bad side of every story, and the other carries that tale to others.

The Spies entered Canaan, a wonderfully fertile land. A cluster of grapes was so large that two of them had to carry it hanging from a pole. As they toured the country, God arranged another miracle on their behalf, timing deaths in various communities to coincide with the Spies' arrival. The populace was so distracted by funerals that they did not confront their visitors.

FACT

The logo of the Israeli Tourism Ministry is a stylized image of two people carrying a huge cluster of grapes on a pole. This recalls the material blessings of the Land of Canaan . . . but it also recalls a sorry episode in Jewish history.

How did the Spies respond? They found the worst possible interpretation of events. With fruits so large, the people were large as well—and the Spies discussed this as if God expected the nation to go in and conquer it on their own, without His help. They confidently proclaimed that such conquest was impossible. And furthermore, they viewed the funerals not as a sign of Heavenly protection, but as an indication that the land was turning upon those who lived on it, telling the nation that if they moved in, they would be its next victims.

A Learning Opportunity

The Torah wants you to see the devastating power of evil, and learn to pursue good. Who can claim never to behave like the Spies? Who among us looks only for the good in other people, refrains from repeating the latest gossip, and attempts to change the subject when gossip comes their way?

Everyone knows how destructive gossip is. If you commit yourself to judging others more favorably, and to refrain from spreading every harsh rumor, you can hardly imagine the amount of good that you can accomplish.

Part 5: Korach—Numbers 16:1–18:32

> And Korach the son of Yitzhar . . . and Dasan and Aviram the
> sons of Eliav, and Ohn the son of Peles, the sons of Reuven, took
> [themselves to the side]; and they rose up against Moshe. (16:1–2)

The Mishnah in the Chapters of the Fathers (5:17) reads, "Which is an argument for the sake of Heaven? This is the argument of Hillel and Shammai. And not for the sake of Heaven? This is the argument of Korach and his entire congregation."

The language of this Mishnah clashes with our expectations. We expect an analogy—Hillel versus Shammai, Korach versus Moshe. Instead, the Mishnah reads "Korach and his entire congregation," and never mentions Moshe at all.

The Medrash Shmuel commentary explains that this actually makes perfect sense. "Which is an argument for the sake of Heaven? This is the argument of Hillel and Shammai," both of whom were motivated entirely for the sake of Heaven. So a comparison between the two is correct and appropriate.

The argument between Korach and Moshe, however, offers no analogy to Hillel and Shammai. The motivations of the two parties were not at all the same—Korach acted "not for the sake of Heaven," but Moshe had pure motivations. So the Mishnah couldn't say that "the argument of Korach and Moshe" was "not for the sake of Heaven," because that would wrongly put Moshe in the same basket with Korach.

There is a simple, yet crucial lesson in this Mishnah: one cannot, upon seeing an argument, assume that both sides are equally wrong. It does not "take two to tango." It takes one person doing the right thing, and another person stirring up trouble, to create an argument. A person can be attacked for doing the right thing, and that doesn't make him or her wrong.

Part 6: Chukas—Numbers 19:1–22:1

> This is the Torah: when a man dies in a tent, all who come into
> the tent and everything in the tent shall be impure for seven days.
> (19:14)

The word *Torah* means "instruction," so it isn't strange that one area of law should be called "the" Torah. It is quite unusual nonetheless, and here the Talmudic Sage Rabbi Shimon ben Lakish finds a *remez*, a "hint," to the nature of Torah study. He says (Talmud Brachos 63b): "How do we know that words of Torah are only well-established within one who kills himself over them? Because it says, 'This is the Torah: a man who dies in a tent . . .'"

The Busy Businessman

Rabbi Yisrael Meyer Kagan explains what this means, using a parable: There was once a great merchant whose business kept him occupied day and night and who rarely found time for himself. But as he grew older, as gray became his predominant hair color and his heart started to bother him, he began to think about the end of his life, and decided to prepare to enter the World to Come.

So one day, he sat down to learn for a few hours before going to work. When he showed up to work three hours late, his wife questioned his delay—the store was besieged by customers, who were quickly disappearing because he wasn't there. But he answered that he had been busy, and was thus unavoidably delayed.

The next day, when he again failed to appear, his wife went herself to see what he was doing. Finding him with an open book, she began to shout at him. "Have you lost your mind? Your store is filled with customers, and I can't handle it alone!"

Dead for an Hour

Her husband replied, "My dear wife: if the Angel of Death were to show up now and tell me it was time to go, would you explain that I didn't have free time just yet, and a store full of customers, and could he please come back tomorrow? Of course not! So you can imagine that during these hours it is as if I am 'dead,' and unavailable—will you mind if I am two hours late?"

This, the Chofetz Chaim explains, is the meaning of this teaching from Rabbi Shimon ben Lakish. A person who truly wishes to learn and grow must dedicate a certain amount of time for learning, "off-limits" to regular distractions—when one is able to concentrate.

Part 7: Balak—Numbers 22:2–25:9

Bilaam was a man obsessed. And since Balak was as well, they made a great combination—and probably the best comedy act found in the Torah.

Balak Asks Bilaam to Curse the Blessed

King Balak sent a delegation, asking Bilaam the Prophet to come curse the Jews. Since Bilaam was truly a Prophet of God, he asked that very night if he could go, and God said no. "You shall not curse the nation, for they are blessed" (22:12).

Now, were Balak and Bilaam rational human beings, that would have been the end of it. We asked, God said no, so sorry, it's over.

King Balak, though, surmised that it was just a matter of politics—Bilaam wouldn't go with a collection of undersecretaries, so Balak had to send princes to ask him to come. And of course, Balak was right. Bilaam was very happy to have these higher officers come to visit, because he truly wanted to go and curse the Jewish People.

So, with a new delegation awaiting his word, he asked God again. God permitted Bilaam to go since he insisted—but not to curse the Jews! "Only the word which I shall speak to you, that shall you do" (22:20).

Bilaam's Donkey

What did Bilaam do? He leaped out of bed in the morning, and ran to saddle his donkey . . . even though he had been told that he could not curse the Jews once he arrived.

Once the journey was underway, God sent an angel to stand in the way, to warn him. Three times Bilaam's donkey, who always obeyed his every instruction, turned aside: It turned away from the path, then it scraped against the wall, and finally it lay down. And then, it started talking! As Rabbi Hirsch points out, if Bilaam were not so totally obsessed, he would certainly have paid attention to these obvious signs. He lived his entire life following signs and omens, and now he ignored them at their most obvious.

Even when his donkey started talking, what did Bilaam do? Did he fall off the donkey? No! He threatened it instead: "I wish I had a sword in my hand, because I would have killed you by now" (22:29). He needed to see the angel himself—and even then, Bilaam didn't get the message.

Curses Turned to Blessings

Once he arrived, the story continued in the same vein. Three times Bilaam attempted to curse the Jews, and three times God made him bless them. And every time, Bilaam and Balak avoided the obvious and logical conclusion.

Balak took Bilaam to a place where he could see the Jewish camp, and Bilaam told Balak to build an altar and offer sacrifices. Balak did so, Bilaam wound up and . . . showered blessings on the Jews. They went to another place (23:13) and did the whole show again. Balak built seven more altars, offered an ox and a ram on each, Bilaam wound up and . . . blessed the Jews once again. If we didn't know this was the Torah, we would suspect that Abbott and Costello had a hand in the plot line.

God was not going to change His mind. Bilaam and Balak were not going to get their wish. He placed His words directly into Bilaam's mouth: "God is not a man that he should twist [his words], or the son of man that he should regret" (23:19).

So, what do this great king and great prophet do next? "Come, please, and I'll take you to another place . . ." (23:27).

The Price of Obsession

It seems ridiculous, but this is what an obsession can do to a person. It doesn't matter how many facts stand up in the way, facts that tell any rational person that the idea is wrong—because an obsessed individual is not being rational. He has made an idol from his ideology, and shall cling to his worship until the end.

Part 8: Pinchas—Numbers 25:10–30:1

Pinchas, the son of Elazar, the son of Aharon the Priest, has turned away My anger from the children of Israel, by being zealous for My vengeance amongst them; and [thus] I did not destroy the children of Israel in My vengeance. Therefore, I say, behold I give to him My Covenant of Peace. (25:11–12)

This is an incredible statement. When God says that Pinchas was "jealous for HaShem," that makes sense. But God also gives Pinchas the "Covenant of Peace"—Pinchas killed someone, yet the Torah calls him a peacemaker.

Pinchas killed Zimri, leader of the tribe of Yaakov's son Shimon (Simeon), and the Midianite princess Kosbi bas Tzur, because the two of them were engaging in (and thus encouraging) immorality.

Rabbi Samson Raphael Hirsch says that a Bris, a covenant, represents an absolute promise from God. God promised that the world will eventually see complete peace and harmony—and with this covenant, affirmed that the actions of Pinchas were a step in the right direction. Rabbi Hirsch notes that the behavior of Pinchas is exactly that which the world likes to condemn as "disturbing the peace"—but this, he explains, is not the failure of Pinchas. The problem lies with a world that fails to respond to evil, and inappropriately labels inactivity and the appeasement of evil as "love of peace."

The Medrash says in the name of Rabbi Simon that when God wanted to create man, the attending angels divided into groups to argue the matter. "Kindness and truth encountered each other; righteousness and peace kissed each other" (Ps. 85:11). Kindness said "Create him, for he will perform acts of kindness." Truth said "Do not create him, for he is full of lies." Righteousness said "Create him, for he will do righteous acts." And Peace said "Do not create him, for he is full of argument." What did God do? He took Truth and threw it on the ground!

The Kotzker Rebbe, famed for his sharp comments, asks the question: What about Peace? Fine, the majority was now in favor, but nonetheless is there not a lack of Peace? He answered that there's no problem; without Truth, Peace is easy to achieve! Sometimes it's impossible to make peace when you care about the truth—the Torah says this isn't always a bad thing.

Part 9: Matos—Numbers 30:2–32:42

> Build for yourselves cities for your small children, and enclosures for your flocks, and that which comes from your mouths, you shall do. (32:24)

The tribes of Reuven and Gad asked to settle on the east of the Jordan River, because they had large flocks. Moshe questioned them, asking if they intended to leave the other tribes to worry about God's Commandment to take over the Land of Israel. The tribes responded that they would merely "build enclosures for our possessions here, and cities for our small children" (32:16), but would lead the way, not returning home until the other tribes received their inheritance. Moshe responded that if they did so, then they would be "clean of sin before God and Israel, and will inherit that land as their inheritance before God" (32:22).

Given that Moshe told them to do as they had promised, their response is surprising. "And the Children of Gad and the Children of Reuven spoke to Moshe, saying, 'Your servants will do as our master commanded'" (32:25). Were they going to do what Moshe commanded, or simply what they themselves pledged to do in the first place?

The *Ksav Sofer* commentary, quoting from the Medrash, finds a very important distinction. The two tribes said "We will build flock-enclosures for our possessions here, and cities for our small children." Moshe, however, reversed the order: "Build for yourselves cities for your small children, and enclosures for your flocks." The tribes of Gad and Reuven worried first about their possessions, and then about their little children; Moshe said to them, "Do not make the trivial central." Put first things first—build cities for your children, and *then* protect your flocks.

The Ksav Sofer warns that when a person is chasing after money, this can cause him to renege on his or her commitments. Only if the tribes of Reuven and Gad could reverse the order, and put their families first, could they be trusted. This is why Moshe concluded, "And that which comes from your mouths, you shall do." If you take care of your families before your flocks, *then* you can be trusted to meet your commitment to the nation as well.

Part 10: Masei—Numbers 33:1-36:13

> Command the Children of Israel, and they shall give the Levites cities from their inherited holdings, cities to dwell in . . . And from the cities that you shall give to the Levites, six Cities of Refuge that you will give for the killer to flee there . . . (35:2, 6)

God commands the nation to set aside Cities of Refuge, three on each side of the Jordan River. These cities were used by those guilty of manslaughter—negligent (but not deliberate) killing. An alleged murderer would be taken from the city and judged, and returned only if the killing was unintentional.

A truly accidental killing was not punished—a person was liable only if he or she might have taken appropriate precautions and avoided the accident. Deliberate murder, on the other hand, could result in a death penalty. The killer was exiled to a City of Refuge only when negligence caused the death.

Placement of the Cities

Putting three cities on each side of the Jordan wasn't, perhaps, "fair": Most people lived in the Land of Canaan on the western side of the Jordan. So why have an equal number of cities on each side?

Abbaye, one of the scholars of the Talmud, provides a very simple answer: There were more cities where there were more murderers. Those areas with more cities also had more people who needed to make use of them, resulting in six cities of roughly the same size.

How Murder Affects Society

There is something wrong with that answer, though. If the cities were only for those guilty of manslaughter, *not* those who deliberately murdered, then why should the number of murderers make a difference? Everyone knows that a city with a high murder rate is likely to have the same in the future. But negligence is another story.

Perhaps the message of this lesson from the Talmud is that negligence isn't so different, after all. In places where there were more murderers, there was less concern for life—and this was something that affected even those who would never contemplate deliberate homicide. Those who were exiled were hardly murderers—they had made a mistake. But this very lack of caution and concern for human life also enabled the lowest members of society to contemplate murder.

An Obvious Lesson

In the world today, street criminals and corporate executives both engage in thievery. The Torah is telling us that this tempts everyone to "borrow" that which is not theirs, because others are doing it. When people witness thousands of murders on television, violence seems less repugnant. People are creatures of their environment. In that kind of world, you need to surround yourself with influences that promote love, life, and holiness.

Chapter 21

Studies in Devarim, the Book of Deuteronomy

The fifth and final book of the Torah features Moshe's retelling of the Israelites' forty-year sojourn in the Sinai desert. Its title is *Devarim*, words, because the first verse begins "These are the words that Moshe spoke"—and indeed, Moshe's words fill the book. The Latin title, Deuteronomy, alludes to the fact that much of the book is Moshe's repetition of earlier history and lessons—in Hebrew as well, the book is called Mishnah Torah, repetition (or relearning) of Torah.

Moshe encourages the people and tries to set them on the right course for the future; in some ways, this could be called the first Mussar lecture. God then dictated Moshe's teachings back to him, to write into the Torah.

Part 1: Devarim—Deuteronomy 1:1–3:22

These are the words that Moshe spoke to the entire nation of Israel . . . (1:1)

The *Sifsei Chachamim* commentary points out that this sentence is constructed in an unusual way—the Torah repeatedly introduces a new topic with something like "Moshe spoke to the entire Nation, saying . . ." Why does the Torah use a less direct reference here, to "the words which Moshe spoke"? Furthermore, Moshe goes on to list various locations where the nation sinned against God, without an explanation of what happened in each place. Why does he not give further detail?

An Implied Rebuke Shows Respect

Rashi explains that the Torah is avoiding direct language *because* Moshe is telling the people where they sinned, and in so doing delivering an implied rebuke. Out of concern for Israel's honor and dignity, the Torah merely hints to the various sins, rather than listing all of the sins themselves.

Rabbi Chaim Shmuelevitz, Dean of the Mirrer Yeshiva in the mid-twentieth century, explains in his *Sichos Mussar* that the Torah teaches us how important it is to honor every person, and care for the dignity of others.

Avoiding Embarrassment

This is not only true concerning an entire congregation of holy people, but even with truly wicked individuals. The Medrash says that Bilaam's donkey died immediately after rebuking his master (as found in the Torah reading called "Balak," in the Book of Numbers). Rashi explains that had the donkey lived, people would have pointed to it and said, "There's the animal which chastised Bilaam!" God was concerned about Bilaam's honor, and thus killed the donkey.

Who is God looking out for? Bilaam! A man who distinguished himself as an evildoer, who attempted to use his God-given spiritual talents to curse the nation that God had blessed. Furthermore, it would have honored God's Name if the donkey were permitted to wander free, with people pointing to it and saying, "This is the animal that God allowed to speak!" Avoiding embarrassment to the wicked Bilaam was more important to God than honoring His Name.

FACT

This Torah portion is always read preceding the Ninth of Av, the fast day commemorating the destruction of the Temples in Jerusalem. The Talmud teaches that the chain of events leading to the Second Temple's fall began with the public humiliation of one individual at a party!

If God passed up that kind of opportunity in order to protect a wicked person, it demonstrates how careful we must be with the honor of others. Every person needs to be treated with honor, dignity, and respect.

Part 2: VaEschanan—Deuteronomy 3:23–7:11

And you shall love HaShem your God, with all your heart, with all your soul, and with all your resources. (6:5)

The Medrash teaches that a person must love God completely. Whether we receive something good or bad, we should accept it with joy. As the Mishnah says in Pirkei Avos, the Chapters of the Fathers, "Who is rich? He who is happy with his portion."

Two aspects of this saying bother Rabbi Yisrael Meyer Kagan. First of all, how can we expect a person who is poor, and who provides for himself with difficulty, to be happy with his situation? And second, why does the saying refer to "his portion," rather than simply "he who is happy with what he has?"

The Carpenter

To answer these questions, the Chofetz Chaim offers a parable. Everyone knows that a carpenter needs a saw. But a carpentry saw is a simple instrument, available from any hardware store for a few dollars. Why not give him something better? Imagine if you were to replace his simple, cheap saw with the type of high-precision cutting instrument used by diamond cutters, worth hundreds of times what the original cost.

Have you done him a favor? Of course not. It may be true that a carpentry saw is inexpensive, but it is a necessity if the carpenter is to do his job. He can't earn a living with a diamond-cutting saw. He can't cut wood with it, and no one would entrust their diamonds to him. In order to get his job done, the carpenter needs his plain, simple instrument—a diamond-cutter is useless.

Answering Our Unique Needs

The Chofetz Chaim says that we must learn to look at the world the same way. The Holy One, Blessed be He, stands over every creature, and He knows exactly what each individual needs, and what tests each person needs to face. Some must be tested with poverty, to see if they will withstand difficult situations. Others must be tested with wealth, to see if they will open their hands to the poor. Every detail of a person's life is designed to respond to his or her unique needs, in order to enable everyone to perfect both themselves and the world.

Were a person to suddenly find himself in someone else's situation, he would certainly be much worse off. This is why the Sages tell us that a wealthy person is one who is happy with his portion—using the language "portion" quite intentionally. That which each of us has is apportioned.

Living the Message

Whenever you find yourself in a difficult situation, even one capable of causing great pain and anguish, don't let it break you—for just the opposite is true: whatever you receive is somehow, at some level, for your benefit. Perhaps no one can explain or even understand why, but you will profit from this test, like all others. It may seem impossible to imagine at the moment, but you may see it in another light entirely in the not-so-distant future.

Obviously it takes a person on an exalted spiritual level to truly feel this way about every situation. But every person can take comfort in recognizing that God never abandons us, and never leaves us in difficult times. Sometimes just the opposite is true: we feel God's closeness during the greatest trials. And, says the Chofetz Chaim, if a person is able to pass through such tests and not despair, this will stand as living testimony to that individual's trust and reliance on God's limitless love, care, and ability to help.

Part 3: Eikev—Deuteronomy 7:12–11:25

> And you shall eat and be satisfied, and you shall bless HaShem your God for the good land which He gave to you. (8:10)

This is not merely a prediction that you will bless God, but a Biblical Commandment to bless God after eating a meal. The specified time for this blessing, however, runs against our intuition. Don't we feel most thankful *before* the meal? Shouldn't we say the blessing when we're hungry? Most blessings, including the blessing on learning Torah, are said before doing something, not after—so saying the blessing before the meal would fit the pattern.

This anomaly reflects the Torah's profound understanding of human nature. Yes, it is easier to thank God before the meal, and that is exactly the point.

Rabbi Gedalyah Schorr comments that the holy Kabbalistic work, the Zohar, says that the Torah frequently relates the positive and the negative. Our reading, he says, is one example of this concept. The Torah goes on to warn us that after we are sated, we can make a tragic mistake.

> Guard yourselves lest you forget HaShem your God . . . lest you eat and be satisfied, and build good houses and dwell therein . . . and you say in your hearts, "My strength and the might of my hand made me all of this great wealth!" (8:11–12, 17)

Say a blessing recognizing that it all comes from God, says Rabbi Schorr, and you will avoid the false claim that your own abilities brought you what you have. That is why the blessing on food comes after the meal.

When it comes to learning Torah, the opposite is true. As the famous Israeli columnist Amnon Denker once commented, "The appetite comes with the eating." The more Torah you learn, the more you *want* to learn. So it is *before* learning that you least appreciate it. Since one must recognize the material and spiritual wealth that God has given, we must bless God at precisely the moments when we are most likely to fail: *after* enjoying material blessing, and *before* dwelling in the spiritual.

Part 4: Re'eh—Deuteronomy 11:26–16:17

> After HaShem your God you will go, Him you shall fear, His Commandments you will guard, to His voice you will listen, Him you will serve, and to Him you will cleave. (13:5)

Chapter 13 of Deuteronomy discusses three distinct influences that attempt to draw a person away from God and His Commandments, in order to serve a false god. The *Avnei Ezel* commentary warns us not to think that the worship of "foreign gods" must literally be idolatry. Rather, *any* ideology that tries to get a Jew to act in a way "foreign" to Torah will qualify. He explains that the three influences listed in this reading have "real-world" applications in our day, and thus we learn from the Torah to be on guard against each one.

The False Prophet

The first of these influences is the "false prophet," who produces signs or wonders that actually come about as predicted. In our own era, says the Avnei Ezel, this corresponds to a convincing, charismatic leader. A guru comes to town, sets up shop, and announces that your life will be filled with meaning and happiness, if you will only give yourself and all of your money to his cult. It sounds ridiculous, but various charlatans have proven extremely successful at doing exactly this. And, as we also know, young Jews without a solid Jewish education have proven susceptible to their influences, promises, and sheer charisma.

The early *kibbutzim* in Israel were not merely communes, but were often both openly hostile to religion and very attached to Lenin, Communist philosophy, and the Soviet Union.

Friends and Family

The next paragraph discusses persuasion by "friends and family," which is expressed today as "peer pressure." If a few of your friends end up in one of these cults, you're likely to find yourself bombarded with love and free gifts—such as books by the guru. Again the Torah warns us, with clear understanding of human nature: Be on guard. The same person who proves resistant to the charismatic leader may be all too dependent upon his or her closest friends and relatives, and may find it extremely difficult to resist their entreaties.

The Streets of the City

The third and final influence discussed by the Torah is the idolatrous city—otherwise known as "the street." You go outside, and this is what "normal" people are doing. This is what newspapers, radio and television, public officials, and general public behavior indicate is normative and appropriate. You don't do this? You don't believe this? You observe the Torah?! Clearly, you are a "throwback to the Middle Ages"!

This is the pressure of the street that the Torah is talking about. This is what bears down upon any person who attempts to follow the path and precepts of the Torah and its demanding moral values, instead of the whims of modern society. This is what the Torah is warning you about, because it's all around you.

Part 5: Shoftim—Deuteronomy 16:18–21:9

Judges and officers shall you place for yourself, in all of your gates which HaShem your God gives you . . . (16:18)

Many commentators apply this verse not only to the community, but to the individual—note that it says that you shall place judges and officers "for yourself," singular, as is emphasized by the *Toldos Yaakov Yosef* commentary. He says that each person is first obligated to judge and correct himself, before getting involved in judging others.

The *Sfas Emes* also applies this verse to the individual, saying that each person must act both as "judge" and as "officer." You must "judge" in your own mind, thinking carefully about your actions and choosing that which is correct and appropriate. And you also need to be an "officer," forcing yourself to behave in accordance with your judgments.

When you aren't involved in other things, that is the time to be thinking about the right way to behave, the right way to act, the right things to do. That's the time to be a "judge." But the Talmud (Nedarim 32b) warns us, "at the time that the Evil Inclination takes control, there is no one to remind you of the Good Inclination." In the middle of a hectic day, when suddenly confronted with a situation, a person barely has time to think "Is this the right thing to do?" That's when you need an "officer," able to control your baser instincts and to actually follow the rules that you laid out for yourself in moments of reflection.

The *Shnei Luchos HaBris* quotes the *Sefer Yetzirah*, an early Kabbalistic work, which says that there are seven "gates" into a person. A person has two ears, two eyes, two nostrils and a mouth. The Torah teaches that a person has to watch everything that passes through the gates. A person needs to think about what he looks at, what he listens to, what he eats, and what he says—judging in advance whether this is appropriate, and then acting as an officer to prevent the wrong sort of traffic from flowing through.

Part 6: Ki Seitzei—Deuteronomy 21:10–25:19

> When you shall go out to wage war against your enemy, and Hashem your God should give him into your hand . . . (21:10)

Note how the subject switches in the middle of the verse: when "you" go out, and "HaShem" gives you . . . Who goes out? You do. But who gives success? God!

The War Within

The Talmud and Kabbalistic sources explain that the most important war in your life is the one you fight against your own inclinations and desires. You have good and bad inclinations fighting within you. So your task is to battle against your bad inclinations and follow the good, and thus become a more perfect and Godly individual.

The *Ksav Sofer* applies the above passage to this most important war, and in so doing explains the cryptic saying of Hillel in the Chapters of the Fathers (1:14), "If I am not for me, who will be for me? And if I am for myself, what am I? And if not now, when?"

God Helps Those Who Help Themselves

In the Talmud (Sukkah 52b), Reish Lakish says that a person's evil inclinations attempt to overpower him or her every day, and if God would not help you, it would be impossible to beat those inclinations back. If so, says the Ksav Sofer, you might imagine that it is better not to fight, or to make any effort at all to bring your desires under control—just trust that God will help you, and fight the great war on your behalf.

The truth, says the Ksav Sofer, is just the opposite. Someone who believes this will never control his or her desires. You must constantly battle your desires to the full extent of your capabilities—and *then* Heaven will help. "One who comes to purify himself, [Heaven] helps him," say our Sages. The person must begin to purify himself first.

The Words of Hillel

So this is what Hillel said: "If I am not for me, who will be for me?" If a person does nothing on his own behalf, and does not stand up to fight his inclinations, then who is going to help him? "And if I am for myself, what am I?" Even after making the effort, what is it? Because alone it is insufficient— you need further help from God. "And if not now, when?" You can't ignore this battle, or wait until you get old. The Talmudic Sages said: Happy is the one who fears God while he still has physical strength, for then he will be able to completely return to God and abandon his misbehavior.

Part 7: Ki Savo—Deuteronomy 26:1–29:8

> And all the blessings will come upon you, and overtake you . . .
> (28:2)

The way the verse reads, it looks as if the blessings will be chasing you, and you're going to be running away! Who runs away from blessings? Everyone wants a happy and healthy family, a comfortable home . . . and probably wouldn't turn down a winning lottery ticket, either. So why does the Torah talk about blessings that "come upon you" as if you weren't looking for them, and "overtaking you" as if you were even running away?

The *Sha'ar Bas Rabim* comments: Many times, people *do* run away—from something that is actually good for them, but that they don't recognize as a blessing. Since they don't see the benefit, they think it is bad and attempt to escape it. The Torah is saying that if they do what God wants of them, then God will ensure that they get the blessing anyway.

FACT

The Sha'ar Bas Rabim explains that this was King David's prayer in Psalm 23:6, "May only good and kindness pursue me all the days of my life." His prayer was: "May good and kindness pursue me, even when I do not see them for what they are, and run away (and, of course, may they be the only things to pursue me!)."

Part 8: Nitzavim—Deuteronomy 29:9–30:20

> And you shall return to HaShem your God, and you shall listen to His voice, like all that I have commanded you today, you and your children, with all your hearts and with all your souls. (30:2)

This Torah portion is read on the last Sabbath of each year. It is followed by Rosh HaShanah, the Day of Judgment, which begins the Ten Days of Repentance that culminate on Yom Kippur, the Day of Atonement.

Return, Rather than Repentance

The truth is that "repentance" is a poor translation of the word *Teshuvah*, and one that tends to be associated in our minds with fire and brimstone. Teshuvah actually means "return," as found in the verse above: "and you shall *return* to HaShem your God." The idea of returning is to go back home, to be the child of God you were created to be, and to live up to your spiritual potential. Fire and brimstone have nothing to do with it!

QUESTION?

Does the Torah believe in Heaven and Hell?
Yes, as you can see in Chapter 4, "Heaven"—or the World to Come—is very much a Jewish concept. While there is also *Gehinnom*, the best translation of that would be purgatory—because a soul may require a process of cleansing, purging it of wrongdoing in this world. But the average person won't need more than several months of "cleansing"— it's not permanent except for uniquely evil individuals.

Fear of God and fear of punishment don't motivate the ideal form of return. True return is motivated by love.

God as Our Father

Most people feel grateful toward their parents, recognizing all that their parents have done for them. If you are like most children (of whatever age), you love your parents, want them to be proud of you, and try to do the favors they ask of you.

The same should be true in the relationship between each person, and God, our Father in Heaven. Trying to go back to doing what He wants, because you recognize that He cares about you, is return motivated by love.

The Power of Return

How powerful is this return? The Sages teach that if a person's return is motivated by fear, then his or her deliberate transgressions are treated as if they were careless errors. But if one is motivated by love, then those same deliberate transgressions are converted into merits.

The Chassidic master, the Ba'al Shem Tov, offers a parable: If a person walks into a dark room and turns on the light, then the darkness disappears. To anyone who walks into the room afterward, it is as if it was never dark at all. Return, he says, is so powerful that it can transform a person in much the same way. Even a past filled with misdeeds can be turned to light.

Part 9: Vayeilech—Deuteronomy 31:1–31:30

> Gather the nation together, the men, the women, the children, and the stranger who is within your gates, in order that they hear and in order that they learn, that they fear HaShem your God, and that they guard, in order to perform, all the words of this Torah. (31:12)

The mitzvah of *Hakhel*, gathering the entire nation together to hear a public Torah reading, afforded the entire Jewish Nation the opportunity to come together to listen to the words of the Torah. Yet in this mitzvah, we find an apparent contradiction—the verse goes out of its way to specify that even small children should come and participate as well. This mitzvah is supposed to offer the opportunity to come together and to listen carefully, to learn—but they were also supposed to bring the kids.

Any parent will tell you that if you want the adults to listen carefully, then you should instruct them to leave their children at home! Small children disturb the adults, preventing them from paying attention and listening properly. So why should little children, who won't understand anyway, not only be tolerated but invited?

In the Talmud (Chagiga 3a), Rabbi Elazar Ben Azaryah asks this very question. "The children—for what purpose are they coming?" And he answers: "In order to give reward to those who bring them." Rabbi Nosson Adler explains: Children, as everyone knows, are extremely impressionable. It may be true that they will not fully understand, but simply being in such a sanctified environment, and seeing so many people brought together for the purpose of hearing the Torah, is an experience that will have a deep and lasting impact in their hearts.

The Torah says that it is worth sacrificing personal growth in order to guide your children toward Torah and good deeds. Should anyone fear that they will "lose out" by bringing their children, the Torah requires that they come—and Rabbi Elazar Ben Azaryah explains that the Torah is promising extra reward to their parents.

The Torah places a high priority on marrying and raising a family. Too often, people regard their careers as the measure of their accomplishments, but a successful marriage and happy, flourishing children as little more than good fortune. This is a mistake—marriages and child-rearing require time and effort.

Educating children requires sacrificing both money and time. Certainly, it is not appropriate to bring young children to every event, or to synagogue in a situation where they will disturb the services. But at other times, we need to weigh the impact upon our children if we do bring them, to see, to hear, and to listen, even if they do not fully understand. What does the Torah tell us? That when you sacrifice for the sake of your children, you will receive extra reward.

Part 10: Ha'azinu—Deuteronomy 32:1–32:52

> The Rock, his works are perfect, for all His ways are just; a faithful Almighty without blemish, straight and righteous is He. (32:4)

It is one thing to believe that God exists. But you see bad things happen to good people, and good things happen to bad people. To believe that God is perfect and just, you need to accept that you'll never know the whole story.

The Wealthy Father

The Chofetz Chaim offers a parable. There was a wealthy businessman who had property, servants, all a man could ask for—but the joy of his life was his only son, David, whom he loved with all his heart. One day, his little boy fell ill—and it soon became clear that it was very serious. After many desperate attempts to diagnose the problem, a leading specialist discovered that David suffered from an intense allergy to red meat. He restored David to health, but the doctor gave his father the strongest of warnings to never permit his child to eat beef or veal.

He was indeed very careful—until he was called out of town on business. He warned his servants repeatedly, but on the last day of his trip, one of the cooks foolishly left a steak sandwich on the table. David wandered in, smelled the meat, grabbed a piece and ran outside. He immediately became sick once again, and his father returned to discover him near death. With great effort, the doctors were able to save David's life once again.

The Thanksgiving Banquet

The father made a special meal of thanksgiving for all his relatives and friends. As they sat down to dinner, they saw that their host had ordered a catered meal that surpassed even his ordinary standards. And of course, not serving meat would have been out of the question, and would have required all sorts of uncomfortable explanations.

Several guests, sitting near the entrance, heard something very surprising—and disturbing: the voice of David himself, crying loudly to be permitted into the dinner hall! They sat there amazed, not understanding the bizarre actions of the "cruel" father who would not permit his own son to enter, when after all it was his health they were celebrating . . .

Often you can't understand why God runs the world as He does. All you can do is realize that we don't know the full story.

Part 11: Zos HaBrachah—Deuteronomy 33:1–34:12

And Moshe, the servant of God died there . . . no man knows of his grave, until this very day. (34:6)

The *Kehillas Yitzchak* asks why the Torah needs to tell us that no one knows where Moshe's grave is—isn't it obvious, since the Torah never told us where it is, and everyone left the area?

Imagine, however, what should have happened at the end of a story like that of Moshe's lifetime. A man came on the scene and demonstrated both moral and national leadership, was responsible for a series of open miracles, rescued an entire nation from slavery, and led them in their encounter with God. And, until his last day, he showed none of the ordinary infirmities of old age.

The story should have continued that he had ascended alive to Heaven. He should be some sort of god, or at least an angel. Since we don't even know where his grave is, the opportunity for personal or national embellishment is wide open.

With Moshe, however, it is very clear—there was no exaggeration. The Torah says that he died, and no one knows where his grave is, in order that there be no mistake. So the Torah was obviously not interested in overstating Moshe's accomplishments in any way. And that, of course, says something about all that the Torah claims Moshe *did* achieve!

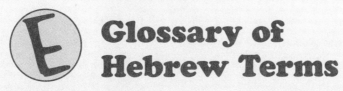

Appendix A

Glossary of Hebrew Terms

Amorah (pl. Amoram):

Scholar of the era when the Talmud (Gamorah) was written.

Ashkenazic:

German/Northern European, regarding both a style of prayer (*Nusach Ashkenaz*) and the community of Jews from Northern Europe, from France to Russia.

Av Bais Din:

Chief Justice (lit., father of the court)

Avraham:

Abraham. The first Avraham was the first of the three generations of patriarchs, and is also called *Avraham Avinu*, Our Father Abraham.

Bais Din:

A religious court.

bar:

Aramaic equivalent of *ben*, son of—e.g., Rabbi Shimon bar Yochai.

ben:

son of—e.g., "Rabbi Moshe ben Maimon" means Rabbi Moshe son of Maimon.

Chanukah:

Eight-day holiday, usually in December, celebrating the re-dedication of the Temple after a small group of faithful Jews were (miraculously) able to push the Greek army away from the Temple site in Jerusalem. Also spelled Hanukkah.

Chassid (pl. Chassidim):

Adherent of Chassidism.

Chassidism:

Movement emphasizing joy, fervent prayer, and attachment to a Rebbe, founded by Rabbi Yisrael Ba'al Shem Tov ("Master of the Good Name") in the early eighteenth century.

Gemarah:

Discussions surrounding the Mishnah and elaborations upon its laws—also known as the Talmud. One was compiled in Israel and a second, later one in Babylon; the second is regarded as more authoritative.

Halachah:

Torah Law.

ibn:

Arabic equivalent of *ben*, son of—e.g., Rabbi Yehudah ibn Tibbon.

Kabbalah:

Literally, that which is received. Refers to the mystical tradition of Torah.

Kohen (pl. Kohanim):

Priest of the Jewish People, a descendant of the male line from Aharon, brother of Moshe.

Kohen HaGadol:

The High Priest.

Kosher:

Fit, or acceptable. In common usage, refers to foods that are acceptable for eating under Torah law. To be Kosher, land animals must both chew their cud and have cloven hooves (pigs are a common example of an animal that has one sign, but not the other), and must be ritually slaughtered with a painless knife cut across the windpipe and esophagus. Fish must have fins and scales, and therefore all shellfish are not Kosher.

Matzah (pl. Matzos):

Unleavened bread, baked extremely fast at high heat, used during the holiday of Pesach. Pesach Matzos may consist of only flour and water, and must be completely baked within eighteen minutes of mixing the two.

Medrash:

Explanations of Torah verses from the Oral Torah. Includes explanations of the stories as well as legal conclusions and references.

Megillas Esther:
The Scroll of Esther. One of the smaller books of the Bible, it tells the story that led to the Purim holiday.

Mishnah:
The first written record of the Oral Law, compiled by Rebbe Yehudah HaNasi in approximately 188 C.E.

Mitzvah:
A Commandment of the Torah.

Moshe:
Moshe. The first Moshe received the Torah from God, and is also called *Moshe Rabbeinu*, Moshe our Rabbi.

Moshiach:
Anointed One. Used especially in reference to the future King of Israel, who will end the exile and rebuild the Holy Temple.

Nasi:
President—Head of the Sanhedrin.

Pesach:
Holiday, during the spring, called Passover in English. During Passover no leavened bread may be eaten or even possessed by a Jewish person, and on the first night the story of the Exodus is told. See also *Matzah*.

Rabban:
Honorific designation for the president (*Nasi*) of the Sanhedrin.

Rabbi:
Anglicized from *Rav*. In modern times, also used as honorific designation of a spiritual leader of a congregation of Jews, similar to Pastor, Minister, or Imam for Catholicism, Protestantism, or Islam, respectively.

Rambam:
Acronym for Rabbi Moshe ben Maimon, the twelfth century (C.E.) codifier and philosopher, also known as Maimonides.

Ramban:

Acronym for Rabbi Moshe ben Nachman, thirteenth century (C.E.) Halachist, also known as Nachmanides.

Rashi:

Acronym for Rabbi Shlomo Yitzchaki (son of Yitzchak), eleventh-century (C.E.) commentator—the pre-eminent commentator on Torah and Talmud.

Rav:

Teacher of Torah.

Rebbe:

In Mishnaic and Talmudic times, honorific designation of one who received true Rabbinic ordination (*semicha*) handed down since Moshe. This lapsed at the end of the era of Palestinian scholarship, in roughly the fourth or fifth century C.E. In modern times, honorific designation of a leader of a Chassidic group.

Rosh HaShanah:

Beginning of the year—the Jewish New Year, also the Day of Judgment.

Sanhedrin:

Supreme religious court of seventy-one sages. The courtroom was on the Temple Mount until the destruction of the Temple.

Seder:

Order or structure. The Mishnah is divided into six *Sedarim*, or Orders. The *Pesach Seder* is the order of the Passover meal.

Sefard:

As an order of prayer, following the Spanish style. *Nusach Sefard* is a variant of *Nusach Ashkenaz* with modifications in accordance with Lurianic Kabbalah, and is used by Chassidim.

Sephardic:

As a community, that of Jews from Spain and Northern Africa.

Shavuos:

Holiday, during the early summer, on the day God spoke from Mt. Sinai. Also called the Festival of Weeks, because it is always seven weeks and one day after the start of Pesach.

Shlomo:

Solomon. The first Shlomo was the son of King David and succeeded him as King, and built the First Temple.

Shofar:

A horn, usually of a ram, blown on Rosh HaShanah, the Jewish New Year.

Sinai:

A small mountain in what is today known as the Sinai Desert, located between ancient Egypt and Israel. The exact location of the mountain is not known.

Sukkah (pl. Sukkos):

A temporary "booth" with a roof composed of unfinished plant products, such as bamboo, tree branches, or thin slats.

Sukkos:

Holiday, during the fall, also called the Festival of Booths. During the holiday Jewish men are commanded to eat and reside in a Sukkah.

Tahor:

Spiritually pure.

Talmud:

The Mishnah and the Gemara, the written records of the Oral Law.

Tameh:

Spiritually impure.

Tanach:

The Jewish Bible. The name is the Hebrew acronym of *Torah, Nevi'im,* and *Kesuvim*—the Torah, Prophets and Writings.

Tanah (pl. Tannaim):

Scholar of the era when the Mishnah was written.

Torah Shebaal Peh:

The Oral Torah, the Oral Law.

Torah Shebichtav:

The Written Torah, the Five Books of Moshe—the first five books of the Bible.

Yaakov:

Jacob. The first Yaakov was the third of the three generations of patriarchs, and is also called *Yaakov Avinu*, Our Father Jacob.

Yetzer HaRa:

The Bad Inclination. A desire inside every person to do the wrong thing, drawing that person away from God and spirituality.

Yetzer HaTov:

The Good Inclination. The opposite desire to the Yetzer HaRa, this one drawing a person to do the right thing.

Yitzchak:

Isaac. The first Isaac was the first of the three generations of patriarchs, and is also called *Yitzchak Avinu*, Our Father Isaac.

Yom Kippur:

The Day of Atonement, the holiest day on the Jewish calendar.

Zohar:

The Book of Splendor, written by Rebbe Shimon bar Yochai at the dawn of the Common Era.

Appendix B

Resources: Books, Web Sites, and More

EverythingTorah.com

The Web site created for this book, ✍*www.everythingtorah.com*, is designed to offer ongoing resources to those who have read this book. For the latest Web sites and book recommendations, please join fellow readers at the site.

Web Sites

✍*www.torah.org* Project Genesis/Torah.org

✍*www.aish.com* operated by Aish HaTorah, a yeshiva for adult beginners

✍*www.ohr.edu* operated by Ohr Somayach, also a yeshiva for adult beginners

✍*www.chabad.org* Chabad Lubavitch

✍*www.613.org* Jewish Torah Audio

✍*www.torahmedia.com* Torah Audio Lectures

✍*www.rainbowcovenant.org* Information on Noahides and the Seven Universal Laws

Books

All the resources listed here are available from Jewish booksellers as well as online. Formal citations with date of publication are omitted here, because there is no ambiguity concerning which work is referenced.

The Basics

The Chumash (Printed Torah): The Stone Chumash from ArtScroll, the Margolin edition from Feldheim Publishers, the Metzudah edition, the Living Torah (with Rabbi Aryeh Kaplan's commentary) from Moznaim, and the Pentateuch with Rabbi Samson Raphael Hirsch's commentary (Judaica Press) are all valuable study editions for the English-speaking student. For those interested in delving deeper, the *Mikraos Gedolos*, in Hebrew, is the standard study edition.

The Siddur (Prayer Book): The ArtScroll Siddur is the standard, and comes in both Nusach Ashkenaz and Nusach Sefard (for Chassidic synagogues).

The Tanach (Jewish Bible): The Stone Tanach from ArtScroll is the recommended English translation for serious study. The Jerusalem Bible (Koren) from Feldheim Publishers is also a valuable reference.

For Study

For Noahides: *The Rainbow Covenant: Torah and the Seven Universal Laws*, by Michael Ellias Dallen, from LightCatcher Books.

Halachah: The *Mishnah Berurah* from Rabbi Yisrael Meyer Kagan, with English translation, from Feldheim Publishers.

History: Rabbi Zechariah Fendel's series from Hashkafa Publications, and Rabbi Berel Wein's series from Shaar Press, both discuss the history of Torah study in great detail.

Mishnah: With commentary by R' Pinchas Kehati, with English translation, from Feldheim Publishers.

Mussar: *Mesilas Yesharim*, the Path of the Just, by Rabbi Moshe Chaim Luzzato, with a new translation by Rabbi Yosef Liebler, from Feldheim Publishers.

Talmud: From ArtScroll in English translation, or any printing of the original Hebrew/Aramaic work.

Index

THE EVERYTHING SERIES!

BUSINESS & PERSONAL FINANCE

Everything® Budgeting Book
Everything® Business Planning Book
Everything® Coaching and Mentoring Book
Everything® Fundraising Book
Everything® Get Out of Debt Book
Everything® Grant Writing Book
Everything® Home-Based Business Book, 2nd Ed.
Everything® Homebuying Book, 2nd Ed.
Everything® Homeselling Book, 2nd Ed.
Everything® Investing Book, 2nd Ed.
Everything® Landlording Book
Everything® Leadership Book
Everything® Managing People Book
Everything® Negotiating Book
Everything® Online Business Book
Everything® Personal Finance Book
Everything® Personal Finance in Your 20s and 30s Book
Everything® Project Management Book
Everything® Real Estate Investing Book
Everything® Robert's Rules Book, $7.95
Everything® Selling Book
Everything® Start Your Own Business Book
Everything® Wills & Estate Planning Book

COMPUTERS

Everything® Online Auctions Book
Everything® Blogging Book

COOKING

Everything® Barbecue Cookbook
Everything® Bartender's Book, $9.95
Everything® Chinese Cookbook
Everything® Cocktail Parties and Drinks Book
Everything® College Cookbook
Everything® Cookbook
Everything® Cooking for Two Cookbook
Everything® Diabetes Cookbook
Everything® Easy Gourmet Cookbook
Everything® Fondue Cookbook
Everything® Gluten-Free Cookbook
Everything® Glycemic Index Cookbook
Everything® Grilling Cookbook

Everything® Healthy Meals in Minutes Cookbook
Everything® Holiday Cookbook
Everything® Indian Cookbook
Everything® Italian Cookbook
Everything® Low-Carb Cookbook
Everything® Low-Fat High-Flavor Cookbook
Everything® Low-Salt Cookbook
Everything® Meals for a Month Cookbook
Everything® Mediterranean Cookbook
Everything® Mexican Cookbook
Everything® One-Pot Cookbook
Everything® Pasta Cookbook
Everything® Quick Meals Cookbook
Everything® Slow Cooker Cookbook
Everything® Slow Cooking for a Crowd Cookbook
Everything® Soup Cookbook
Everything® Tex-Mex Cookbook
Everything® Thai Cookbook
Everything® Vegetarian Cookbook
Everything® Wild Game Cookbook
Everything® Wine Book, 2nd Ed.

CRAFT SERIES

Everything® Crafts—Baby Scrapbooking
Everything® Crafts—Bead Your Own Jewelry
Everything® Crafts—Create Your Own Greeting Cards
Everything® Crafts—Easy Projects
Everything® Crafts—Polymer Clay for Beginners
Everything® Crafts—Rubber Stamping Made Easy
Everything® Crafts—Wedding Decorations and Keepsakes

HEALTH

Everything® Alzheimer's Book
Everything® Diabetes Book
Everything® Health Guide to Adult Bipolar Disorder
Everything® Health Guide to Controlling Anxiety
Everything® Health Guide to Fibromyalgia
Everything® Hypnosis Book

Everything® Low Cholesterol Book
Everything® Massage Book
Everything® Menopause Book
Everything® Nutrition Book
Everything® Reflexology Book
Everything® Stress Management Book

HISTORY

Everything® American Government Book
Everything® American History Book
Everything® Civil War Book
Everything® Irish History & Heritage Book
Everything® Middle East Book

GAMES

Everything® 15-Minute Sudoku Book, $9.95
Everything® 30-Minute Sudoku Book, $9.95
Everything® Blackjack Strategy Book
Everything® Brain Strain Book, $9.95
Everything® Bridge Book
Everything® Card Games Book
Everything® Card Tricks Book, $9.95
Everything® Casino Gambling Book, 2nd Ed.
Everything® Chess Basics Book
Everything® Craps Strategy Book
Everything® Crossword and Puzzle Book
Everything® Crossword Challenge Book
Everything® Cryptograms Book, $9.95
Everything® Easy Crosswords Book
Everything® Easy Kakuro Book, $9.95
Everything® Games Book, 2nd Ed.
Everything® Giant Sudoku Book, $9.95
Everything® Kakuro Challenge Book, $9.95
Everything® Large-Print Crosswords Book
Everything® Lateral Thinking Puzzles Book, $9.95
Everything® Pencil Puzzles Book, $9.95
Everything® Poker Strategy Book
Everything® Pool & Billiards Book
Everything® Test Your IQ Book, $9.95
Everything® Texas Hold 'Em Book, $9.95
Everything® Travel Crosswords Book, $9.95
Everything® Word Games Challenge Book
Everything® Word Search Book

Bolded titles are new additions to the series.
All Everything® books are priced at $12.95 or $14.95, unless otherwise stated. Prices subject to change without notice.

HOBBIES

Everything® Candlemaking Book
Everything® Cartooning Book
Everything® Drawing Book
Everything® Family Tree Book, 2nd Ed.
Everything® Knitting Book
Everything® Knots Book
Everything® Photography Book
Everything® Quilting Book
Everything® Scrapbooking Book
Everything® Sewing Book
Everything® Woodworking Book

HOME IMPROVEMENT

Everything® Feng Shui Book
Everything® Feng Shui Decluttering Book, $9.95
Everything® Fix-It Book
Everything® Home Decorating Book
Everything® Homebuilding Book
Everything® Lawn Care Book
Everything® Organize Your Home Book

KIDS' BOOKS

All titles are $7.95

Everything® Kids' Animal Puzzle &
    Activity Book
Everything® Kids' Baseball Book, 4th Ed.
Everything® Kids' Bible Trivia Book
Everything® Kids' Bugs Book
Everything® Kids' Christmas Puzzle
    & Activity Book
Everything® Kids' Cookbook
Everything® Kids' Crazy Puzzles Book
Everything® Kids' Dinosaurs Book
**Everything® Kids' Gross Hidden Pictures
    Book**
Everything® Kids' Gross Jokes Book
Everything® Kids' Gross Mazes Book
Everything® Kids' Gross Puzzle and
    Activity Book
Everything® Kids' Halloween Puzzle
    & Activity Book
Everything® Kids' Hidden Pictures Book
Everything® Kids' Horses Book
Everything® Kids' Joke Book
Everything® Kids' Knock Knock Book
Everything® Kids' Math Puzzles Book
Everything® Kids' Mazes Book
Everything® Kids' Money Book
Everything® Kids' Nature Book

Everything® Kids' Pirates Puzzle and
    Activity Book
Everything® Kids' Puzzle Book
Everything® Kids' Riddles & Brain Teasers Book
Everything® Kids' Science Experiments Book
Everything® Kids' Sharks Book
Everything® Kids' Soccer Book
Everything® Kids' Travel Activity Book

KIDS' STORY BOOKS

Everything® Fairy Tales Book

LANGUAGE

Everything® Conversational Japanese Book
    (with CD), $19.95
Everything® French Grammar Book
Everything® French Phrase Book, $9.95
Everything® French Verb Book, $9.95
**Everything® German Practice Book with
    CD, $19.95**
Everything® Inglés Book
Everything® Learning French Book
Everything® Learning German Book
Everything® Learning Italian Book
Everything® Learning Latin Book
Everything® Learning Spanish Book
Everything® Sign Language Book
Everything® Spanish Grammar Book
Everything® Spanish Phrase Book, $9.95
Everything® Spanish Practice Book
    (with CD), $19.95
Everything® Spanish Verb Book, $9.95

MUSIC

Everything® Drums Book (with CD), $19.95
Everything® Guitar Book
**Everything® Guitar Chords Book with CD,
    $19.95**
Everything® Home Recording Book
Everything® Playing Piano and Keyboards
    Book
Everything® Reading Music Book (with CD),
    $19.95
Everything® Rock & Blues Guitar Book
    (with CD), $19.95
Everything® Songwriting Book

NEW AGE

Everything® Astrology Book, 2nd Ed.
Everything® Dreams Book, 2nd Ed.
Everything® Love Signs Book, $9.95

Everything® Numerology Book
Everything® Paganism Book
Everything® Palmistry Book
Everything® Psychic Book
Everything® Reiki Book
Everything® Tarot Book
Everything® Wicca and Witchcraft Book

PARENTING

Everything® Baby Names Book, 2nd Ed.
Everything® Baby Shower Book
Everything® Baby's First Food Book
Everything® Baby's First Year Book
Everything® Birthing Book
Everything® Breastfeeding Book
Everything® Father-to-Be Book
Everything® Father's First Year Book
Everything® Get Ready for Baby Book
Everything® Get Your Baby to Sleep Book,
    $9.95
Everything® Getting Pregnant Book
Everything® Homeschooling Book
Everything® Mother's First Year Book
Everything® Parent's Guide to Children
    and Divorce
Everything® Parent's Guide to Children
    with ADD/ADHD
Everything® Parent's Guide to Children
    with Asperger's Syndrome
Everything® Parent's Guide to Children
    with Autism
Everything® Parent's Guide to Children with
    Bipolar Disorder
Everything® Parent's Guide to Children
    with Dyslexia
Everything® Parent's Guide to Positive
    Discipline
Everything® Parent's Guide to Raising a
    Successful Child
**Everything® Parent's Guide to Raising
    Boys**
**Everything® Parent's Guide to Raising
    Siblings**
Everything® Parent's Guide to Tantrums
Everything® Parent's Guide to the Overweight
    Child
Everything® Parent's Guide to the Strong-
    Willed Child
Everything® Parenting a Teenager Book
Everything® Potty Training Book, $9.95
Everything® Pregnancy Book, 2nd Ed.

Bolded titles are new additions to the series.
All Everything® books are priced at $12.95 or $14.95, unless otherwise stated. Prices subject to change without notice.

Everything® Pregnancy Fitness Book
Everything® Pregnancy Nutrition Book
Everything® Pregnancy Organizer, $15.00
Everything® Toddler Book
Everything® Toddler Activities Book
Everything® Tween Book
Everything® Twins, Triplets, and More Book

PETS

Everything® Boxer Book
Everything® Cat Book, 2nd Ed.
Everything® Chihuahua Book
Everything® Dachshund Book
Everything® Dog Book
Everything® Dog Health Book
Everything® Dog Training and Tricks Book
Everything® German Shepherd Book
Everything® Golden Retriever Book
Everything® Horse Book
Everything® Horse Care Book
Everything® Horseback Riding Book
Everything® Labrador Retriever Book
Everything® Poodle Book
Everything® Pug Book
Everything® Puppy Book
Everything® Rottweiler Book
Everything® Small Dogs Book
Everything® Tropical Fish Book
Everything® Yorkshire Terrier Book

REFERENCE

Everything® Car Care Book
Everything® Classical Mythology Book
Everything® Computer Book
Everything® Divorce Book
Everything® Einstein Book
Everything® Etiquette Book, 2nd Ed.
Everything® Inventions and Patents Book
Everything® Mafia Book
Everything® Mary Magdalene Book
Everything® Philosophy Book
Everything® Psychology Book
Everything® Shakespeare Book

RELIGION

Everything® Angels Book
Everything® Bible Book
Everything® Buddhism Book
Everything® Catholicism Book

Everything® Christianity Book
Everything® Freemasons Book
Everything® History of the Bible Book
Everything® Jewish History & Heritage Book
Everything® Judaism Book
Everything® Kabbalah Book
Everything® Koran Book
Everything® Prayer Book
Everything® Saints Book
Everything® Torah Book
Everything® Understanding Islam Book
Everything® World's Religions Book
Everything® Zen Book

SCHOOL & CAREERS

Everything® Alternative Careers Book
Everything® College Major Test Book
Everything® College Survival Book, 2nd Ed.
Everything® Cover Letter Book, 2nd Ed.
Everything® Get-a-Job Book
Everything® Guide to Being a Paralegal
Everything® Guide to Being a Real Estate
  Agent
Everything® Guide to Starting and Running
  a Restaurant
Everything® Job Interview Book
Everything® New Nurse Book
Everything® New Teacher Book
Everything® Paying for College Book
Everything® Practice Interview Book
Everything® Resume Book, 2nd Ed.
Everything® Study Book
Everything® Teacher's Organizer, $16.95

SELF-HELP

Everything® Dating Book, 2nd Ed.
Everything® Great Sex Book
Everything® Kama Sutra Book
Everything® Self-Esteem Book

SPORTS & FITNESS

Everything® Fishing Book
Everything® Golf Instruction Book
Everything® Pilates Book
Everything® Running Book
Everything® Total Fitness Book
Everything® Weight Training Book
Everything® Yoga Book

TRAVEL

Everything® Family Guide to Hawaii
Everything® Family Guide to Las Vegas,
  2nd Ed.
Everything® Family Guide to New York City,
  2nd Ed.
Everything® Family Guide to RV Travel &
  Campgrounds
Everything® Family Guide to the Walt Disney
  World Resort®, Universal Studios®,
  and Greater Orlando, 4th Ed.
Everything® Family Guide to Cruise Vacations
Everything® Family Guide to the Caribbean
Everything® Family Guide to Washington
  D.C., 2nd Ed.
Everything® Guide to New England
Everything® Travel Guide to the Disneyland
  Resort®, California Adventure®,
  Universal Studios®, and the
  Anaheim Area

WEDDINGS

Everything® Bachelorette Party Book, $9.95
Everything® Bridesmaid Book, $9.95
Everything® Elopement Book, $9.95
Everything® Father of the Bride Book, $9.95
Everything® Groom Book, $9.95
Everything® Mother of the Bride Book, $9.95
Everything® Outdoor Wedding Book
Everything® Wedding Book, 3rd Ed.
Everything® Wedding Checklist, $9.95
Everything® Wedding Etiquette Book, $9.95
Everything® Wedding Organizer, $15.00
Everything® Wedding Shower Book, $9.95
Everything® Wedding Vows Book, $9.95
Everything® Weddings on a Budget Book, $9.95

WRITING

Everything® Creative Writing Book
Everything® Get Published Book, 2nd Ed.
Everything® Grammar and Style Book
Everything® Guide to Writing a Book Proposal
Everything® Guide to Writing a Novel
Everything® Guide to Writing Children's Books
Everything® Guide to Writing Research Papers
Everything® Screenwriting Book
Everything® Writing Poetry Book
Everything® Writing Well Book

Available wherever books are sold!
To order, call 800-289-0963, or visit us at *www.everything.com*
Everything® and everything.com® are registered trademarks of F+W Publications, Inc.